GREAT JEWS IN SPORTS

GREAT JEWS IN SPORTS

by

ROBERT SLATER

Introduction by
RED AUERBACH

 JONATHAN DAVID PUBLISHERS, INC.
MIDDLE VILLAGE, NY 11379

GREAT JEWS IN SPORTS

Copyright © 1983

by

Robert Slater

Jonathan David Publishers, Inc.
68-22 Eliot Avenue
Middle Village, New York 11379

10 9 8 7 6 5 4 3 2

Library of Congress Cataloging in Publication Data

Slater, Robert, 1943-
Great Jews in sports.

Includes index.
1. Jewish athletes—Biography. 2. Jews—Biography.
I. Title.
GV697.A1S53 1983   796'.089924 [B]   82-19953
ISBN O-8246-0285-4

Book design by Arlene Schleifer Goldberg

Printed in the United States of America

For My Children

MIRIAM, ADAM, and RACHEL

ACKNOWLEDGMENTS

While the writing of this book was done largely in Israel, where I have lived for the past 10 years, the research was carried out, to a large extent, during two visits to the United States. No single research facility was more important to my work than the sports branch of the *Time Inc.* Library in the Time-Life Building in New York City. The main library for *Sports Illustrated* is described proudly by its staff as "the greatest sports library in the world." It proved immensely helpful in tracking down the thousands of tiny details required for a book of this kind. I want to thank Lester Annenberg, Peter Miller, and Harry Peckham, the research librarians there, for their generosity with their time and general helpfulness.

Bruce Liebman works in the Time Sports Library, and he became my personal research aide for this book; I owe him a special debt of gratitude. His skill in finding just the right material and answers to my many questions quickly and his enthusiasm for this project made my own work throughout that much easier and added significantly to whatever success this book enjoys.

It was something of a joyful coincidence for me that the founders of the Jewish Sports Hall of Fame at the Wingate Institute in Netanya, Israel, were getting their relatively new enterprise into high gear just as I began research on this book. I wish to thank one and all connected with the Hall of Fame for their cooperation, both in Israel and in the United States. Especially I want to pay tribute to Dr. Uri Simri, the executive director of the Jewish Sports Hall of Fame, who became more than simply a valuable fount of knowledge; in fact, Dr. Simri willingly came to be an informal adviser on which Jewish sports figures to include. Others at the Jewish Sports Hall of Fame had their impact on this book: Zipporah Zeidner, public relations director at the Wingate Institute in Netanya; Shlomo Korlandchik, archivist at the Wingate Institute; and the capable staff of the Wingate Institute sports library. I thank them as well.

Arthur Hannak, the archivist for the World Maccabi Union at Kfar Maccabiah, Ramat Gan, was particularly helpful; he spent many hours describing Jewish athletes, digging up research material, and providing many useful leads for further investigation.

Joseph Siegman, the international chairman of the Jewish Sports Hall of Fame, offered advice and provided research materials during my visit to Los Angeles in the spring 1982, and for his constant interest and guidance, I wish to thank him.

Few men are as knowledgeable about the subject of Jews in sports as Haskell Cohen, the Sports Editor of the Jewish Telegraphic Agency. Fortunately for me, he gave me some of his valuable time to assess and offer new perspectives on various research lines in this book. His advice was especially important at crucial times during the researching of this book, and I am very grateful to him.

I am, of course, aware of the major contribution to the subject of Jews in sports played by the *Encyclopedia of Jews in Sports,* published in 1965 by Bloch Publishing Company, New York, and written by Bernard Postal, Jesse Silver, and Roy Silver. Naturally, the book has been an excellent reference for me. I would also like to mention as particularly helpful *The Jewish Almanac,* published by Bantam in October 1980, compiled and edited by Richard Siegel and Carl Rheins. I have benefited greatly from the *Almanac's* excellent chapter on Jews in sports. In the course of my work I have perused hundreds of books on sports, far too numerous to name here. I have also read many newspaper articles to acquire details about the personalities in this book.

Researching the section on Israeli sports figures required the continuing help of several people: Shmuel Lalkin, the director-general of the Sports Federation of Israel; Uri Afek, the deputy director of the Israel Government Sports Authority; and Israel Paz, the editor of *Hadashot Hasport* (Sports News), the Israeli sports newspaper. I thank them all for taking so much time and for suggesting just which figures should be mentioned.

I am grateful to Dorothy Resnik for her good-natured help in translating material from Hebrew to English and for a host of other efforts that facilitated my work on this book. I thank also Jennifer Frey for typing parts of this manuscript.

Other people and institutions whom I wish to thank are: Andrea Schwartz, Israel Tennis Centers Association, New York; Ian Froman, executive director of the Israel Tennis Center, Ramat Hasharon, Israel; Blanche Blumberg, public relations, Israel Tennis Center, Ramat Hasharon; Lloyd Wagner, Office of Public Relations, City College of New York, New York City; Clifford Kachline, Historian, National Baseball Hall of Fame and Museum, Cooperstown, New York; Pro Football Hall of Fame, Canton, Ohio; Bud Fisher, Public Relations Director, Professional Bowlers Association, Akron, Ohio; Mary Anne Marenna, *Meriden Record-Journal,* Meriden, Connecticut; Los Angeles County Sheriff's Department, Los Angeles, California; Meyer F. Steinglass, New York City; Mac DeMere, News Department Manager, Sports Car Club of America, Englewood, Colorado; Louis Geseltzer, World Maccabi Union, Kfar Maccabiah, Israel; Robert Spivak, President, U.S. Committee Sports for Israel; Suzie Adams, Editor-in-Chief, *World Tennis* Magazine, New York City; Nat Lobet, former *Ring Magazine* publisher and editor; Joseph Telecki, Haifa, Israel; Bruce Pluckhahn, Curator, National Bowling Hall of Fame and Museum, Greendale, Wisconsin; Ray Nelson, Press Relations Manager, American Bowling Congress, Greendale, Wisconsin; and Bess Resnik, New York City.

I would also like to mention those sports figures mentioned in the book with whom I had personal contact: Sid Gillman, Victor Hershkowitz, Sandy Koufax, Red Holzman, Agnes Keleti, Angelica Rozeanu, Al Rosen, Esther Roth, Marshall Goldberg, Red Auerbach, Dolph Schayes, Harry Litwack, Tal Brody, Hank Greenberg, Brian Teacher, Shlomo Glickstein, Ken Holtzman, Angela Buxton, Henry Wittenberg, Julie Heldman, Benny Friedman, Art Heyman, Gretel Bergmann, Eva Szekely, Shimshon Brockman, Eitan Friedlander, and Dick Savitt.

The following were especially helpful in providing photographs: Michael P.

Aronstein, President, TCMA Ltd., Amawalk, New York; W. R. "Bill" Schroeder, Managing Director, First Interstate Bank Athletic Foundation, Los Angeles, California; Israel Government Press Office; Jewish Sports Hall of Fame; June Harrison Steitz, Library Director, Naismith Memorial Basketball Hall of Fame, Springfield, Massachusetts; Lev Borodulin, Tel Aviv; Eli Hershkowitz, Jerusalem; Rich Eng, NYRA Photo Services, New York Racing Association, Jamaica, New York; Burt Sugar, *Ring Magazine*; Debbie Harmison, Sports Information Director, Old Dominion University, Norfolk, Virginia; United Press International; Haskell Cohen.

Finally, no one was more important to this book than my wife, Elinor. Its shape and its content owe much to her. She has patiently edited drafts, collected photographs, offered advice, and made the entire enterprise one that contained few major burdens and many, many joys.

CONTENTS

MAJOR BIOGRAPHIES

THUMBNAIL SKETCHES

ISRAELI SPORTS FIGURES

PHOTO CREDITS

Acknowledgments and thanks are due to the following institutions and persons for having kindly permitted their photographs to be used in this book:

Professional Bowlers Association—pages 9, 103, 188; Basketball Hall of Fame—pages xiii, 56, 68, 82, 90, 101, 169, 200, 203; Jewish Sports Hall of Fame, Netanya, Israel—pages 6, 17, 24, 27, 37 (with *Daily Mirror*), 42, 51, 92, 105 (top, bottom right), 112, 115, 120, 123, 125, 130, 162, 179, 193, 195, 218, 219, 225, 232, 237(left), 239, 242 (right), 243 (left), 245 (left top, bottom), 255, 278 (bottom), 279, 280, 281; *Ring Magazine*—pages 11, 53, 61, 118, 133, 135, 139, 154, 177, 183, 234; Boston Celtics—page 14; Haskell Cohen—page 19; TCMA—pages 22, 29, 40, 78, 85, 107, 121, 127, 152, 166, 171, 173, 214; Shimshon Brockman and Eitan Friedlander—page 31; Israel Government Press Office—pages 34, 186, 242 (left), 243 (right), 252, 253, 255 (left), 258, 260, 261, 263, 264, 265, 266; First Interstate Bank Athletic Foundation—pages 45, 65, 148, 159, 163, 175; Pittsburgh Pirates—page 49; Harold O. Zimman/Haskell Cohen—page 57; World Maccabi Union—page 59; Philadelphia Eagles—page 70; Israel Tennis Center, Ramat Hasharon, Israel—pages 73, 165, 198, 208 (with Uzi Keren)—221, 223; Marshall Goldberg—page 76; Harold O. Zimman—pages 81, 95, 137; Pittsburgh Steelers—page 87; Victor Hershkowitz—page 98; Professional Bowlers Association—pages 103, 188; City College of New York—page 105 (bottom left); New York Knickerbockers—page 109; New York Racing Association—page 111; Old Dominion University—page 142; American Bowling Congress—pages 144, 227; Temple University—page 146; Women's Professional Bowling Association—page 150; Angelica Rozeanu—page 190; Los Angeles Dodgers—page 205; United Press International—page 212; Baltimore Orioles—page 216; Pinky Danilowitz—page 237 (right); New York Mets—page 245 (right); Wingate Institute of Sport, Netanya, Israel—page 278 (top).

FOREWORD

by

RED AUERBACH

A long two-handed set shot by Dolph Schayes. Eddie Gottlieb, lovable, ex-owner, schedule-maker, rules-maker and a member of the Basketball Hall of Fame. And many other great players running with the best of the pros, I guess that's what a book like this is all about.

Great Jews in sports: Nat Holman, perhaps the greatest player of the Original Celtics back in the '20s. Red Holzman did a fantastic job while coaching the New York Knicks. I remember the great track star and famous announcer, Marty Glickman, who represented the Jews in the confrontation with Hitler back in 1936. Those are the things that stick with me.

The question of just who are the greatest Jews in sports grows on you. Everybody knows Sandy Koufax, Mark Spitz, and Hank Greenberg. Anyone who's followed boxing knows Barney Ross and Benny Leonard. These were unquestionably athletes who ranked at the top of their sports. Jews, however, have been reaching the pinnacle in sports far more broadly than the mention of these few names would suggest.

As I leafed through the pages of *Great Jews in Sports,* I felt a sense of pride that Jews have had such an impact. It's people like the Hungarian ping pong player, Victor Barna. Like the Hungarian swimmer, Eva Szekely. Like the British sprinter, Harold Abrahams. Each of them has a wonderful story.

What makes this book distinctive is that it is not merely a review of sports statistics. The men and women whose stories comprise this volume lived lives filled with a mixture of heartbreak (Barney Ross toward the end of his life) and of poignancy (Gretel Bergmann losing out on a chance to compete in the 1936 Berlin Olympics because of Hitler) as well as the story of victory.

Of course, a major theme strikes the reader throughout the sketches of these athletes and coaches: for the parents of many of these men and women sports were a real taboo. Jews just didn't aspire to careers in athletics. A lawyer or a doctor or an engineer, yes. But, not a bowler, a football player, or a ping pong player. Those were not the spheres in which Jews strove to excel.

But what the older generation couldn't realize was that sports was a passport to a better life for some of the people in this book. Sports gave them a chance to excel, to make a living. Furthermore, in some cases at least, like Benny Leonard or Sid Gordon, sports was all they ate, drank, and breathed. I know how the older generation must have felt, but I have to admit that I side with their children, the ones who wanted to skip the free professions, to head for the tennis court, or the football stadium, or the boxing ring.

Of course, in some sports Jews have reached the heights, while in others they have not. In ping pong, handball, and even boxing, Jews have climbed to the top. But, they've had a difficult time in golf, and in tennis for that matter. And, of course, in my own sport, basketball, only a relative handful have made it big in college and in the pros. Moreover, while there were quite a number of Jews playing basketball in the 1920s, 1930s, and 1940s, that number has dwindled to only a few in the 1980s. I don't know why it's that way. It just is.

If this book has done one thing for me, it's aroused my interest in the whole subject of Jewish sportsmen. Like many others, I guess I had thought I knew who would naturally be in this book. Well, some of the sports figures included here I hadn't heard of, while some that I thought would belong really don't.

I'd like to think that youngsters, and oldsters for that matter, who read *Great Jews in Sports,* will find new heroes to emulate. These are, after all, men and women who have achieved a great deal, who have overcome intense pressures, great injustice here and there, and much physical wear and tear. They have made something of themselves, and if a youngster finds in one or more of them a worthy model, I believe he's making a good choice.

INTRODUCTION

As a young boy, I had the same obsession with major league baseball as most American youngsters. But I also had a grandfather who, every time Sid Gordon (the great National Leaguer of the 1940s and 1950s) came to bat, reminded me that "Gordon is Jewish." I could not possibly have figured out—nor did I bother to ask my grandfather—how Sid's religious heritage could have been related to his "socking" the ball out of the park. I was mostly interested in the number of home runs Gordon hit that particular season. But my grandfather's "hang up" about Gordon's Jewishness was the stimulus that started me in search of great Jews in sports.

Common knowledge has it that few Jews have had noteworthy sports careers. This may have been true for a long time. Indeed, Judaism traditionally eschewed a sports culture. In antiquity, sports were associated with pagan worship, and for centuries Jews did not regard sports as an area of life to be pursued or a realm in which success should or could be sought. So Jewish parents encouraged their children to become lawyers, doctors, engineers, and teachers. The parents of many of those who people this book offered this traditional advice, but their sons and daughters still sought success and glory in the gym or on the playing field. And, over the years, these "rebels" from the traditional Jewish pursuits have accumulated impressive records of achievement in sports.

The point is—and I'm certainly not the first to make it—that Jews have been doing quite well in the sports world dating back to the nineteenth century. Their achievements have not received the acclaim they deserve. Indeed, until the *Encyclopedia of Jews in Sports* appeared in 1965 (a book to which I am greatly indebted), no one had really focused on the Jew in sports. Since the *Encyclopedia*, Jews have continued to succeed in sports in even larger numbers than in the period before the 1960s.

So, now there is ample room for another look at Jewish sports figures. And, it seemed to me, there was good reason not to just attempt another encyclopedia look at the subject (*Encyclopedia* authors Bernard Postal, Jesse Silver, and Roy Silver did that quite well), but to pick 100 or so of the most interesting and most important Jewish athletes and coaches in history, to tell their stories, and by doing so, to demonstrate that Jews have triumphed in the world of sports time and time again.

This book is not just a list of people. Instead, *Great Jews in Sports* is designed to entertain and enlighten by telling some of the most heartwarming and fascinating

1

stories of the best Jewish athletes ever. The reader may be surprised to discover that Jews have, in several sports, actually climbed to the top. Some of these athletes are famous. One thinks not only of Mark Spitz, the Olympic swimmer who outdid almost every Olympian who had come before him. There was also Sandy Koufax, the gutsy left-hander for the Brooklyn Dodgers. And Hank Greenberg, the famous baseball power-hitter of the 1930s and 1940s. And Sid Luckman, the great pro football quarterback of the 1940s.

Some of the athletes in this book became known outside sports circles only after their personal stories were popularized. Harold Abrahams, the British track star at the 1924 Olympics, was probably known only to track enthusiasts until the 1981 movie *Chariots of Fire* recounted his story. Boxing fans may have been aware of Barney Ross, but the public at large came to know him when his autobiography, *Monkey on My Back,* was made into a film. And, there are those who have remained less well-known, but who nonetheless reached the pinnacle in their sports—figures like Jimmy Jacobs and Victor Hershkowitz, the great handball players of the 1950s; Victor Barna, a Hungarian, and one of the greatest male table tennis players of all time; Angelica Rozeanu, a Romanian who was unquestionably the greatest female table tennis player ever.

The roles played by Jews in sports reflect the change in the social and economic roles played by Jews in society in general. The 1920s and 1930s produced many Jewish boxers and 17 champions. As for other minority groups, boxing was a way to escape the slums. So Ted "Kid" Lewis, Battling Levinsky, Barney Ross, and others used their fists to get ahead. By the 1970s tennis, once a province of the elite, had become a sport in which Jews excelled. Though there have been some great Jewish baseball players (such as Hank Greenberg, Sandy Koufax, and Johnny Kling), relatively speaking the number of Jews in that sport has never been large.

Some Jewish sports stars have been caught up in the history of their times. Gretel Bergmann might have won an Olympic gold medal if she had not been a victim of Nazi anti-Semitism in 1936. Elias Katz was killed fighting for the State of Israel in that country's war of liberation. Eva Szekely joined many of her fellow Hungarian athletes in defecting after the 1956 Olympics (though she later returned). And Esther Roth reached the semifinals of the 100-meter race, but had to bow out when Palestinian Arab terrorists murdered 11 of her Israeli teammates at those Olympics in Munich.

Of course, anti-Semitism has always been experienced by Jews in sports as in other fields. Gretel Bergmann had to face the devastating anti-Semitic policies of the Nazis, as mentioned above. Louis Rubenstein, the figure skater, had enormous difficulty trying to compete in the unofficial World Figure Skating Championships in Moscow in 1890. Tennis ace Angela Buxton, the only Jewish Wimbledon finalist, had her application to join the All-England Club rejected for years. Dick Savitt, the Wimbledon champion of the early 1950s, was passed over for Davis Cup play. In each instance, anti-Semitism was thought to have played a role, major or minor.

Getting the stories of the greatest Jewish sports figures down on paper has been challenging. Perhaps my most difficult task was to determine which figures to include. I decided to enlist the aid of experts in the field of sports. Of course, each expert has his own biases, and I was offered many varying opinions. When a seemingly worthwhile name was brought up, I would look into the life and career of the person suggested. On occasion, I would discover that the person wasn't even Jewish! I realized fairly early that some criteria would have to be established to determine which "Jewish" athletes would be included in the book. If I were to limit the book to approximately 100 sports figures, then I would have to be fairly rigid about who is and who isn't a Jew. I chose to go along with the Orthodox definition of a Jew: A Jew is someone born of a Jewish mother. In only one case did an overriding consideration lead me to include someone who didn't fit that definition. Tennis star Tom Okker's mother is not Jewish but his father is. But because Okker has so clearly identified himself as a Jew, I felt he should be included. He is the only exception, and as far as I have been able to determine, all the other stars fit my rigid definition.

By adhering to this definition, I felt compelled to exclude a number of athletes whom others have counted as Jewish or who are known as Jewish. I'm thinking of the great fighter of the 1930s, Max Baer, considered Jewish by virtue of everything about him but his mother. He wore a Jewish Star of David on his boxing trunks, and he called himself a Jew. But, in fact, his closest Jewish relative was his paternal grandfather. Emil "Bus" Mosbacher, the yachting champion, was born a Jew but became a Christian. I have chosen to exclude athletes who were born Jewish but did not identify themselves as Jewish throughout their lives. Thus I had to exclude a leading Princeton University football player of the early 1900s, Phil King, who turned to Christian Science later in life, as well as Peter Revson, the racing driver of the early 1960s, who was buried as a Christian. Then, there is the intriguing example of Rod Carew, a Panamanian baseball player (what a player!) married to a Jewish woman. His children are being raised as Jews, and he says he plans to convert to Judaism when he quits baseball. But I've left Carew, seventimes batting champion, off the list.

I expect that some sports lovers will take issue with which personalities I have chosen to include or exclude from the book. But to them I make the following comment: When limiting oneself to selecting 100 or so of the Jewish greats (the list could have easily grown much larger), there is no way to satisfy everyone. I regret if a favorite player or coach of yours has been excluded.

Another point. I've deliberately weighted the list toward the Americans. I have tried my best not to minimize the contributions of non-Americans, and a substantial number of these do appear. But the reader will quickly perceive that preference has been given to American sports and sportsmen. One reason is my feeling that most readers of this book would be more familiar with American sports and sports figures than with non-Americans.

In this volume, the baseball world is well represented, as is the world of football, basketball, and tennis. This is no accident. These are the sports where Jews have really made a mark. Still, I have included figures prominent in the lesser known sports with the intention of offering the reader information about athletes of whom he might have heard little and about whom he would like to know more.

I hope you, the reader, get as much enjoyment and satisfaction from reading these profiles as I did in researching and writing them.

Robert Slater

Jerusalem, Israel

March 1983

GREAT JEWS
IN SPORTS

HAROLD ABRAHAMS

A Chariot of Fire

ABRAHAMS, HAROLD MAURICE (born December 15, 1899, in Bedford, England; died January 14, 1978) English sprinter. One of the leading sprinters in English track history. By winning the 100-meter dash in the 1924 Paris Olympics, he became the first European to win an Olympic sprint title, as well as the first and only Briton to capture such a title. A lawyer by profession, Abrahams was admitted to the bar in 1924 and practiced until 1940. He also became one of England's most important sports administrators.

The product of a wealthy, athletic family, Harold Abrahams took up track at eight years of age. In 1911 he won his first 100-yard race. His time was 14.0 seconds. By age 19 he had won both the 100-yard dash and the long jump at the British public schools championships. A law student at Cambridge University from 1920 to 1923, he became one of the school's greatest athletes. The secret of his success in running, he once quipped, was being born with long legs.

But it was more than that, obviously. Abrahams competed in the 1920 Antwerp Olympics, managed to win his 100-meter heat in 11.0 seconds, but was eliminated in the next round. In the long jump, he came in twentieth. After the Olympics, Abrahams decided to concentrate on sprinting.

Though he spoke little of the subject, Abrahams was conscious of the subtle discrimination against him because he was a Jew. Sprinting afforded him an opportunity to prove to those gentlemen who practiced anti-Semitism that he could beat them at their own sport. With this in mind, he took the then-unusual step of hiring a personal coach for the six months before the 1924 Olympics. Such a tactic, if not against the formal rules, was certainly against the unwritten code of amateur sport. The man he hired, Sam Mussabini, half-Arab, half-French, was considered to be the best sprinting coach in Britain.

Harold agreed with Sam that it was important to concentrate on the 100-meter dash at the Paris Olympics, and that the 200-meter race was secondary. Three times a week the two men went through a rigorous training schedule. Abrahams worked meticulously on perfecting the start, the arm action, the placing and digging of starting holes (there were no starting blocks in those days), and on controlling the accuracy of the first few strides. "I always carried a piece of string the length of the first stride," Abrahams once explained, "and marked the spot on the track at which I gazed intently when I heard the word *set.*"

The intense training had its side benefit when, on June 7, 1924, a month before Paris, Abrahams set the English long-jump record of 7.38 meters (24 feet, 2½ inches), a mark that stood for 32 years. That same afternoon he ran the 100-yard dash in 9.6 seconds, but the record was not submitted for recognition because the track was on a slight downgrade.

To his chagrin, Harold Abrahams was selected to compete in the 100 meters, 200 meters, long jump, and relay in Paris. Unconventionally, he penned an anonymous letter to the *Daily Express* (signing it "A Famous International Athlete"), in which he suggested that it was "unfortunate" that Abrahams should have to compete in four events; he should at least have been allowed to drop out of the long jump. The "Famous International Athlete" added: "The authorities surely do not imagine that he can perform at long jumping at two o'clock and run 200 meters at 2:30 on the same afternoon." The letter, closing with a plea that

Abrahams be permitted to focus on the 100 meters, had its intended effect: Harold was excused from long jumping.

With four American speedsters competing among the 75 entries for the 100-meter race in Paris on July 6, 1924, Abrahams thought little of his chances. But in the first round he breezed to an easy triumph in 11.0 seconds. Remarkably, in the second round he equaled the Olympic record of 10.6 seconds. Could he maintain his top form in the semifinals and finals the next day?

Settling in his holes for the semifinals at 3:15 P.M., July 6, 1924, Abrahams nearly lost the race at the outset. Noticing a runner on his right move slightly, he started badly, figuring there would be a recall. There wasn't. He still won the race in 10.6 seconds. Then he prepared for the final. For those next four hours, he felt "like a condemned man feels just before going to the scaffold."

At 7:05 P.M., Harold Maurice Abrahams went to his mark for the final. An eyewitness, Bernard Darwin, described Abrahams in midcourse as "scudding along like some vast bird with outstretched wings, a spectacle positively appalling in its grandeur." He had managed to get in an extra stride (46 instead of 45). Coupled with his now-famous "drop finish," this provided enough spurt for him to take the race by a full two yards in 10.6 seconds. It was the third time in 26 hours that Harold Abrahams had equaled the Olympic record! In Harold's view, his victory was not only a triumph for Britain, but also a fitting rebuttal to the anti-Semitism that he had discerned within the British establishment.

Harold was not as successful in the 200-meter race. He reached the finals after clocking a personal best of 22.0 seconds in a heat, but came in last in the final. He did, however, win a silver medal in the 4 × 100-meter relay.

Harold Abraham's track career came to an end prematurely. In May 1925, he broke his leg while long jumping. He would never compete again. The accident eliminated his chance of becoming Europe's first 25-footer in the long jump.

After his track days, Abrahams became an athletics administrator as well as a sportswriter. From 1925 to 1967, Abrahams was athletics correspondent for the *Sunday Times* and one of the BBC's first broadcasters. A 1955 profile of him in the *Sunday Times* described Abrahams as a prophet and hero to the younger generation.

Abrahams had a passion for Gilbert and Sullivan (he could quote passages from their plays at ease). He also had the unusual hobby of holding a stopwatch on anything that could be timed. He timed Wimbledon rallies, after-dinner speeches, concert applause, and moving stairways. He even admitted to having "been conceited enough" to time the applause for one of his own speeches.

He was one of the three official timekeepers when British miler Roger Bannister ran his historic four-minute mile in 1954 (Harold later presented his Omega Chronometer, stopped at Bannister's record time of 3 minutes, 59.4 seconds, to Bannister).

Harold was something of a male chauvinist when it came to the issue of female participation in track and field competition. In 1928, he observed: "I do not consider that women are built for really violent exercise of the kind that is the essence of competition. One has only to see them practicing to realize how awkward they are on the running track."

He was one of the most influential members of the British Amateur Athletics Board, serving as its treasurer from 1948 to 1968. The public and press came to regard Abrahams and secretary Jack Crump as the two men who virtually ran British athletics. Both came under heavy criticism for writing and broadcasting on athletics while holding the highest official posts. Abrahams served as chairman of the Board from 1968 to 1975. In November 1976, he fulfilled a life's ambition by being elected president of the AAA.

Harold Abrahams' only civil honor was awarded him for his work as a civil servant: from 1930 to 1963 he had been secretary of the National Parks Commission. In 1981, three years after his death, Abrahams was the subject of a major movie, *Chariots of Fire,* which portrayed the influence of religion on athletes.

Abrahams is a member of the Jewish Sports Hall of Fame in Israel.

BARRY ASHER

The Best Unknown Bowler in the Country

ASHER, BARRY (born July 14, 1946, in Costa Mesa, California-   )
American bowler. In 1976, he became the fifteenth man in the history
of the Professional Bowlers Association tour to win 10 or more titles.
His most successful year was 1973 when he won two PBA tournaments and $57,196 in prize money.

Barry took up bowling at age eight when a friend volunteered to pay Barry's
way if he would bowl with him. At age 10 Barry was averaging 170, and at age 11,
180.

His father died the next year, 1958. "His last words to me," said Barry, "were
about bowling. From that time on, I devoted my life to becoming a pro bowler."
Barry and his mother—who had become his biggest fan—moved to Santa Ana,
California.

Bowling in adult competition at age 14, Asher averaged 200 for the first time in
1959 at the Orange County (California) Open League. He continued to average
200 that year, considered quite respectable even for a pro. "By then," said the
Californian, "I thought I knew all there was to know about bowling." But at age 15,
he fared poorly in some tournaments: "It could have been the best thing that
happened to me. I then knew what I didn't know."

By age 16, he was back in form, and he produced the first of three career 300
games at Maple Lanes in Garden Grove, California.

He turned professional in 1964 at age 18, the earliest age possible for pro
status. He became the youngest person ever to win a PBA-sponsored tournament
when he won the Pacific Coast PBA Open in January 1965, in Santa Ana,
California. Barry then went on the summer tour without much luck, but in 1966 his
fortunes changed: "All of a sudden I got the right help and won. I guess I had the
right conditions. I didn't average much to win, but I beat some great bowlers. It just
happened."

He won the tenth time he bowled on the PBA circuit. That was in Encino,
California, in 1966. That same year he took a second PBA title in New Orleans.
Joining the pro tour full-time in 1968, he did moderately well: in 1969, he won
$12,635; in 1970, $17,710; and in 1971, his first really successful year, $34,528.

In 1971, Barry Asher assured a place for himself in the record books when he
won the PBA tournament at the Chippewa Lanes in South Bend, Indiana. There,
on September 13, he won the highest-scoring championship in PBA history with a
record 247 average for 42 games. In his first six games he scored an incredible
264 average. He also rolled one of the 11 perfect games recorded in the
tournament.

Three weeks later, in St. Louis, Missouri, Barry won another PBA title.

In 1972, he won two more PBA titles, the Japan Gold Cup, and the Cranston,
Rhode Island, tournament. Financially, his best year was 1973, when he was
second on the winnings list with $57,196. He won PBA titles that year in Las
Vegas, Nevada, and Tucson, Arizona.

In 1974, Asher's career went into a slump that he attributed to pressure, tension, and possibly a loss of ambition. The slump was most conspicuous on his approach, where he consistently balked. Instead of taking the usual smooth steps to the line, he would often hesitate, stumble and draw back. In the spring of that year, Asher acknowledged that he was seeking the help of a hypnotist in the Los Angeles area. His winnings that year totaled only $16,773, and he won no PBA titles.

The following year was only slightly better. Asher did win a PBA tournament in Alameda, California, his first since his excellent 1973 year. He also finished second in the Firestone Tournament of Champions. But he bowled in only 15 tournaments and earned $29,310.

In 1976, Barry cut down further on his PBA tour activity. He did bowl in Tucson, Arizona, near his home in Costa Mesa, California, and took the tournament for the tenth PBA title of his career. Winning there depressed him as much as it excited him, for few people around the country would know about his feat since bowling was not brought via TV into the homes of millions of Americans.

Asher recalled how he felt after the Tucson victory: "Mark (Roth) and Joe (Berardi) were with me and we drove all night to make a practice session for the Best Ball Doubles the next day. At one point, Mark was sleeping in the back seat and Joey was driving and I was thinking about the fact that only a few hours earlier

I was the best bowler in the country, yet nobody was going to know it because it was only on Home Box Office TV." He made $25,000 on the tour in 1976.

After 1976, Barry stopped his membership in the PBA, and the curly-haired bowler said he has few regrets: "I liked bowling on the tour. But the tour itself is just one big, constant hassle." Added Barry: "I wonder what would have happened if I had listened to my mother and been a nice Jewish boy and gone to college. At my present age, I'd probably be a CPA or a lawyer and be making $40,000 or $50,000 a year. So there's pros and cons to bowling as a career. I made my bed and I'm sleeping in it."

In 1976, Asher started a new career, going into partnership with Dick and Diane Braasch to form Braascher Distributors, a clothing apparel business. Clothing had always been important to Asher. He had been known for his sartorial elegance as a bowler. In 1970, his fellow-players voted him one of the "best-dressed players" on the tour. He wore custom-made pants with lightning streaks, bowling pins and bowling balls as part of the decorative scheme.

"Often," Barry noted in 1970, "especially when my game is off and I'm feeling low, I dress for dinner. Dressed up, I feel better. It's like a tonic. It peps me up and I come back for the night (bowling) action a new man." His wardrobe was one of the most extensive and expensive of any athlete. His specially-designed slacks cost almost $500 for three pairs.

Though he renewed his PBA membership in 1980, Barry has done relatively little bowling since retiring from the tour in 1976.

ABE ATTELL

San Francisco's Little Champ

ATTELL, ABE "THE LITTLE CHAMP" (born February 22, 1884, in San Francisco, California; died February 6, 1969) American boxer. World featherweight champion from 1901 to 1912. Damon Runyon called Abe one of the five best fighters of all time. Nat Fleischer said he was the third best ever in his class. Attell's career record: 167 pro bouts, 91 wins (47 by knockout), 10 losses, 17 draws, and 49 no decisions.

Attell was born Albert Knoehr on George Washington's birthday but was named Abe for Abraham Lincoln. A poor boy from a large San Francisco family, he learned to fight at an early age. "We were Jews living in an Irish neighborhood," he recalled. "You can guess the rest. I used to fight three, four, five, 10 times a day." On the street, in the vacant lots, on the docks, a little of Abie's blood stained every street in Frisco.

But then he learned that he could get paid for fighting, and so he quickly gave up the streets and went over to the "amateur" clubs. He was only 5 feet, 4 inches and weighed 122 pounds, but he was a hard hitter. "When I started I was only 16 years old," Abe observed, "and I thought the easy way was to knock 'em out." That's exactly what he did. He enjoyed the work at the clubs because he could trade the medals he won for cash from the club promoters: a winner's medal then was worth $15, a hefty sum for a poor 16-year-old at the turn of the twentieth century.

Abe turned pro when he was almost 17. In his first pro fight he received $100 for fighting a 10-round draw with one Jockey Bozeman. Attell was working as a Western Union delivery boy at the time. His mother had been against his fighting, and demanded that he give up the ring for good. When he brought home $15 from one fight and showed it to her, she relented, becoming his number-one fan. A nice Jewish boy had no business mixing with the boxing game, but the Attell family could certainly use those handsome sums Abe started bringing in.

Abe's career began with an incredible number of knockouts. He won the first 24 of his 29 fights by felling his opponents for the count of 10. "I was a conceited fighter," acknowledged Attell. "I thought I could lick anybody. For a long time, I was right."

But the price for the knockouts was high; Abe was constantly being injured. He admired the way James J. Corbett and George Dixon boxed: skipping, blocking, ducking, and sidestepping punches. Abe realized there was more to boxing than just trying to knock one's opponent out and getting injured far too often in the process. "The light dawned," noted Attell. "A fellow could be a prizefighter and not get hurt, provided he was smart enough. I learned that lesson way back in 1900 and I remembered it until I quit boxing in 1915."

His first important triumph was a 20-round decision over Jack Dempsey in Pueblo, Colorado, in September 1901. He reported the win to his mother with a wire: "Dear Mother win in 20 rounds easy Abe." Instead of telegraphing his punches, he was telegraphing his victories.

Attell won the featherweight title the next month, surviving a four-man elimination contest for the crown; he defeated George Dixon in a 15-round decision in St. Louis to take the prize.

He successfully defended his title 12 times over the next 10 years until he finally lost to Johnny Kilbane in 20 rounds on February 22, 1912, in Vernon, California. The setback occurred on Abe's 28th birthday. For losing that bout he received $15,500, the biggest purse of his career.

Attell claimed that his greatest thrill was in defeating Battling Nelson, though the record books (for reasons that have not been properly explained) indicate that the fight, held in San Francisco in 1908, ended in a draw after 15 rounds. It may well be that Abe convinced himself thereafter that he *should have won* the match—and subsequently tried to rewrite history ever so slightly.

Attell's name was mentioned frequently during the probe that followed the infamous 1919 Chicago White Sox World Series baseball scandal. Attell was first linked to the scandal when a magazine story described him as sitting in the bar of a Cincinnati hotel with a bale of hundred dollar bills on his lap, trying to bet on the Cincinnati Reds—against the White Sox in the World Series.

He was indicted in Chicago on a conspiracy charge in connection with allegations that ball players and gamblers had conspired to fix the World Series. But, because of insufficient evidence, he was exonerated. Abe called the charges against him lies.

Abe was indeed a gambling man. He had spent his free time at racetracks, dice games, sporting events—anywhere a bet could be made. "I have always gambled and I'm no angel," he said after the scandal, "but I was born on Washington's birthday and have tried to live up to the reputation of the father of our country where truth and honesty are concerned."

Attell's business life and his private life were not successful. His first marriage ended in divorce. During the long spells between title bouts, Abe fought six-round bouts in small cities, offering $100 to any local youngster who could stay the distance. It brought in the crowds and filled his pockets with some cash.

Abe's business fortunes improved after 1939 with his marriage to the former Mae O'Brien who helped him manage a tavern on the East side of New York. Though long retired from boxing, he was a regular figure at Madison Square Garden bouts until he had to enter a nursing home. During those years he liked to refer to himself as "the oldest living ex-champion."

The Jewish Sports Hall of Fame in Israel announced on December 1, 1982 that Abe Attell had become a member of the Hall of Fame and would be inducted in the spring, 1983.

ARNOLD AUERBACH

Most Successful Coach in Basketball History

AUERBACH, ARNOLD J. "RED" (born September 20, 1917, in Brooklyn, New York-) American basketball coach. Coach and later general manager and president of the Boston Celtics of the

National Basketball Association. He was the most successful basketball coach in history, establishing the Celtics as one of the great sports organizations. As Celtics' head coach between 1950 and 1966, Auerbach led his team to nine NBA titles (eight in succession), and 11 division titles. His overall coaching record was 1,037–548, the best ever recorded by an NBA coach.

Auerbach's father, Hyman, was a Russian immigrant and his mother, Marie, American-born. Red began playing basketball at P.S. 122 in the Williamsburg section of Brooklyn, and became a guard for the Eastern District High School varsity team. As a senior he captained the team and made All-Scholastic second team. He also captained the handball team.

In February 1936, Red entered Seth Low Junior College on an athletic scholarship. The school was the Brooklyn branch of Columbia University. In 1937, he went on to George Washington University and was a star basketball player there until 1940. In his last year, Red was the leading college scorer in the Washington, D.C. area, averaging 10.6 points per game. His major field of study was physical education with a biology minor.

After college, Auerbach coached St. Albans Prep School and Roosevelt High School in Washington, D.C. In 1941, he married Dorothy Lewis and received his M.A. from George Washington University. His thesis was on physical education programs for junior high schools. From 1943 to 1946, he served in the U.S. navy. As an ensign he directed intramural sports at the Norfolk, Virginia, naval base. Later, promoted to lieutenant, Auerbach served as rehabilitation officer at the Bethesda, Maryland Naval Hospital.

When Mike Uline, owner of the Washington, D.C., Arena, decided to create a Washington-based pro basketball club in 1946, Auerbach successfully persuaded the owner to hire him as a founding coach. "It cost me less than $500 in phone calls to assemble that club," Auerbach recalled with a smile. In their first three seasons, the Washington Capitals won 115 and lost 53. Ironically, one of Auerbach's first decisions as coach was to pass over a popular All-American guard from Holy Cross named Bob Cousy. The Capitals' head coach felt that he had to build up his team so he acquired three players instead of taking only Cousy. Cousy ended up playing for the Boston Celtics.

In 1946–47, Red's team finished in first place in the Eastern division of the Basketball Association of America (the forerunner of the NBA). His 49–11 record was the best won-lost percentage in the league's history. After three successful seasons with the Capitals, Auerbach moved to the Tri-City (Moline and Rock Island, Illinois, and Davenport, Iowa) Blackhawks as coach. The team, a member of the new NBA, was 28–29 for the 1949–50 season, the only year an Auerbach team lost more games than it won. The Blackhawks' owner made a trade without informing Auerbach, a trade Auerbach opposed, and he quit in protest. Mutual friends brought Auerbach and the Boston Celtics owner Walter Brown together. Auerbach agreed to move to Boston, and an historic association began. Brown gave his new coach free rein to choose his players. In April 1950, Red replaced Alvin Julian as head coach of the Celtics.

Auerbach had his work cut out for him: the Celtics had finished last in the Eastern Division the previous season, with the third worst record in NBA history.

Things changed under Auerbach. In his first six seasons, the team finished second in the Eastern division four times. Then in 1956–57, with Bill Russell added to the lineup, the Celtics won their first NBA title.

The next season they lost to St. Louis in the NBA Championship final, but then the Celtics went on a winning spree unprecedented in NBA history. With Russell, Bob Cousy, Bill Sharman, Frank Ramsey, Tom Heinsohn, John Havlicek, and the Jones boys—K.C. and Sam—the Celtics won the league title eight straight times—from 1959 to 1966. Auerbach built a team, not just individual players—the sixth man could start, if necessary. Red was not a good loser: "Show me a good loser," he liked to say, "and I'll show you a loser."

His coaching techniques included fining players for every minute they were late for practice. "I have a $.25 fine for every minute a guy's late. If (Bill) Russell comes in at 10:10 A.M., it costs him $2.50. I'd rather fine the big guys. Hell, anybody can fine a rookie."

Instinct guided his coaching technique as much as anything else. He would know when to substitute, when a player had soured. He could get more from players than other coaches. "You take a washed-up guy," he once said, "and if you instill in him his pride again and create desire, you can squeeze a good year or two out of him."

He infuriated fans when he complained about bad calls, and was often pounded with eggs and vegetables. He was assessed $17,000 in fines during his career. His practice of lighting a cigar when victory appeared assured infuriated the opposition.

He was ahead of his time on the racial issue. He brought the first black player, Chuck Cooper, into the NBA and in 1966 he made Bill Russell the Boston Celtic coach. Auerbach was inducted into the Basketball Hall of Fame in 1968.

He has given basketball clinics around the world, including Eastern Europe. In 1964, for example, he took a pro All-Star team, which included Oscar Robertson, Bob Cousy, and Bill Russell, on a visit to Egypt, Romania, and Poland.

When Walter Brown, co-owner of the Celtics, died in 1964, Red Auerbach succeeded him as vice president and general manager. Lou Pieri, co-owner, remained in the presidency. In 1965, Auerbach was named NBA Coach of the Year, an honor voted him for the first time only after winning eight NBA titles. One complaint against him was that anyone could have won with Bill Russell, a charge many thought unfair.

When Red retired from coaching in 1966, he had led his team to division and world titles in nine of his last 10 seasons. To appreciate just how great a coach Red was, it is worth noting that only five other NBA coaches have recorded 500 or more victories in their careers. As vice president and president (beginning in 1971), as well as general manager of the Celtics between 1966 and 1981, Auerbach presided over Celtic teams which won another five NBA titles. Boston won NBA championships in 1968 (the year Red was elected to the Basketball Hall of Fame), 1969, 1974, 1980, and 1981 (the year he was chosen NBA Executive of the Year).

Bill Russell pointed out the greatness of his coach and mentor in his autobiography, *Second Wind:*

"Red would never let things get very far out of focus. He thought about winning more than I thought about eating when I was little. He ached when we didn't win: his whole body would be thrown out of whack when we lost. He didn't care about a player's statistics or reputation in the newspapers: all he thought about was the final score and who had helped put it on the board. He was our gyroscope, programmed solely for winning, and it was difficult for any of us to deviate from the course he set for us."

Auerbach is a member of the Jewish Sports Hall of Fame in Israel.

GYOZO VICTOR BARNA

The Greatest Table Tennis Player Who Ever Lived

BARNA, GYOZO VICTOR (born August 24, 1911, in Budapest, Hungary; died February 28, 1972) Hungarian table tennis player. Barna won 16 world championships, including five singles titles. He accumulated more than 1,000 prizes and won nearly every national championship. Ivor Montagu, president of the International Table Tennis Federation from 1926 to 1966, called Victor "the greatest table tennis player who ever lived."

Victor came upon table tennis—or as he called it, *"Tisch tennis"*—as a youngster when his friend (and subsequent rival) Laci Bellak discovered a ping-pong table among his Bar Mitzvah presents. The two boys practiced with one another frequently. "The very first time I took a bat (paddle) in my hand," recalled Victor, "I knew that this was the game for me."

Two events helped make table tennis Victor Barna's game. The first occurred when he watched the two top table tennis clubs in Budapest play. "There's nothing to it," the young Victor told himself. "You can do it just as well."

The second event happened while he was playing football (soccer) for a local sports club, even though youngsters were barred from membership in such clubs.

If a youngster were caught playing for a club, he risked expulsion from school. Although Victor played under an assumed name, he was nevertheless discovered and, to avoid being expelled, promised the school authorities that he would never play football again.

From that time on Barna concentrated on his "bat" and the little, celluloid ball. He played in his first table tennis tournament on December 25, 1925, coming in third and receiving a small bronze plaque which he carried with him for a long time thereafter. For his fifteenth birthday he was given a ping-pong table, and sixteen months later—December 26, 1927—Victor enjoyed his first tournament triumph by winning the Hungarian Junior National Championship.

In 1929, Barna was a member of the Hungarian team which won the Swaythling Cup, symbolic of the men's world team championship. (The Cup was donated by Lady Swaythling, mother of table tennis administrator Ivor Montagu.) The following season he won the first of his five world singles championships in Berlin.

In Budapest the next year (1931), he lost in the finals of the world singles championship. But he won the title back in 1932 in Prague, and kept it for the next three years. The year 1932 was a great disappointment for Barna. Though he won both the world singles and men's doubles, his Hungarian team lost the Swaythling Cup competition to Czechoslovakia. Victor was convinced his teammates could have done better.

Afterwards in the dressing room, speaking to them, he had some simple advice: "Forget about the crowd, even your opponent, his style and even yours. All you must see is the ball as it leaves your opponent's bat, and then return it. Place it so that it is out of his reach. It is all very simple; you have to keep the ball in play just one hit more than the other fellow does."

He himself tried to increase his own power of concentration: the results were impressive. He won the singles title and the men's doubles title in 1933, 1934, and 1935. Victor also helped his Hungarian teammates gain the Swaythling Cup team championship. (He was in fact the men's double champion each year from 1929 to 1935 and again in 1939. He was also mixed doubles champ in 1932 and 1935.)

Barna's greatest performance came in February 1935, when during the world championships at the Empire Pool and Sports Stadium in Wembley, England, he took the world singles, doubles, and mixed doubles. His native Hungary also retained the Swaythling Cup that year.

Victor Barna was small, fleet-footed, and wiry, returning almost impossible shots with ease. His backhand was especially effective, and he played nine out of every 10 strokes backhand. Victor and his Jewish colleagues played all over Europe in the early 1930s, helping to popularize a sport that was then little-known. In 1933, he and another Hungarian Jew, Sandor Glancz, joined to win the world doubles title. As a result, the following year the two were invited to tour the United States for four weeks, becoming the first foreign table tennis players ever to reach the U.S. In Chicago, they played before an enthusiastic crowd of 4,000.

Unfortunately, an accident cost Victor Barna the chance to continue his championship play. On May 10, 1935, he was injured in an auto crash in France, where he had been living for a year. His right arm, the one he used in table tennis, was so badly injured that the doctors could repair the fracture only by implanting in his arm a silver plate, held by four screws. Those same doctors told him he

would never play again. Barna did play, however, though the caliber of his singles game was seriously affected.

On April 27, 1939, he married the former Susie Arany, and he and his wife had some success in a few mixed doubles tournaments. They were semifinalists in a Wembley open tournament in 1940, and runners-up in the East India Open Championship in Calcutta in 1949, as well as in the Irish Open in 1950.

Victor retired from singles competition in 1949, and five years later, he quit competitive doubles as well. Until the end of his career, Barna had the experts mesmerized. Table tennis administrator Montagu wrote that Barna's "backhand was so spectacular that few spectators appreciated that the winning rally position had often been opened by his forehand. His positioning was so perfect that with the slightest change of foot angle and body balance his flick could instantly and invisibly alter the direction of the kill from diagonal to straight or vice versa. . . ."

During World War II, Victor gave table tennis exhibitions for the British Red Cross and the troops. He also joined the British army's commando unit.

In 1946, Barna joined the Dunlop Sports Company, helping this major sports equipment firm market its own line of table tennis equipment, including tables, nets, and a "Barna Super Ball." Barna eventually became head of all Dunlop sporting equipment for the international market.

In 1947, he became a British national.

Barna suffered a fatal heart attack on one of his frequent overseas tours promoting Dunlop Sports equipment in Lima, Peru in 1972.

Gyozo Barna is a member of the Jewish Sports Hall of Fame in Israel.

HERMAN BARRON

The Greatest Jewish Golfer

BARRON, HERMAN (born December 23, 1909, in Port Chester, New York; died June 9, 1976) American golfer. Considered the greatest Jewish golfer ever. His greatest years of accomplishment were the 1930s and 1940s, after which he retired to become a teaching pro.

Herman Barron was a member of the U.S. Ryder Cup team in 1947 and won a number of major tournaments, including the Goodall Round Robin (1948) and the Professional Golf Association Seniors and World Seniors in February 1963. In 1963, he also captured the unofficial senior championship of the world at St. Anne's, England.

He grew up in Port Chester, New York, and was introduced to golf as a caddie, toting his first golf bag at the Port Chester Country Club when he was only nine. Herman, along with the other caddies, got a chance to hit a few when the greens were unoccupied.

Barron's skill was noticeable at an early age. At 11, he astounded the golfing world by shooting a 70 to break the Port Chester course record. The local *Port Chester Daily Item* ran his picture and the story on page one. A few weeks later, he won his first tournament—the Metropolitan Caddie Championship.

At age 13, Herman had a strong aversion to mathematics, and was expelled from school for missing mathematics classes. On the same day that his formal education ended, he was named assistant pro at the Port Chester Club. There he began instructing his elders in the fine points of the game.

The next year, playing at the Lakeville Club in Flushing, New York, Barron captured the Metropolitan Assistant-Pro Championship. He became head pro at Port Chester at age 15.

In 1934, the young protégé won his first major tournament, the Philadelphia Open. On each of the first three days of the tournament, Barron equaled the competitive course record of 60 for the Philmont Club Course.

In 1935, Barron became the pro at the Fenway Golf Club in White Plains, New York, and began alternating his time between Fenway and Palm Beach (Florida) Country Club where he spent his winters as a golf host.

In 1946, Barron earned $30,000 in prize money and Ben Hogan was the only golfer to win more. In one three-week span, Herman took the rich *Philadelphia Inquirer* tournament, lost the National Open by one stroke, and captured Chicago's All-American pro championship at the Tam O'Shanter Country Club. The highlight of his career was being named to the U.S. Ryder Cup team in 1947, the year in which the Americans totally overwhelmed the British.

Herman attributed his achievements to a key decision taken in the early part of the 1930s: "Success came when I discarded the whippy shafts I had used for so many years and switched to stiff-shafted clubs. The more powerful clubs stepped up my distance off the tee. I used to be a short driver, though pretty straight. Back in the early '30s they argued that direction was more important than distance off the tee, but, brother, you can't get anywhere in golf today unless you're long off the tee."

Barron is proud of being the first Jewish golfer to do well. Once Byron Nelson, the great golf pro, advised Herman to "advertise the fact that you are Jewish. Cash in on being the first great Jewish golfer. There's money in it for you." Nelson then pointed to other Jewish sports stars: Hank Greenberg, Sid Luckman, Benny Leonard, and Nat Holman. "You can earn the same sort of (moral) support from Jewish folks who yearn for a golf champion." Barron took his advice, practiced twice as much, sought solid coaching, and became determined to do well in the sport so that Jewish fans would have someone to follow.

Among the other major crowns Herman won are the Canadian Open, the Western Open, the Metropolitan PGA, and the Westchester PGA. He rated Byron Nelson as the greatest player he ever faced, with Ben Hogan a close second. Nelson said of Herman: "He had one of the finest short games in the business."

Herman Barron gave up the winter competitive pro tour in 1948 after four bouts with pneumonia. Had Herman not quit, he might have gone on to dizzying heights. But he never regretted doing so and going into teaching: "There is as much satisfaction in that as I ever enjoyed in competition," he noted.

In November 1964, Barron scored his 11th hole-in-one. His best score in competition was 64. In 1975, he retired from his job at Fenway to live in Palm Beach, Florida, with his wife Carla, a former model. When he died in 1976, he had been a golf pro for over 50 years.

MORRIS BERG

The Baseball Player Who Knew Twelve Languages

BERG, MORRIS "MOE" (born March 2, 1902, in New York City; died May 30, 1972) American baseball player. He was considered the best educated man ever to play in the major leagues. Moe was a catcher for the Brooklyn Dodgers in 1923, the Chicago White Sox from 1926 to 1930, the Cleveland Indians in 1931 and 1934, the Washington Senators in 1932 and 1934, and the Boston Red Sox from 1935 to 1939. In 663 games he had a career batting average of .243. The classic remark, "good field, no hit," was coined by scout Mike Gonzales in assessing Berg.

Moe was born on East 121st Street in New York City in a cold-water tenement, the second son of immigrants from the Ukraine. His father, a pharmacist, decided to move from New York City to Newark, New Jersey, because he thought the environment was better.

At the age of three, Moe displayed athletic tendencies. Sometimes he would squat down, like a catcher, behind a manhole cover which served as home plate while a policeman on the beat would throw to him. Moe caught everything thrown his way, and soon crowds began to gather to watch.

At the age of seven, Moe caught the attention of Newark's Rose Methodist baseball team. The team's coaches wanted Moe to play for them, but for obvious reasons wanted him to change his name. Moe agreed, and played for Rose Methodist as Runt Wolfe. In 1909, Moe's pseudonym was mentioned for the first time in the *Newark Evening News* sports section.

Moe's father was upset over his son's devotion to baseball. He preferred that he devote himself to schoolwork and help in the family pharmacy.

Moe did well in his studies at South Eighth Street Public School. The only criticism of his schoolwork, duly noted in his report card, was that he sang off-key. After school, Moe ran off to play ball, seldom returning home before dark. Baseball continued to cause tension in the Berg home, and once Moe even ran away. He didn't stay away long, however. In a few hours he trudged home, his bat slung over his shoulder.

At Newark's Barringer High School, Moe's athletic prowess received some public attention. He played third base for the high school baseball team and was its star. In 1920, upon graduation, he enrolled at Princeton University and played baseball with a Princeton team acclaimed the greatest in its history. He was a crack shortstop on the team which won 19 games in a row, a record that stood for many years.

After graduating in 1923, Princeton offered Berg a teaching position, but he wanted to study romance languages at the Sorbonne in Paris. But, when Moe received an offer to join the Brooklyn Dodgers, he did the practical thing: he signed with the Dodgers and managed to sandwich in his schooling during the baseball off-season. In 1925, he went to Columbia Law School. (He received his law degree in 1928.)

In 1926, Berg became a catcher with the Chicago White Sox. He broke into the lineup by accident. His manager Ray Shalk, also a catcher, broke a finger and so did the second-string catcher. Shalk yelled to his road secretary, "Call a Class D club and get us a catcher, quick." Moe Berg turned to Shalk and said, "What do you mean, get a catcher? We have a catcher on this bench."

"Okay," said Shalk, "get in and catch, wise guy." Moe Berg then made his debut as a major league catcher. "The funniest thing about it," Berg said later, "is that when I said we had a catcher, I didn't mean myself. Earl Sheely, a first baseman, was a pretty good backstop and I had him in mind."

In 1931, playing for the Cleveland Indians, Berg batted .350 and played errorless ball. Walter Johnson, one of the major league's greatest pitchers, thought Moe was one of the major league's better catchers. Later, Moe played for the Boston Red Sox. Joe Cronin, pilot of the team, said, "Book sense and baseball sense don't always go together, but this fellow's got more than his share of both."

Moe Berg knew more languages than any other ball player: French, Spanish, Latin, Portuguese, Italian, Russian, Yiddish, Japanese, and Greek, among others. The total number was actually 12. Yet he was sensitive about publicity that portrayed him as a scholar: "I don't want to be known as a ball player who reads a book."

Reminiscing about the game, Moe said, "In baseball a player stands on his own feet, and the fact that he can talk in five or six languages avails him nothing when he is up there at the plate with the bases filled and two out."

In 1941, he was appointed "good will ambassador" to South America by Nelson Rockefeller, then coordinator of inter-American affairs. During World War II, Berg broadcast to the Japanese and became a counterintelligence agent in Europe.

Much of his life after World War II has been cloaked in mystery, and the suspicion that he had remained within the counterintelligence community has remained strong. In 1951, he officially reentered government service. The government had asked him to confer with European scientists at a time when reports of dramatic Soviet scientific advances were current. According to a biography of Berg (*Moe Berg: Athlete, Scholar,* by Louis Kaufman, Barbara Fitzgerald, and Tom Sewall, 1974), he had a contractual relationship with the CIA at the time.

After the Soviets launched Sputnik I in 1957, Berg agreed to accept a role in the NATO defense structure, joining the staff of the head of NATO's advisory group for aeronautical research and development. He worked with scientists and

military personnel of other nations to determine where NATO's missile-launching base should be centered.

In February 1963, Berg was invited to the White House to attend an award ceremony for his boss at the NATO advisory group. "Moe," President John F. Kennedy had said, "baseball hasn't been the same without you." To which Moe replied, "Thank you, Mr. President. I'd like to think that was true."

Berg worked little during the last seven years of his life. An occasional law case provided pocket money. He would rise early and walk to various newsstands to buy newspapers. In 1972, he was taken to Clara Mass Hospital in Newark, New Jersey, after suffering injuries in a fall at home. He was 70 years old. Minutes before he died he turned to a nurse and spoke his last words: "How did the [New York] Mets do today?"

ISAAC BERGER

First Featherweight to Lift 800 Pounds

BERGER, ISAAC "IKE" (born November 16, 1936, in Jerusalem-   )
American weightlifter. He won three Olympic medals in the featherweight class: a gold in 1956 and silvers in 1960 and 1964. Berger was
the first featherweight to lift over 800 pounds and the first to press
double his body weight. His 1964 Olympic record of 336 pounds in
the jerk at a body weight of 130 pounds made him pound-for-pound
the strongest man in the world, a record that stood for nine years. His
1958 victories over Russian opponents won him recognition as the
finest weightlifter in the world at the time.

Isaac lived in Jerusalem until age 12 where he attended a yeshiva (Jewish
religious school). His father, a deeply religious man, was a rabbi and a diamond
setter. During the 1948 Israeli War of Independence, Isaac recalled that he would
go out each day to get food for his family and the neighbors. He had to walk about
three miles each way and had to contend with occasional artillery shelling and
snipers. Once he was nicked in the back by shrapnel. And another time when he
returned three hours late, his mother was certain that she would find him in the
morgue.

With his family, Isaac emigrated to the United States in 1949, when he was 13
years old. They settled in New York City. In 1952 "Ike" Berger, as he was called by
now, started lifting weights at Shaffer's gym in Brooklyn, New York. He studied
auto mechanics for three years at East New York Vocational School, and later also
studied voice and trained to be a cantor in a synagogue.

When Isaac began lifting weights he was small. He weighed 102 pounds, and
was 4 feet, 11 inches tall which made him a target for bullies. This bothered him
quite a bit. One afternoon as he was standing in front of the Adonis Health Club, he
noticed some girls admiring the pictures of muscular, good-looking men. Berger
decided then and there to start lifting weights.

Isaac was always a competitive lifter, never a body builder. Eventually he
developed what some called the most perfect proportionate form for all weightlifters, except for his slightly large 16½-inch neck. His chest measured 40 inches;
his waist, 28½ inches; and his hips, 36 inches. Part of his training included
tumbling and hand balancing. As a youngster, Ike spent considerable time in
playgrounds, doing acrobatics, playing softball, basketball, and even getting in
some boxing at the Hebrew Educational Alliance in New York.

In 1955, Berger, then 19, won the senior United States weightlifting title, a feat
he repeated the next two years. At the end of that year he became an American
citizen. Berger represented his adopted country at the 1956 Melbourne Olympics
and won a gold medal by lifting a total of 777 pounds. At age 18, he was the
youngest competitor at the games. He returned to his native country for the 1957
Maccabiah Games. There he broke the world featherweight record for the press.
It was the first world record established in Israel. Ike pressed 258 pounds (117.1

kilograms). In doing this, he became the first man ever to press double his body weight. David Ben-Gurion, Israel's prime minister at the time, was among the spectators. The crowd watched silently as Berger lifted the bar to his chest. His groans were audible as he strained to raise the weight over his head. A deafening roar erupted when the judges raised white flags to indicate Ike Berger had succeeded.

Over the course of the next year, Berger defeated the Russian weightlifters on all four occasions that he met them: in Chicago, Detroit, and New York and at the world championships at Stockholm. At Stockholm, Berger won the featherweight title with a recordbreaking performance. He broke the world mark with a total lift of 804.7 pounds and then bettered that record with 821.2 pounds for the press, snatch, and jerk. He also established a world standard for the jerk with a lift of 335.1 pounds.

In October 1958, the *New York Times* noted that "this 21-year-old package of puissance is the major stumbling block to Soviet domination of the weightlifting field." At that point, Berger had beaten the Russians five out of five times in international competition. At one of those events, in Stockholm, one of the Russian coaches, a Jew, confided to Berger in Yiddish, "You're the only one (of the weightlifters) who's given us trouble. And you happen to be Jewish." In other words, the coach was delighted that at least it had taken one Jew to beat another Jew (the coach). That, at least, was how Berger interpreted the coach's remark. During this period, to earn his living, he worked in the food distribution section of Olympic coach Bob Hoffman's York, Pennsylvania, barbell firm.

Berger spent relatively little time training. He worked out for 90 minutes at a time three times each week. He was not overly careful about his diet. He would consume as many hot dogs, hamburgers, and milkshakes as any Coney Island youngster. Before a match, he was moody and jittery. Some believed a weightlifter should avoid sex before competing. "That was silly," noted Berger. "I didn't. I needed it to relax me." He thought of the weights as the enemies he had to defeat. Lifting them was his conquest. Once he had accomplished the feat and heard the applause, the weights became his friends again.

Berger thinks that weightlifters are more relaxed than other athletes. He feels that all weightlifters are well-adjusted extroverts who never take more than five minutes to fall asleep at night. He has had to suffer a certain amount of unexpected abuse from the opposite sex. He noted that women may stare and make derogatory comments about lifters and body builders and consider them dull, vain, and horrible. But, he has also noticed that women will date the athletes they criticized.

Overconfidence cost Berger the featherweight title in the 1960 Rome Olympics. Four days before the Games he broke four world records: in the press (264 pounds), the snatch (253 pounds), the clean and jerk (336 pounds), and the total (853 pounds). As a result, he hurt his muscles and received only a silver medal behind Eugen Miniev of the Soviet Union (Miniev had won the silver medal in 1956). Berger admitted that he should have concentrated more on the Olympics and less on breaking the world records, but he had been certain that he could win at both. He partially avenged his Rome defeat by whipping Miniev in the 1961 World Championships in Vienna. Berger retired in 1962 but returned the following year. In the 1964 Olympics he captured a silver medal lifting 841½ pounds. His U.S. Olympic teammates nicknamed him Mighty Mouse.

Ike Berger retired from weightlifting after the Tokyo Olympics in 1964. That year he began a mail-order firm in New York, selling an exerciser that promised to help people lose weight. The following year, 1965, he invented a product called Waste-a-Way, a belt for losing weight, that was marketed quite successfully.

Ike was inducted into the United States Weightlifters Hall of Fame in 1965. And in that same year he began a three-year training period at the New York College of Music to become a cantor. Since then he has officiated in synagogues in Florida, Missouri, and New York.

In 1970 Ike started to concentrate his attention on a business venture (called Ike Berger Enterprises) which was devoted largely to the sale of weightlifting and exercise products.

Ike Berger is a member of the Jewish Sports Hall of Fame in Israel.

MARGARETHE "GRETEL" BERGMANN

An Outstanding Athlete Crushed by the Nazis

BERGMANN, MARGARETHE "GRETEL" (born April 12, 1914, in Lauphein, Germany–   ). German high jumper. Forced off the 1936 German Olympic team by the Nazi government, she never received the rewards she merited. In 1980 the Jewish Sports Hall of Fame honored her with a commemorative award.

As a child, Gretel (the diminutive of Margarethe) loved sports and all physical activities. She was the only girl in her class in Lauphein, and for the first nine years of her schooling she played soccer and field-handball on the boys' teams.

She loved winter sports, particularly skiing. She even went shopping on ice skates.

In 1930, when she began her secondary education in Ulm (now part of West Germany) Gretel joined that town's athletic club. With the improved coaching available, she excelled in track and field and sometimes won six different events in one day. Her specialty was the high jump.

In the spring of 1933, shortly after Hitler had come to power, she completed her studies at Ulm. She wanted to become a physical education teacher and was accepted by the university in Berlin. But immediately thereafter, when they learned that she was Jewish, she was advised not to attend classes until the political situation changed. During that same spring, the UFV club (the Ulm Soccer Club) where she had won many medals, notified her that she was no longer welcome.

As the Nazis intensified their discrimination against the Jews of Germany, Jews formed their own social and athletic clubs. In Gretel's hometown, she and her Jewish friends leveled a potato field to play soccer. Gretel was the coach and the only female member.

Realizing that there was no future for her in Germany, Gretel and her parents decided that she should go to England to pursue a degree in physical education. Gretel hoped that she might qualify to represent England at the 1936 Olympics, which were to be held in Berlin. In England she found no suitable school in her chosen field so instead she enrolled in the London Polytechnic to study English.

In June 1934, competing for her school, Gretel won the British high jump championship. Her father was in England at the time on what his daughter believed to be a business trip. After she won in the competition, her father took her aside and informed her that he was actually in England to deliver an important message: she was to return to Germany to try out for the German Olympic team. If she refused, not only would her family in Germany suffer the consequences, but all the Jewish athletes in Germany would also suffer. Gretel had no alternative and she returned to Germany.

In America, a groundswell of protest against American participation in the 1936 Olympics had arisen. The American Olympic Committee had sought assurances that everyone, no matter what his religion, could participate in the 1936 Games. But in 1933 Germany had decreed that Jews would be excluded from joining. Fearful that the United States might boycott the Berlin games, the Nazis announced in June 1934, that 21 Jews, including Gretel, had been nominated to attend German Olympic training camp.

On Gretel's return to Germany, she was placed on the so-called Olympic nucleus team from which the three best for every event would be chosen. Gretel later noted ironically that at a time when Jews were not permitted in restaurants, resorts, movies, or concerts, she was being considered for a place on the German Olympic team!

Gretel was sent with the rest of the nucleus team to training camp twice a year. She experienced no overt anti-Semitism from her fellow athletes (although the officials were not so restrained) and was grateful for the opportunity to train properly. But she was not permitted to compete with her non-Jewish German teammates at the same meets. The reason: She was not a member of the German Track and Field Association. Still, she often achieved results as good as or better than those teammates.

Gretel's roommate at the training sessions was Doro Ratjen. Gretel later noted that she doubted Ratjen's femininity, but dared not voice these thoughts outside her family circle. (Ratjen competed in the Olympics but did not win a medal. Years later Ratjen was barred from all women's competition and in 1966 emerged as Hermann Ratjen, confessing that he had been forced to pose as a female during those years in the hope of winning an Olympic medal.) Putting the two together served the Nazis' purpose: Gretel could not afford to betray Ratjen and, "she" dared not make advances toward Gretel as Aryan men could be severely punished for cavorting with a Jewish woman.

In June 1935, Gretel and a group of Jewish athletes began training at Baden. Of the entire group, Gretel was the only one who measured up to Olympic standards. There, Gretel met her future husband, Bruno Lambert.

As the fall of 1935 approached, the American Olympic Committee's membership still appeared ready to stay away from Berlin. To offset this possibility, the Nazis invited Gretel and one other Jew, Helene Mayer, to join the Olympic team. Mayer was a winner of a gold medal in fencing (foil) at the 1928 Olympics and a silver one in the 1932 Los Angeles Olympic Games. Mayer's father was Jewish; her mother was not. Helene remained in California after the 1932 Olympics.

The admission of the two Jewish athletes to the German team tipped the scales in favor of having the American team go to Berlin.

On June 30, 1936, Gretel equaled the German high-jump record with a mark of 5 feet 3 inches, an achievement that would have sufficed to win either a gold or silver medal that summer in Berlin. But on July 16th, she received a letter from the German sports authorities informing her that her achievements were inadequate. She was terribly disappointed because participating in the Olympics had been extremely important to her. She had been eager to refute the Nazi caricature of the Jew as "fat, bowlegged, and miserable."

Helene Mayer did participate in those 1936 Games. She won a silver medal in fencing. During the medal award ceremony, Helene wore a swastika on her sweater and raised her arm in the Nazi salute.

Gretel arrived in New York in May 1937, with $10 in her pocket, all the money she had been permitted to take. She began using the American version of her name, Margaret. At first she worked as a maid for $10 a week and later as a masseuse. But soon thereafter she found work as a physiotherapist in an orthopedist's office where she earned $100 a month, and began to feel rich.

Bruno Lambert, whom Gretel had met in 1935, joined her in August 1938. He had been studying medicine in Switzerland, because the Germans would not let him take his state boards in Germany. They were married in 1939. That fall, Bruno became the first foreign intern to be accepted at Wyckoff Heights Hospital in Brooklyn, New York. He received no salary, so the couple had to live on Gretel's salary.

In the late 1930s, she began training again at the private athletic club she had joined: the Park Central Athletic Association. Weighing only 112 pounds she managed, in that same year, to win the American championship in the high jump and shot put.

In 1938, Gretel again won the American championship in the high jump. The following year, she had already begun to prepare for another championship try, but decided against it when war broke out. Her family was still in Europe and she could no longer concentrate on sports. When her husband joined the U.S. Army, she moved with him to the various army posts where he was stationed. They returned to New York when the war was over, where Dr. Lambert, an internist, reestablished his private practice. They have two sons.

In February 1980, Gretel Bergmann was given a special commemorative award by the Jewish Sports Hall of Fame in Israel.

RON BLOMBERG

A New York Yankee Jewish Hero

BLOMBERG, RONALD MARK (born August 23, 1948, in Atlanta, Georgia–   ) American baseball player. A major leaguer for eight years, mostly in the 1970s. He was baseball's number-one draft pick in 1967. Blomberg became a Jewish sports hero in New York while playing for the New York Yankees in 1969, and again from 1971 to 1976. He played for the Chicago White Sox in 1978. In 1973, he was the first designated hitter. In 461 games, Blomberg had 391 hits, 52 home runs, and a career batting average of .293.

In high school, Ron not only won four letters in both baseball and basketball, he also earned four letters in track, excelling in the sprints. To make money as a youngster he collected returnable bottles, sold Kool-Aid, and had a newspaper route. Ron began playing Little League baseball at the relatively late age of 12, and claims that he began his basketball career two years later, when he picked up a basketball and dunked it in a ninth-grade physical education class.

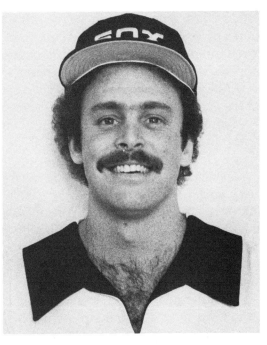

After graduating from Druid Hills High School in Atlanta, Georgia, in 1967, Ron spurned numerous college basketball scholarships to play baseball. He enrolled in DeKalb Junior College in Atlanta that year (attending the school for another two years), but devoted himself principally to his baseball career.

The 205-pound athlete was the Yankees' number-one selection in the 1967 free-agent draft. He broke into pro baseball in 1967 in the Yankee farm chain with Johnson City of the Appalachian League, hitting 10 home runs in 66 games, with a .297 average. In 1968, playing for Kingston in the Carolina League, he hit only .251 in 105 games, with seven homers. But in 1969 he hit .284 and 19 homers for Manchester in the Eastern League and was brought up to the Yankees very briefly that season. He played in only four games and had three hits in six at bats. In 1970 he played for Syracuse in the International League, the highest level minor league. In 92 games, he hit .273, with 10 home runs and 38 runs batted in.

The following year, 1971, Blomberg hit .326 and six homers in 48 games for Syracuse before being brought up again to the Yankees, this time for good. In 64 games for the Yankees that season, he hit .322, with seven homers.

While playing for the Yankees, Blomberg resumed his college studies, majoring in psychology at Fairleigh Dickinson University in Teaneck, New Jersey.

Ron Blomberg had some excellent years with the Yankees. In 1972 he slammed 14 homers in 107 games, though he hit only .268 as a first baseman and an outfielder. In 1973, in 100 games, he batted .329 with 12 homers and 57 runs batted in. In 1974, he hit .311 and 10 homers in 90 games. Then the injury jinx struck him.

His problems began in 1975 with a shoulder injury. He went to bat only 106 times in 1975, only twice in 1976, and not at all in 1977. Blomberg injured his knee running into a fence in pursuit of a fly ball in 1977 spring training and that kept him out for the entire season. He played in only 35 games between 1975 and 1977 because of injuries. He had two operations, one in 1976 to redirect tendons in his shoulder and one in 1977 to reassemble his shattered knee.

Blomberg remembers his playing days in New York fondly. New York's Jewish fans had dubbed him the Messiah. He liked to succeed for them just as black and Hispanic players like to be heroes for their people.

His attitude toward playing on Jewish High Holidays seemed ambiguous. He once said that he would not play baseball on the High Holidays because Jewish fans would have difficulty understanding such behavior. But when reminded that this could have caused him to miss the World Series opener in 1978 if the White Sox were playing, he observed: "In that case, I've talked to a couple of rabbis who say they'll pray for me at the ballpark." The White Sox, however, did not make the World Series.

Blomberg received his nickname of "Boomer" when he hit a towering home run on his third trip to the plate in his first major league game—and the name stuck.

Blomberg's last team—the Chicago White Sox—obtained him through the reentry draft in 1978. Six teams had picked him in the free-agent draft but the White Sox offered him the security of a four-year guaranteed contract in which he was to receive $600,000 over four years. On opening day of 1978 he hit a home run to help the White Sox beat the Boston Red Sox. But injury again marred that season. In August, he pulled a groin muscle and played in only 61 games that year. He managed to hit only .231 with five home runs. Blomberg had been a designated hitter that year.

He was released by the White Sox in March 1979. Later that year, Ron and his wife moved to Atlanta where he worked as a public relations representative for a firm run by the former New York Football Giant quarterback, Fran Tarkenton; the firm provided advice to Atlanta-based industries. In 1980 he joined Robert Jameson Associates, also of Atlanta, a firm which finds jobs for people wishing to switch careers.

Ron Blomberg is married and has a son, Adam, age five.

SHIMSHON BROCKMAN & EITAN FRIEDLANDER

Outstanding Israeli Sailing Team

BROCKMAN, SHIMSHON (born September 21, 1958, in Tel Aviv, Israel–) and **FRIEDLANDER, EITAN** (born September 16, 1957, in Kibbutz Rosh Hanikra, Israel–), Israeli sailors. They won the world sailing championship in the 420 non-Olympic class in France in 1980.

Shimshon Brockman (left) and Eitan Friedlander

Both Brockman and Friedlander came from sailing families. Brockman's father represented Israel in two world championships, the last one in 1968.

In 1970, Shimshon's father decided to train his 12-year-old son in sailing. The boy began as a member of his father's sailing crew and a year later, the 13-year-old Shimshon joined the crew of the Israeli national sailing team.

Like Shimshon, Eitan Friedlander also acquired his interest in sailing from his father, a man who loved the sea. Eitan's father was a sailing coach for many years. By 1970, Eitan was sailing for Hapoel Ashkelon and Hapoel Bat Yam, two sailing clubs.

Shimshon and Eitan did not know each other before 1971. Eitan was sailing off of Bat Yam, south of Tel Aviv, and Shimshon did his sailing off of Haifa. The distance between Bat Yam and Haifa is not great, 60 miles (100 kilometers) or so, but far enough to require some matchmaking.

The matchmaker was Aryeh Harel, an Israeli sailing coach. Sensing that the two men had a unique combination of vision and desire, he brought the young

sailing enthusiasts together. While normally a youngster must take courses in sailing to become a competent sailor, both Eitan and Shimshon, thanks to the training they received from their fathers, skipped this preliminary stage.

The two Israeli sailors encountered a range of problems as they worked to further their careers. For one thing, until 1977, no funding was available for competitive sailors and, for another, good coaches were hard to find. Fortunately, they were helped by Robert Mann, a Jewish-American sailing champion in the late 1950s and 1960s, and Yair Michaeli, who had represented Israel in sailing in the 1972 Munich Olympics. Michaeli has served as their coach since 1972.

Acquiring equipment was another problem. The cost of equipment was high and there was little funding available in Israel for serious sailors. But the two enjoyed one advantage that sailors elsewhere did not have. In Israel they could sail virtually throughout the entire year. Only California, Florida, southern France, and Spain offer similar conditions.

Brockman graduated from high school in 1975 and then served in the Israeli navy for the next five years—until 1980. He then began studying for a B.A. in aeronautical engineering. Friedlander served in the Israeli navy from 1977 to 1980. Their navy service did not hurt their sailing careers. Being on the water as much as they were while in the navy was only an advantage. In addition, they managed to train twice a week.

By 1975, the two sailors were confident that they were ready to challenge the best in the world. Many in Israel remained skeptical and thought that they were dreamers, that Brockman and Friedlander could never succeed on an Olympic level. But the two men were convinced that they could sail with the best not only in the non-Olympic 420 class, but also in the Olympic 470 class.

Still, they had to prove themselves. Slowly but surely, they did just that. In event after event, while winning very few, they showed a talent for the seas and a willingness to work hard. The real turning point came in 1977. In June of that year they took third place in the European championships in Rust, near Vienna, Austria. Then, two weeks later, they won the Kiel Week competition in Germany, considered the Wimbledon of sailing. From then on, they sensed that they had a chance to win a gold medal at the next Olympics in 1980. At this time, financial help was becoming more readily available and they set their sights on Moscow and a shot at the Olympic prize.

The Israeli sailors continued to win races. In 1978, Brockman and Friedlander won the world championship in the 420 non-Olympic class at Hyere, in France. In April of that year, they also won at Weymouth, and by year's end were the 1978 winners of the World Cup, given to the sailing team with the highest points in the six most important races each year. Brockman and Friedlander were now recognized and respected in the international sphere.

In July 1979, the two went on to win the European championships at Dania, Spain, near Valencia on the Mediterranean. The event was second in importance only to taking the world championship or the Olympic gold medal itself.

But their dream of an Olympic victory was not to be, at least not in the summer of 1980. Israel, taking its cue from the United States, boycotted the games as a protest against the Soviet invasion of Afghanistan. Both sailors were bitterly disappointed, first because they felt their chances of taking the gold medal were good, and second, because they believed that sports and athletes should be above politics.

They were indeed in a quandary about their futures. One part of them wanted to quit sailing, disappointed that they had invested so much time and energy for nothing. But another part urged them to continue, because there would be another Olympics in Los Angeles in 1984, and because they loved the sport of sailing.

In September 1980, Brockman and Friedlander reached the zenith of their careers by winning the world championship at Quiberon, France, in the 420 non-Olympic class. To win, they had to compete in six races during one week against 80 other boats. The team which had the highest score in five of the six races triumphed.

Spurred by their win at Quiberon, the two sailors decided to stay in sailing competition. In 1981, they entered the world championships which were again in Quiberon, but were disqualified this time when their boat collided with another. A week before the world championship, they had won the Open French Championship at the same locale, an event in which all those competing in the world championships, plus others, took part—200 boats in all.

In a decision that may sound strange to an outsider, Brockman and Friedlander decided to pass up the 1982 European Championships in Switzerland, claiming that weather conditions would make it too difficult for them to race successfully. In truth, they felt they had little to gain by competing.

Brockman and Friedlander achieved their greatest success in 1982 at the European Championships at Lake Balton, Hungary, in September of that year, where they finished as runners-up. In November 1982, they were named "Israeli Sportsmen of the Year" by the Israeli newspaper *Yediot Aharonot*.

When he is not sailing, Eitan Friedlander runs a Tel Aviv sailing equipment firm. Shimshon Brockman is studying aeronautical engineering at Haifa's Technion.

TAL BRODY

American-born Israeli Basketball Player

BRODY, TAL (born August 30, 1943, in Trenton, New Jersey-   ) American-born Israeli basketball player. An All-American basketball star in the 1960s at the University of Illinois, Brody emigrated to Israel and captained Maccabi Tel Aviv to Israel's first European basketball title in 1977. He is credited with introducing fast-paced American-style basketball into the Israeli game.

At age 10, Brody played basketball at the Trenton, New Jersey Jewish Community Center. He graduated from Trenton Central High School in 1961, as a member of the undefeated state champion. Brody was selected for the All-State team. He continued to show his talent at the University of Illinois where between

(Left) Tal Brody shakes hands with the late Moshe Dayan at Yad Eliahu (Maccabi Tel Aviv's home court) on January 16, 1975. Dayan, former Israeli Defense Minister (1967-74) and Foreign Minister (1977-80), rarely missed a Maccabi Tel Aviv home game. (Below left) Tal Brody, holding ball, playing for Maccabi Tel Aviv on January 9, 1975. (Below right) Tal Brody, holding European Cup won three days earlier by Maccabi Tel Aviv. Photo was taken on April 10, 1977. Brody was team captain. Maccabi Tel Aviv won first European Cup ever for an Israeli basketball team.

1961 and 1965, the 6-foot, 1½-inch guard won All-America, All-Academic, and All Big-Ten honors.

In the summer of 1965, Tal went to Israel for the Maccabiah Games and helped the United States team win a gold medal in basketball. He was approached by the Israeli Ministry of Education and the managers of the Tel Aviv Maccabi basketball team about living in Israel and playing basketball for Maccabi. "I liked what I saw," Brody said later. "They hit just the right note." He was asked to return to Israel to set up sports programs.

But first he returned to Illinois, took his masters (in 1965–66) in educational psychology and turned down a chance to play with the Baltimore Bullets. He was the Bullets' second draft choice that year. In 1966, Brody returned to Israel: "They didn't try to sell me on how good things were," observed Tal. "They approached me with the challenge of helping to build basketball and sports in the country."

Tal's family was no stranger to Israel. Earlier, Tal's father had spent two years in Palestine en route from Eastern Europe to the United States and one of Tal's grandfathers had helped to build an electric station and an airfield in Palestine.

After completing his studies, Tal returned to Israel and played for Maccabi Tel Aviv from 1966 to 1968. In 1967, he nearly led the team (runner-up that year) to the European title, and was named Israel's Sportsman of the Year.

Though he had decided to settle in Israel permanently, Brody returned to the United States in 1968 to fulfill his military obligation. For the next two years, while serving in the U.S. army, he played for the Armed Forces All-Star teams in national and international competitions. The army team for which he played also represented the U.S. in the World Championships in Belgrade, Yugoslavia, in 1970, and came in third.

Brody returned to Israel late in 1970, becoming an instructor at the Wingate Institute of Physical Education in Netanya. He established a sporting goods business and married an Israeli. His guest of honor at the wedding was Moshe Dayan, then Minister of Defense, who was an enthusiastic basketball fan. That same year, Tal rejoined the Maccabi Tel Aviv club. He became an Israeli citizen and served for a time in the Israel Defense Forces.

One wintry evening in 1977, in Virton, a small Belgian town, Brody led Maccabi Tel Aviv in a game against the mighty Red Army team of Moscow. The winner would play in the European Cup finals. In a startling upset, Maccabi won 91–79, and Brody, as team captain, was carried shoulder-high from the court by ecstatic fans. It was then that he made his now-famous remark, "We are on the map. We are staying on the map, not only in sport, but in everything." He succeeded because of a combination of excellent playmaking, shooting, and aggressive defense.

Later that same year, Maccabi Tel Aviv went on to win the European Cup, a tournament matching 23 national champion club teams. To everyone's surprise, on April 7, 1977, Maccabi defeated Mobil Girgi of Varese, Italy, 78–77 in Belgrade, Yugoslavia, for the title.

Soon thereafter, Brody retired from basketball when, as he put it, "I realized that I was running on the court with guys half my age." He declared that he would continue to coach and establish sports programs for Israeli youth. In keeping with that, he reached out to some 200,000 Israeli youngsters by giving basketball clinics in schools, development towns, and in the army.

He has twice been named Israeli basketball player of the year. Sporting goods dealers who used to sell six soccer balls to one basketball now say that this ratio has been reversed, and they credit Tal Brody largely for the turnabout.

Brody had come to Israel, as he said, to make a contribution. "Since I was Jewish, I thought I'd take a year out of my life and see what was going on in the world. One year turned out to be 16." He knew that he could have had a good life in the U.S., "but I felt that in Israel I could do something special."

Brody has spent a lot of time giving lectures to overseas Jewish groups—Israel Bonds, the United Jewish Appeal, etc.—to try to encourage businessmen and others to get involved in Israel. In 1979, President Yitzhak Navon of Israel awarded Brody the nation's highest honor: the Israel Prize, in recognition of his contribution to youth and sportsmanship.

In 1980, Brody sold his sporting goods business to his partner and opened his own life insurance agency which gave him more free time to devote to his great love: basketball. During the 1981–82 season, he again became deeply involved in the game and began serving as assistant coach for Maccabi Tel Aviv.

He and his wife, Ronit, have two children, a boy and a girl.

ANGELA BUXTON

1956 Wimbledon Doubles Champion

BUXTON, ANGELA (born August 16, 1934, in Liverpool, England-) British tennis player. The first British woman to reach a Wimbledon final since 1939. In 1956 she was Wimbledon doubles champion (with Althea Gibson).

Both of Angela's parents were born in Britain. In 1940, during World War II, Angela, then six years old, was evacuated from England, to Capetown, South Africa, together with her mother and brother; her father remained behind. Angela attended a convent school in Johannesburg for four years and while there, at age eight, began playing tennis. She played every day on the convent's tennis courts, instructed by a visiting coach.

When she returned to England in 1946, at age 12, she discovered that she was a far better tennis player than her English contemporaries who, because of the war, had missed out on tennis altogether. Her parents divorced shortly after the war, and Angela and her mother moved to Llandudno, North Wales, where her maternal grandparents were living.

At the school she attended in Llandudno, opportunities to play tennis barely existed. Tennis lessons were given to a few select pupils, Angela included, but only for a half hour a week. But the tennis instructor recognized Angela's potential and advised her parents to enter the youngster in tournaments. Mrs. Buxton asked if he meant Wimbledon. The instructor laughed, and suggested starting with lesser tournaments.

Although her father couldn't even score a tennis match, he offered to finance Angela's tennis career. The first step was to help Angela and her mother move to London in 1950. Angela worked at her tennis and in 1952, she studied for one year at the Polytechnic in London, specializing in domestic science.

Angela played in her first Wimbledon tournament in the spring of 1952. She was one of two players to win a lottery permitting her to play in Wimbledon. The lottery was drawn from players who had lost in the final qualifying round and therefore became known as the "Lucky Loser" lottery. Angela went out in the first round. But she managed to reach the quarterfinals of the Plate event for first-round losers.

Realizing that she needed to improve, Angela convinced her father to send her and her mother to California for six months. The two women chose an apartment overlooking the Los Angeles Tennis Club, but Angela was surprised to find that the club would not permit her to play. She blamed it on anti-Semitism. So, mornings, she played at the La Cienega public courts; afternoons, she worked in Arzy's tennis shop; and nights, she attended typing courses at Fairfax High School. She was coached by Bill Tilden, the great American star, during the last months of his life. Buxton played in a few tournaments, doing well in some. In March 1953, expecting to begin a brilliant career, she returned to England.

In April of that year she played in the Bournemouth Hardcourt Championships and lost to Doris Hart, the 1952 Wimbledon champion, 6-0, 6-0. She was utterly crushed and felt that she had wasted all of her father's money. In the Bournemouth clubhouse, she came upon *Daily Mirror* sportswriter Jimmy Jones, who cautioned her not to read the newspapers the next day. He offered to help her with her tennis, but she declined, figuring he may have had other motives. Jones also ran a tennis magazine.

Angela had decided to play out the 1953 season and then go into dress designing. By the end of 1953, she obtained a degree in dress designing from the Katinka Dress Designing School of London.

Despite her humiliation at Bournemouth, she worked on improving her tennis.

In October 1953, she traveled to Israel for the Maccabiah Games in what she was sure would be her "swan song" (her own phrase) in tennis. To everyone's surprise, Angela defeated Anita Kanter, of California, then ranked eighth in the world, 6-2, 6-3 in the finals. (Kanter had just beaten Doris Hart.) Buxton picked up a second gold medal by winning the Maccabiah doubles.

Sailing back to Europe on the *Artza*, Angela decided that she would look up Jimmy Jones for the tennis lessons of which he had spoken. The lessons took place at two courts at Lincoln's Inns Field behind Cheshire House, where Jones had an office. Jones introduced Angela to the psychology of tennis and its tactics (elements of the game she had never considered before). Until then, she had learned only that one had to return the ball over the net.

In December 1953, two months after the lessons began, Angela was defeating opponents whom she had never defeated before. In 1954 she improved so much that she managed to achieve the No. 4 ranking in England by the year's end. No one ever before had come from such total obscurity to so high a rank in so short a time. In 1954 and 1955 she represented Britain in the Wightman Cup matches against the United States. She did not do well in either year, and the U.S. won both times. In 1955 she reached the quarterfinals of the Wimbledon singles, and was ranked No. 9 in the world.

The year 1956 was her best. She won the English Indoor and Grass championships, as well as the hardcourt doubles title (with Darlene Hard). She also won the doubles (with Althea Gibson) of both Wimbledon and the French Open. Her crowning achievement was reaching the singles final at Wimbledon that year, but she lost the match to the American Shirley Fry in the finals.

Wimbledon singles winners have automatically been invited to join the All-England Lawn Tennis Club (Wimbledon) and doubles winners, when they applied, were usually accepted. But Angela's application was refused. She applied in August 1956, and reapplied years later, but was told to wait patiently. Trying to uncover the real answer why she had not been asked, she came up with the conclusion: anti-Semitism.

In June of 1981, on the *Nationwide* English TV program, Angela was asked why she had never been admitted to the club: "I'm Jewish; it's as simple as that." When the chairman of the club was asked the same question, he replied that he did not know and that he had never really looked into the matter.

In 1956, with great tennis potential in her future, Angela was forced to curtail her playing career prematurely. In August of that year, while playing in a tournament in New Jersey, the wrist on her (right) playing hand suddenly swelled up and had to be placed in a cast for six weeks. She thought she would be able to return to her previous playing level when she recovered, but discovered that after practicing more than two or three times a week the injury recurred. In 1957 she did manage to win the French coveted court title, and that same year she won the Maccabiah singles event easily.

Even before her wrist problems began, Buxton had worked for Lilywhites, the famous English sports shop located at Picadilly Circus in London. She worked for them between 1954 and 1958, first as a typist, then as a receptionist. Afterwards, she worked in the shop's tennis department, and later represented the store in India and the U.S.

In February 1959, Buxton married Donald Silk, an attorney. They have three children: Benjamin, 22, Joseph, 21, and Rebecca, 16.

From 1960 to 1967, Angela was involved in dress designing.

Angela Buxton went to Israel after the 1967 Six-Day War, and spent six months there. She considered settling there and setting up a tennis school. But when she returned to England in early 1968, she discovered that her husband, who had been an ardent Zionist until then, did not want to leave England. (She separated from him in 1970.) So she and Jones began the Angela Buxton Center, a tennis school in London's Hampstead section. The school today handles some 3,000 pupils over the course of a year.

During the last 10 years, Angela visited Israel several times and has given free courses in tennis at the Wingate Institute for Sport, Netanya, Israel. She is a member of the Jewish Sports Hall of Fame in Israel.

ANDREW COHEN

The Jewish Ball Player John McGraw
Was Anxious to Recruit

COHEN, ANDREW HOWARD (born October 25, 1904, in Baltimore, Maryland-   ) American baseball player. He was the player New York Giant manager John McGraw chose when he searched long for a Jewish baseball star. Cohen played for the Giants in 1926, 1928, and 1929. For his career total of 262 games, he had a .281 batting average.

At the age of 16, Andy Cohen was a high school star in El Paso, Texas. A natural athlete, he could have joined a professional ball team upon graduation, but he wanted an education. So, he went to the University of Alabama where he earned letters in football, basketball, and baseball.

During his last year at Alabama, he left school to play baseball. In 1925, he signed on with Waco, but in 1926 was acquired by the New York Giants. He appeared in 32 games as an infielder. The following year (1927), he was farmed to Buffalo where he hit .353 for the season.

In 1928, John McGraw's Giants traded the legendary star Rogers Hornsby to the Boston Braves. Andy Cohen was given the tough assignment of filling in at second base.

In the early days of the 1928 season, the New York fans grew excited at the prospect of "the Jewish hope" in New York and a number of amusing suggestions heralding Andy Cohen's arrival surfaced. One fan wanted to change the name of Coogan's Bluff, overlooking the Giants' stadium, the Polo Grounds, to Cohen's Bluff. An owner of the refreshment concession at the Polo Grounds gave the following order to his sales force: "Remember, in the Polo Grounds you are no longer selling ice cream cones, but ice cream Cohens."

The newspapers contributed to the excitement as well. *The New York Times* ran an editorial on the second day of the season entitled, "A Daniel Comes to Judgment." It read in part: "Francis Hogan played well for the Giants in their opening game, but the Hogans have always played good baseball; so have the Kellys and the Caseys, the Delahantys and the Bresnahans, so have the Wagners and the Zimmers. And the Lazzeris, the Lajoies and the Chances have contributed stars for many years. But the Cohens? . . . None of their kinfolk has ornamented the professional diamond in New York. Therefore, when Andy Cohen carried off nearly all the honors when the Giants met the Braves Wednesday at the Polo Grounds, there was much more than just a baseball game at stake."

That very day, Cohen had two hits which produced the runs that helped the Giants win; he was also responsible for the last putout. The fans carried him off the field on their shoulders and tore his uniform in pieces in pursuit of souvenirs.

"Don't let it turn your head, boy," John McGraw advised Cohen in the dressing room afterward. "It's just one ball game."

There was more of that to come, though. By May, Andy Cohen was hitting a phenomenal .350 while Hornsby, now with the Braves, was in an unusual slump and hitting below .250. One New York newspaper ran a daily box comparing "What the Rajah (Hornsby) did" with "What our Andy did." Hornsby was furious. "That's a pretty shabby trick they're pulling on the kid [Andy was then 23]," he grumbled. "Sure I'm not hitting. But you know it won't be long before I will and where will that leave him?"

Hornsby turned out to be correct. Andy dipped to .274 at season's end while the Rajah won his seventh batting title with a .387 average.

Cohen recalled that brief, colorful year: "They said I was the Jewish ballplayer John McGraw always wanted. But McGraw was primarily interested in good ball players, although I know he felt that a Jewish one wouldn't do any harm at the gate." Cohen raised his batting average to .294 in 1929, but because Andy was slow afoot, McGraw sent him to the minors; Andy never returned to the majors as a ball player.

During the off-season months in the late 1920s, Cohen teamed up with a 265-pound catcher for the Giants named Shanty Hogan in a vaudeville act. They called themselves "Cohen and Hogan," except when they appeared in Boston, where it changed to "Hogan and Cohen" because of its large Irish immigrant population. They told stories and sang parodies, receiving the then-huge sum of $1,800 a week.

In 1930, McGraw considered bringing Andy back to the Giants from the minor league club in Newark, but Cohen had a torn muscle in his leg and thus lost his last chance to return to the majors to play. For the next 25 years he kept busy in the minors, playing and later managing. He played for Minneapolis in the American Association from 1932 to 1941. Then, between 1941 and 1951, he piloted teams in towns such as Pine Bluff, Arkansas; Dayton, Ohio; New Orleans, Louisiana; and Memphis, Tennessee.

From 1951 to 1954, he managed Denver in the Western Association, winning pennants in 1952 and 1954. In 1956 he managed Indianapolis, and in 1957 he managed Denver.

In March 1960, Andy was back in the majors after a 31-year absence, coaching the Philadelphia Phillies. On April 14, 1960, he served as Phillies' manager for one game, and beat the Milwaukee Braves. The reason: Gene Mauch, who had been appointed to replace Eddie Sawyer as Phillies' manager, was only to arrive a few days later to take up his new job. Cohen went on to become a vice president and coach of the El Paso club in the Texas League.

LILLIAN COPELAND

Outstanding American Track and Field Star

COPELAND, LILLIAN (born November 25, 1904, in New York City; died February 7, 1964) American track and field star. Outstanding competitor in the shot put, discus, and javelin. In 1926 she was touted as one of the world's greatest women athletes. She was the winner of a silver medal in the discus throw in the 1928 Olympics and of a gold medal in the same event in the 1932 Olympics.

Lillian was an all-around athlete during her college years at the University of Southern California, where she played tennis and basketball as well as competed in track and field. Her college record was spectacular, and she won every woman's track event she entered while at USC.

Copeland won the first of her nine national titles in 1925 with a victory in the shot put. In 1926, when she won three national titles in the shot put, discus, and javelin, she broke two world records by throwing the javelin 112 feet, 5½ inches and the discus, 101 feet, 1 inch. A four-time national champion in the shot put, Lillian had to face disappointment because this event was not part of the women's schedule for the 1928 Olympics. So she entered the discus contest and placed second at the Amsterdam Games, reaching 121 feet, 7⅞ inches (setting a world record).

Copeland won national titles in 1931 in the shot put and javelin in preparation for the Los Angeles Olympics the following year.

The 1932 Olympics provided Copeland with the triumph of her athletic career. She won a gold medal in the discus and set a world's record, hurling it 133 feet, 1⅝ inches.

Three years later, Copeland was so eager to participate in the 1935 Maccabiah Games held in Palestine that she did not even wait for an invitation. Instead, she paid her own way, and won each of her three specialties.

Lillian is a member of the Helms Athletic Hall of Fame and of the Jewish Sports Hall of Fame in Israel.

Copeland worked with the Los Angeles County Sheriff's Department from August 11, 1936, to January 31, 1960, most of the time as a juvenile officer.

HARRY DANNING

The New York Giants Outstanding Jewish Player

DANNING, HARRY "THE HORSE" (born September 6, 1911, in Los Angeles, California–   ) American baseball player. Considered to be the best Jewish player to play for the New York Giants. In 890 games, he hit .285.

Harry's older brother Ike was an inspiration to him. Ike played as a catcher for the St. Louis Browns in only two games in 1928, but it was enough to encourage Harry to be a catcher.

For a while, Danning was a rug salesman. His baseball interest was sparked when his brother Ike was doing well at semipro baseball in Mexico. Harry decided that he, too, would play there, and he did so successfully.

In 1931, Harry got into organized ball in the United States by signing with the Bridgeport team in the Eastern League. In his first year, he hit .324. The following year, 1932, he got off to a quick start, hitting .320. In midseason, he moved to

Winston-Salem (North Carolina) of the Piedmont League. There, he became the regular catcher and finished the season at .313.

In 1933 Harry moved up to the International League and became the starting catcher for the Buffalo Bisons, hitting .349 for half a season's play. He reached the major leagues midway through the 1933 season, playing for the New York Giants.

For the rest of the 1933 season, Danning was on the bench, where he watched the Giants participate in the World Series. The National League pennant-winning Giants of 1933 had two veteran catchers, Gus Mancuso and Paul Richards, and Harry couldn't displace either of them. In 1934 he was used, but only sparingly. In 53 games, he hit .330.

When the next two years followed the same pattern, Harry grew unhappy playing second-string catcher to Mancuso. In 1937, Danning asked Giants' manager, Bill Terry, for a chance to catch. Terry's Giants had failed to win pennants in 1934 or 1935, and Danning was a stronger hitter than Mancuso, so Terry relented. The Giant pitching staff at that time had such stars as Hal Schumacher, Fred Fitzsimmons, and Carl Hubbell.

On June 9, 1937, Danning hit a two-run homer to help the Giants defeat the St. Louis Cardinals in New York's Polo Grounds. That homer gave Harry the chance to play regularly. On July 13, he hit a homer in each game of a doubleheader, showing his power. By July 24, he had become a regular, catching the next 35 games in a row.

In the 1937 World Series against the New York Yankees, Harry split the catching chores with Mancuso. Harry was the batting star of the fourth game, going three for four to help beat the Yankees. (The Yankees won the Series four games to one.) The following season, Danning became the team's number-one catcher.

For the next four years (1938 to 1941), Harry caught at least 120 games each season. In 1938, he hit .306; in 1939, .313; and in 1940, .300. In one game on June 15, 1940, he hit a single, double, triple, and home run.

Danning served in the U.S. Army during World War II, and when he was discharged, announced that he was retiring from baseball.

It was sports announcer Ted Husing, a reader of Damon Runyon, who created the character named "Harry the Horse." Husing, thinking of the Runyon character, gave that nickname to Harry, and it stuck.

After retirement, Harry Danning went into the automobile business in Los Angeles, his hometown.

AL DAVIS

Mastermind of the Oakland Raiders

DAVIS, AL (born July 4, 1929, in Brockton, Massachusetts–) American football coach and owner. Beginning in 1963 Davis built the Oakland Raiders into a football powerhouse that has won more games and lost fewer than any other team in professional football. They garnered two Super Bowl championships (1977 and 1981) and emerged victorious in more than 70 percent of their games—a record unsurpassed by any club in pro football.

Al Davis' career began in Brooklyn, New York. His father, Louis Davis, owned a clothing store and other businesses. Al considered his father a brilliant, competitive, and politically conservative man. He was pleased that his father always encouraged him to think for himself.

Growing up in Brooklyn was not without difficulties. Davis had to cope with street gang fights, and he learned early that it is much better to win than to be beaten up.

At Erasmus High School in Brooklyn, Davis played football, baseball, and basketball and was chosen the most popular boy in his senior class (1947). Upon graduation, he attended Wittenberg College in Ohio on an athletic scholarship, but then transferred to Syracuse University in upstate New York where he played football, basketball, and baseball. He graduated in 1950.

Al's family wanted him to go into business, but Al wanted to be a football coach. So at age 21, in the fall of 1950, he joined the football staff at Adelphi University, in Garden City, New York. He distinguished himself there by becoming the first coach to advocate a four-man line in football. His idea was not readily acceptable at that time, but since then it has become widely accepted.

In addition to coaching, Al published technical articles in coaching magazines which gained him attention from other coaches.

Davis joined the U.S. Army in 1952 and was assigned to organize a football team at Fort Belvoir, Virginia. His team was so good it beat the national college champion, University of Maryland team in a practice game.

In the years that followed, Al scouted for the Baltimore Colts of the National Football League and served as coach at The Citadel, a college in Charleston, South Carolina. In 1957, he moved to the University of Southern California where he became assistant coach responsible for the line. Davis was a fanatic about studying game films, and often could be seen with a film projector under his arm on his way to study the replay of a game. He remained with USC until 1959.

In 1960, the American Football League, financed by millionaire Lamar Hunt, began its first season. Sid Gillman, coach of the Los Angeles Chargers, hired Davis as offensive coach.

During the early 1960s, the Oakland Raiders were not having much success. They won only two games in 1961 and in 1962 won one and lost 13. In an attempt to turn this around, Davis was brought in from the Chargers to become head coach of the Raiders. He insisted on full control, which meant becoming general manager as well. He was given full reign, and overnight the Raiders shocked their fans by posting a 10-4 record, second only to San Diego's 11-3 record that season.

For the next 18 years, except for the first year, the Raiders suffered only one losing season (in 1964). And even in that year, when they failed to win in their first six games, it was because of injuries, with the Raiders bouncing back to win five of their last eight games.

Davis reacted to the 1964 season by signing eight of his first 10 draft choices, thereby helping the club return to a respectable 8–5–1 record in 1965, again coming in second to San Diego.

In April 1966, Davis became commissioner of the American Football League (which had been founded in 1959). For six years a bitter struggle ensued between the fledgling AFL and the NFL as they competed for players. Davis was particularly interested in wooing star quarterbacks from the NFL. When the AFL owners negotiated a merger of the two leagues, Pete Rozelle, the NFL commissioner, not Davis, was named commissioner of the newly-formed National Football League. Davis returned to Oakland in his former roles of coach and general manager. Some have argued that Davis has never been satisfied with the merger, wishing that the AFL were still independent.

In 1968, the Oakland Raiders lost to the Green Bay Packers 33–14 in the Super Bowl game at the Orange Bowl in Miami, Florida. For six years in the 1970s (1970, 1972, 1973, 1974, 1975, and 1976), Oakland won the Western Division, but lost in the playoffs. But, in 1977, the jinx was finally broken and Oakland won its first Super Bowl, defeating the Minnesota Vikings 32–14 at the Rose Bowl, in Pasadena, California.

First as head coach and general manager and then as principal owner of the Raiders (he holds 25 percent of the stock) Davis built Raider teams that were aggressive and physical, violent, as well as technically sophisticated.

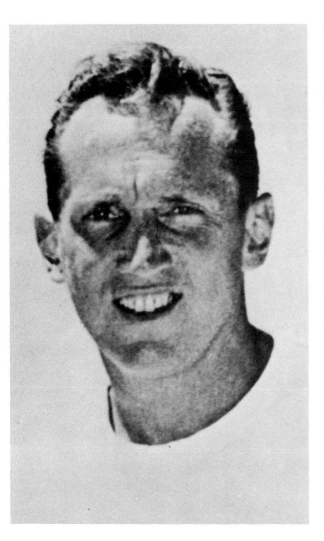

Davis developed what he calls "pressure football," which includes a solid running game that focuses mostly on the long pass. He pioneered the use of the "bump and run" by receivers. He also developed such strong-armed quarterbacks as Tom Flores, Frank Davidson, Daryle Lamonica, George Blanda, and Kenny Stabler.

He is sensitive about aspersions that he interferes with the day-to-day running of the team. When an article appeared in a Miami newspaper in January 1968, which suggested that Davis was undermining the authority of his coach, Johnny Rauch, Davis sent a messenger to the Miami airport to buy up all the newspapers on the stands so Rauch wouldn't see it.

Davis, who believes in taking castoffs and building these players into a winning team, claims that he got the idea by reading Theodore Dreiser, especially *Sister Carrie*. He believes that people respond to the pressures of their environment and change in keeping with their surroundings. In *Sister Carrie* a wealthy businessman who fell on hard times was rejected by his poor girlfriend who had become wealthy. Davis reflected that the girl rejected the man because his environment had changed. Similarly, football players can fare poorly on one team (not get along with a coach, develop an image of being lazy or a troublemaker), but when their environment is changed, Davis says, and players join a new team with a new coach, they often become self-confident again and even Super Bowl heroes.

The Davis record at Oakland is mostly a story of triumph after triumph. In 20 years, Al's teams have had only two losing seasons. His overall record (through the 1982 season) has been 194-78-11. In 1982, the Raiders led the American Football Conference at 8-1, but then lost the conference semifinal playoff to the New York Jets 17-14.

Davis had tried to move his team from Oakland to Los Angeles where the potential pay-TV market for professional football was thought to be enormous. (He wanted to play in the Coliseum which the Lost Angeles Rams left in 1979 for suburban Anaheim.) The NFL objected to Davis' plans suggesting that chaos would result if individual owners could simply move teams wherever and whenever they wanted. The dispute went to the courts. There was a mistrial in 1981. But, on May 7, 1982 a Federal District Court in Los Angeles, retrying the case, sided with Davis, ruling that the NFL had no right to keep the Raiders from moving to Los Angeles. The decision paved the way for Davis to transfer his team to Los Angeles.

Davis left football only once: when his wife Carol had a massive heart attack in 1979 and went into a coma. He moved into the hospital during that football season and turned the team over to coach Tom Flores. After she recovered, Davis reminded her that he had once told her that only a matter of life and death would take him away from football, but he had not expected her to put him to the test.

RENÉ DREYFUS

Winner of Ten Grand Prix Races

DREYFUS, RENÉ (born May 6, 1905, in Paris, France–   ) French racing driver. He drove professionally between 1924 and 1940 and won 36 races highlighted by the 1930 Grand Prix of Monaco. He won nine other Grand Prix races, including those of Belgium, Rheims, Florence, Dieppe, Cork, Pau, and Tripoli. He finished 106 races out of the 148 he started. In addition to his 36 victories, René came in second 19 times and third, 17 times.

The lure of cars was strong even when René was very young. At age six, he rode a pedal car into the Seine in Paris. His older brother, Maurice, his sister, and another youngster were with him in the car. All survived.

At age nine, feeling the urge to race, he began driving his father's Clement-

Bayard car. But for the next few years, his racing was confined to bicycles and, later, motorcycles.

The Dreyfus family had moved to Nice in southern France when René's father died in 1923. René and Maurice took over the family fabric business. Deciding that he needed a car to sell fabrics on the road, René obtained a 6-horsepower Mathis. René drove in an auto race for the first time at Gatthieres, near Nice, with brother Maurice seated next to him. He was victorious in his class, but that was no great accomplishment since his Mathis was the only one registered in the class!

In 1925, René traded his Mathis for a Hotchkiss and, a year later, bought (in his words) "a really beautiful little four-seater Brescia Bugatti." Then he acquired a supercharged 4-cylinder Bugatti Type 37A. For two seasons, 1925 and 1926, he dominated auto racing in southern France, winning 60 starts; but these were still not major competitions like the Grand Prix races.

In 1928, René spent six months in military training, as was required of every Frenchman. He was stationed in Marseille, in the Transportation Corps, and he brought his Bugatti along to give demonstrations for the troops.

He returned to racing in 1929. Driving his Bugatti, he came in fifth in the first Monaco Grand Prix. (He finished first in his class.) That same year he won the Dieppe Grand Prix.

In 1930, René won the Monaco Grand Prix. Many fans accused him and the runner-up, Louis Chiron, of fixing the race. Betting on the outcome was permitted until the race reached the fortieth lap. Chiron was the local favorite so most bet on him. During the sixtieth lap, René took the lead from Chiron because Chiron had stopped in the pit to refuel. René, with a spare tank installed on the seat beside him, had no need to refuel. "When I passed Chiron, people realized I had a chance to win, but they could do nothing because the betting had stopped on the fortieth lap."

After the race, the fans screamed and grew excited. "Some people," René remembered, "congratulated me, but many others shook their fists. They could not understand why Chiron stopped at the pit and I did not. To them the Bugattis (the cars the two men were driving) were alike, and so they thought it was a trick, a fix between Chiron and myself." The promoters, fearing a riot, did not allow betting on that race the following year.

The following years were a bit disappointing for Dreyfus. He had a second in the Marne Grand Prix and a third in the Rome race in 1931. Two years later he was second in the Dieppe Grand Prix, and third at Monaco and Belgium. In 1934, he was third at Monaco, and in the Belgian Grand Prix. Some said there was something missing in René's makeup to which he replied, "Aggressiveness was not one of my major characteristics." In 1938, he won the title, "Champion of France."

When France mobilized in 1939, Dreyfus was back in the army driving transport trucks.

In May 1940, during the "Phony War" period before the Germans overran France, Corporal Dreyfus and another soldier, Private René LeBegue, were sent by the French government to the United States on a 45-day leave to represent their country at the Indianapolis Speedway Memorial Day 500 race. It was meant to be a gesture of good will to America.

Assuming that speeds above 118 miles per hour would guarantee them starting posts in the race, the two qualified in Maseratis, but Dreyfus was eliminated soon thereafter. LeBegue started the famous race and then turned it over to Dreyfus (who was permitted to act as a relief driver) after 250 miles. Dreyfus finished tenth (the winner was Wilbur Shaw in a Boyle Special).

With the Germans overruning France, the French ambassador in Washington told Dreyfus to stay in the United States. While in the U.S., he was discharged from the French army.

The American army was not eager to accept René because he was French, but it finally relented. In 1942, he enlisted in the U.S. army and became fluent in English in an army school. He interrogated war prisoners. The army offered him a commission, but he turned it down. Serving as a sergeant, he participated in the North African and Italian invasions. At one stage he ran an army motor pool in Naples, Italy.

In 1945, the war over, René opened a restaurant on West 55th Street in New York City called Le Gourmet. His brother, Maurice, who had been living in the U.S. since 1940, was his partner. René's 14 years as a pro driver on European race courses had allowed him to sample the culinary art of the continent's best hostelries and this led him into the world of restaurant ownership. In 1952 the brothers closed Le Gourmet and in 1953 opened a restaurant called Le Chanteclair on East 49th Street, off Manhattan's Fifth Avenue. This was a more ambitious venture. Emblems of automobile clubs from all over the world and the signed portraits of famous racing drivers adorned the walls.

René did some driving in the 1950s. In 1952 he and a Parisian banker ran a Ferrari at Le Mans for four hours before a clutch broke. In 1953 René captained a three-car Arnolt-Bristol team that finished first, second, and fourth in their class at the Sebring 12-hour race, at Sebring, Florida. Then he quit racing.

In April 1959, President Charles DeGaulle of France notified Dreyfus of his appointment as a Chevalier of the French Légion d'Honneur, conferred on him "for his feats as a driver and his contributions to the greater glory of his native country over a period of thirty years."

In 1976, Dreyfus sadly noted the passing of decency in auto racing. He assailed the current practice of using sticky, short-lived qualifying tires to achieve better times in lap trials: "A racing car," he said, "should go round the track in the condition in which it will race."

What he missed most among the more modern drivers was the camaraderie of his 1930 Grand Prix days. "Life," he explained, "was less fast. We had time to enjoy ourselves. We drove fewer races a season—10 or 12—and between races we would drive from one country to the next, meeting at inns and hotels on the way.

"And in our cases not only would we carry a suit and a dinner jacket for the evening, but also tails for some of the important parties given in our honor. Now drivers rush off to planes in their blue jeans and La Costes."

BARNEY DREYFUSS

A Great Innovative
Baseball Executive

DREYFUSS, BARNEY (born February 23, 1865, in Freiberg, Germany; died February 5, 1932) American baseball executive. Owner of the Pittsburgh Pirates from 1900 to 1932, creator of the modern World Series, and builder of the major leagues' first stadium. At the time of his death he was vice president of the National League as well as Pirates' owner.

The slightly-built Dreyfuss was born in Germany, but his father was an American citizen. To avoid being conscripted into the German army, Barney came to the U.S. when he was 16, settling in Paducah, Kentucky. Finding work at the Bernheim whiskey distillery there, he cleaned whiskey barrels at first. Soon, his innate intelligence was recognized and he was assigned an office position. In time, he became the distillery's head bookkeeper.

Dreyfuss worked nine hours a day, and then studied English and other subjects until midnight. He soon suffered from headaches, poor digestion, and a

generally run-down condition. A doctor, concerned about the new immigrant's poor health, suggested that Dreyfuss take up outdoor activity. Barney chose baseball and soon organized a semipro team and played second base.

In 1900, the distillery moved to Louisville, Kentucky, and so did Barney Dreyfuss. He obtained part ownership of the American Association team, the Louisville Colonels, then a major league club. He was elected treasurer of the club in 1890 and became its president nine years later.

In 1899, Dreyfuss acquired the Pittsburgh Pirates and served as owner and general manager of the team until his death 32 years later. From Louisville, he brought such great baseball stars as Honus Wagner, Fred Clarke, and Rube Waddell, all Hall-of-Famers, to Pittsburgh.

Dreyfuss ran the Pirates without delegating much authority. He was his own scout. He carried with him a little black book filled with the names of minor league players and their statistics—at least those whom he considered potential players for his Pittsburgh team. Dreyfuss was considered the best judge of baseball talent at the time.

By nature Dreyfuss had little tolerance for losing. "We are a first-division town," he would say, "and I'm a first-division club owner." More often than not he was right. In his 32 years as Pirates owner, his clubs finished in the first division 26 times and landed in the second division (which he considered a sin) only six times. Before he came to Pittsburgh in 1900, the Pirates had never won a National League pennant.

Barney soon changed that. Under his stewardship, the Pirates won six National League pennants—in 1901, 1902, 1903, 1909, 1925, and 1927. They also won the World Series twice: in 1909 and 1925.

In 1903, Dreyfuss arranged the first modern World Series. The Boston Pilgrims, the American League champions, accepted his challenge to meet the National League champion team in a postseason tournament. Boston won that first eight-game Series (it is now seven games), but the Pirate players earned more money than their rivals. In addition to receiving their players' shares for participating in the Series, they were given an extra amount which Dreyfuss contributed from the club's own receipts. Hence, each Pirate wound up with the sum of $1,316 against the Boston share of $1,182 per man. (Total Series receipts were $55,000.)

In 1909, Dreyfuss built Forbes Field which could seat 25,000 spectators. It was the first of the modern triple-tier ballparks. Construction started March 1st and the first game was played June 30th. The stadium was located in Pittsburgh's choice Oakland neighborhood. Barney faced cynicism at first. "When I first selected the Forbes Field site for a new ballpark," he recalled, "people laughed at me. They said I'd never fill our 25,000 seats, but I knew better. One friend bet me a $150 suit that the park would never be filled, but he was wrong." On opening day, 30,338 fans packed the stadium (extra room had to be found by blocking off part of the outfield with rope). In the first five weeks, the park was filled another four times.

Dreyfuss forbade advertisements inside the ballpark to preserve the stadium's beauty. However, during World War I, he yielded to pressure from the government and allowed war-bond posters to be mounted. Hating what he called "cheap homers," Barney had left field extended in 1918. To do this, he had to lease land from the City of Pittsburgh and blast out the concrete wall which had been put up in 1909.

Barney Dreyfuss was also a pioneer in pro football. He was the co-owner and manager of the Pittsburgh Athletic Club which captured pro football's championship in 1898. Pro football was only four years old at the time.

Dreyfuss groomed his son to inherit the ownership of the Pirates. In 1930, the elder Dreyfuss stepped down as the owner, turning the reins over to his son, Sam. But in February 1931, the son died unexpectedly of pneumonia. Barney, having no other choice, resumed command of the Pirates, but he never recovered from the shock of his son's death. Barney Dreyfuss also died of pneumonia, just a year later. At the time of his death, the *Sporting News* called him "the last of the generation of history makers." He is a member of the Jewish Sports Hall of Fame at the Wingate Institute in Israel.

CHARLOTTE EPSTEIN

Mother of Women's Swimming in America

EPSTEIN, CHARLOTTE "EPPY" (born September, 1884, in New York City; died August 27, 1938) American swimming administrator. Considered the mother of American women's swimming, Charlotte Epstein established women's swimming as a sport in the United States, and was largely responsible for the inclusion of the first American women's swimming team in the Olympics when a delegation participated in the Antwerp Games in 1920.

Shortly after the 1912 Stockholm Olympics, in which women competed in swimming events for the first time, Charlotte developed an interest in competitive swimming although she herself was not a particularly strong swimmer.

In 1914, she founded the National Women's Life Saving League, which provided a place for women to meet and swim; it offered competitive swimming as well as lessons. In the autumn of that year, Charlotte persuaded the Board of Directors of the Amateur Athletic Union to permit women for the first time to register as athletes with the AAU (as swimmers only). This led to a large increase in local and national swimmming events for women.

In October 1919, Charlotte's League became the New York Women's Swimming Association. This tiny group of business women built the WSA into the world's greatest swimming organization.

Charlotte's first great coup was to get women's swimming recognized as an international sport. She successfully pushed for its inclusion in the 1920 Antwerp Olympics. The true beginning of American female participation in the Olympics was in Antwerp. Other than the appearance of women archers and golfers in 1900 and 1904, this marked the first time American women were truly involved in competitive athletics at the Olympic Games. The difference this time was that swimming, unlike archery and golf, counted as a major sport in the eyes of the International Olympic Committee.

At the 1920 Olympics, U.S. women swimmers won an unprecedented four out of five races; they also finished first, second, and third in three events and set two world and Olympic records (many of these women were Charlotte Epstein's WSA swimmers).

The success of the 1920 Olympic experiment led to the inclusion of track and field and other sports for American women in future Olympic Games.

Charlotte did not actually coach the women at the Olympics. She had been appointed head of the women's team largely on the strength of being chief executive of the WSA. She again headed the women's Olympic team at the 1924 Paris games and at the 1932 Los Angeles games. (She was present at the 1928 Amsterdam games in an unofficial capacity.) American female swimmers dominated the Olympic swimming events during all of these Olympics.

Among Charlotte's protégés were Gertrude Ederle, Aileen Riggin, and Eleanor Holm. Ederle was the first woman to swim the English Channel, doing so on August 6, 1926, in a time (14 hours and 39 minutes) that was faster than any male swimmer had achieved to that point. Aileen Riggin won the springboard diving competition at the 1920 Olympics. Eleanor Holm won a gold medal in the 100-meter backstroke at the 1932 Olympic Games.

In 1935, Charlotte Epstein served as chairman of the swimming committee in charge of the trials and selection of teams for the second Maccabiah Games, to be held in Tel Aviv.

During her 22 years with the Women's Swimming Association, Charlotte's swimmers held 51 world records and put together 30 national champion relay teams. By profession, Charlotte Epstein was a court stenographer and legal secretary. She had been a court stenographer for 10 years prior to the illness that led to her death in 1938. She never married. Her last assignment was at the Court of Domestic Relations in Brooklyn.

Charlotte Epstein is a member of the Jewish Sports Hall of Fame in Israel.

JACKIE FIELDS

The Youngest Athlete to Win an Olympic Gold Medal

FIELDS, JACKIE (born February 9, 1908, in Chicago, Illinois–   ) American boxer. The youngest athlete to win an Olympic gold medal. He won 51 out of 54 amateur bouts, including the gold medal in the 1924 Paris Olympics, and held the welterweight title twice: 1929–30 and 1932–33. Jack Kearns, Fields' fight manager, said of him: "The best all-around battler in the United States, and he never received credit for the champion he was." His career record in 84 bouts was: 70 wins (28 by knockout), nine losses (one by knockout), two draws, two no-decisions, one no-contest.

Born Jacob Finkelstein, Fields grew up in a Jewish neighborhood in Chicago. "Being in the ghetto," he once recalled, "you had to fight." Fields' father was a

butcher who had contracted tuberculosis and was forced to move to a warmer climate. The family moved to Los Angeles when Jackie was 14. There his father tried his luck in the restaurant business, but the venture was not particularly successful.

A pro fighter named Irving Glazer who had befriended Jackie introduced him to boxing. He advised the youngster to approach George Blake at the Los Angeles Athletic Club for boxing lessons. Fields lied his way through the interview with Blake by telling him that he had fought previously in the Chicago Athletic Club. Blake, having been a boxing instructor there, knew that Jackie was lying, but still gave him a chance.

The lessons began in September 1921. Soon thereafter, Fields fought Fidel LaBarba, the Pacific Coast flyweight champion, and the newcomer was soundly beaten in a three-round decision. In 1924 Fields competed in the pre-Olympic AAU Nationals in Boston and, despite a broken hand, won the preliminaries, reaching the semifinals. Still, he earned a place on the Olympic team as an alternate.

During the voyage to the Paris Olympics, Jackie fought another alternate and defeated him, but it still appeared unlikely that he would fight in Paris. However, at the Paris training camp, Fields impressed the coaches by defeating another Olympic candidate, Harry Wallach. Jackie was therefore chosen as one of the two entrants (along with National AAU champ Joe Salas).

He and Salas reached the finals. Fields, then only 16 years old, won the fight and the gold medal. He was now the Olympic featherweight champion! "When they started to play the national anthem I burst out crying," Jackie recalled.

Joe Salas remained convinced that he should have won in Paris. Bearing a grudge, he challenged Fields to another fight in the U.S. Fields agreed, but only on the condition that the promoter pay him (Jackie) the then-huge sum of $500. Fields was victorious again and, according to Jackie, that fight "just broke his [Salas'] heart." Salas refused to talk to Fields ever again.

Upon his return to the United States, Fields decided to turn professional. He was not yet 17 years old. His first pro fight, for which he earned $5,000, was held in February 1925. He was not only badly beaten, but also suffered a broken jaw.

He returned home to a surprise: his mother administered a spanking to Jackie for fighting in the ring. "You know how Jewish mothers are," Fields explained. Acceding to his mother's wishes, he announced that he would hang up his gloves, but when his friends taunted him, saying that he lacked guts, he decided to return to the ring.

Fields wanted to fight Mushy Callahan, the reigning junior welterweight champion, and offered him a large sum (about $25,000) to contend for Callahan's title. It was billed as the Jewish championship of Boyle Heights and Central Avenue (Callahan was born Jewish, but converted to Catholicism). Fields later recalled: "I kicked the hell out of him. That was the first time I ever bet on myself and we won it. He never spoke to me for years afterward."

Fields' next fight was against Sammy Baker in Los Angeles. In the second round, coming out of a clinch, Fields landed a left hook: "I caught him on the chin and he dropped. I didn't walk to the corner; I ran to the corner. When they started to count and they got up to four, and five I started to pray, I really did." Baker stayed down for the count of 10.

On March 25, 1929, Fields won the National Boxing Association welterweight title from Jack Thompson. Then, four months later, on July 29th, Jackie fought Joe Dundee—then recognized in New York as title holder—for the world championship. Dundee was clearly losing the fight until the second round when he fouled Fields with a blow to the genitals, knocking him out. When Jackie woke up in the dressing room, he was informed that he was champion. Fields believed later that Dundee had fouled him deliberately so that his manager and friends would not lose a $50,000 bet placed on Dundee. Since Dundee lost on a foul (and not by a knockout or a decision), all bets were considered off.

On May 9, 1930, Fields lost the welterweight title to Young Jack Thompson by a decision in Detroit. Fields explained: "It was one of those nights when I was overtrained. I couldn't lift my hands up." So, Fields retired—again. But his manager Jack Kearns encouraged him to challenge Thompson one more time for the title. Meanwhile, Thompson lost the title to Lou Brouillard. Trying to earn back his self-respect, Fields prepared well for the match and beat Brouillard in Chicago on January 28, 1932, in 10 rounds. Thus Jackie Fields became welterweight champion for the second time.

In 1932 Jackie was involved in an automobile accident in Hammond, Indiana, on a trip from Louisville, Kentucky. He lost sight in one eye but told no one about it.

On February 22, 1933, Fields lost the world crown by losing a 10-round decision to Young Corbett III in San Francisco. When the referee, Jack Kennedy, raised Corbett's hand at the end of the fight, Fields and many others were amazed. In the dressing room after the fight Kennedy admitted to Fields' manager, "I made a mistake." The referee said he had raised the wrong hand. Kearns hit Kennedy, sending him to the floor.

Fields fought once more, winning a decision over Young Peter Jackson on May 2, 1933, in Los Angeles. He retired after that triumph mainly because his eye injury was becoming too troublesome.

Jackie's prizefighting encounters with Joe Salas during the 1924 Olympics and afterward were made into a 1939 movie entitled, *The Crowd Roars.*

Fields worked for Twentieth Century-Fox as an assistant unit manager and then as a film editor for MGM from 1934 to 1940. Following this he became the distributor for Wurlitzer jukeboxes in Pennsylvania from 1940 to 1949.

In the early 1950s, he represented the J&B Scotch Whiskey Company in the Chicago area. Then, in 1957, he became part-owner of the Tropicana Hotel in Las Vegas. He later sold his interest and became the hotel's public relations director.

In 1965, Jackie coached the U.S. boxing team at the Maccabiah Games in Israel. He also served in the 1960s as chairman of the Nevada State Athletic Commission. In 1972 he was elected to the United Savings-Helms Athletic Foundation Boxing Hall of Fame.

Jackie Fields is a member of the Jewish Sports Hall of Fame in Israel.

HARRY FISHER

Outstanding Basketball Coach
at Columbia and West Point

FISHER, HARRY A. (born February 6, 1882, in New York City; died December 29, 1967). An All-American basketball player at Columbia University in the early 1900s, and later an outstanding basketball coach at Columbia and the United States Military Academy at West Point.

At Columbia University, Fisher was team leader and scoring star from 1902 to 1905. Early in his career he set the field-goal record of 13, a record which stayed

on the books for 48 years. During his final two years as a player, the team lost only twice, and he was one of the players named All-American in 1905. In that same year he was appointed to a committee established to rewrite the rules of college basketball.

While serving as coach at Columbia University (from 1906 to 1916), he guided the team to three Eastern Invitational League titles, two of which were the reward for undefeated seasons. His overall record was a sensational 101 wins and 39 losses. From 1911 to 1917, Fisher also served as graduate manager of athletics at Columbia.

Fisher retired from Columbia and athletics in 1917, but five years later (in 1922) General Douglas MacArthur convinced him to become head basketball coach at the Military Academy at West Point. The 1922 and 1923 seasons were outstanding and closed out a great period of his career. In those two seasons he won 46 of 51 games. Army defeated Navy in each of those years.

Harry Fisher is a member of the College Basketball Hall of Fame.

HERBERT FLAM

Outstanding Tennis Player of the 1950s

FLAM, HERBERT (born November 7, 1928, in New York City, New York-) American tennis player. One of the outstanding American tennis players in the early 1950s, he was the first Jewish netman to reach the finals of the United States Nationals at Forest Hills when he lost to Art Larsen in 1950. No other Jewish player had as high a world ranking as Herb Flam until that time.

Flam began to play tennis at age 10 and won his first tournament two years later. With his father as his coach, Herb earned his reputation in California as a junior player. In 1948 he came to prominence in national tennis when, as an unseeded player, he reached the semifinals of the National singles competition. On the way he knocked out the third-seed, Gardner Mulloy, and the sixth, Harry Likas. Flam was ranked No. 9 in the U.S. that year.

Herb reached the quarterfinals in six national singles championships. In 1951, he was a semifinalist at the first Wimbledon tournament he played. He won his quarterfinal match in that tournament against Frank Sedgman after losing the first two sets. Flam was ranked No. 6 in the world that year.

Flam was American Clay Court champion in singles in 1950 and 1956 and Clay Court doubles champion in 1950. He played 14 Davis Cup rubbers for the U.S. from 1951 to 1957, winning 12.

In 1952, Herb reached the semifinals at Wimbledon and was ranked No. 10 in the world. He reached the last eight at Wimbledon three times in all. He was ranked No. 7 in the world in 1956 and No. 5 in 1957.

Flam's style of play has been labeled "retriever" with negative implications. A "retriever" in this sense is a tennis player who plays defensively, simply returning the ball without acting aggressively to try to win the point. Flam was not thrilled at that label. He contended that he did rush the net more than others. He realized that

he didn't hit the ball that hard but played subtly, for control, to get his opponent off balance. He tried to work into position to win the point.

Flam acknowledged that he started using the "retriever" style because of his small size as a youngster. As a teen-ager he grew to be 6 feet tall.

After Herb Flam retired from active tennis, he attempted several small businesses in Los Angeles with little success. Intermittently, he gave private tennis lessons. For the past few years he has not been well and is now confined to a hospital.

ALFRED FLATOW

Famous Member of the Berlin Gymnasts Club

FLATOW, ALFRED (born 1869, in Germany; died during World War II, exact date unknown) German gymnast. He won the parallel bars competition in the 1896 Athens Olympics and was awarded a silver medal (gold medals were not given then). He also placed second on the horizontal bars (no medal was given for this in 1896).

Alfred Flatow became involved in athletics at the age of eight when he joined the Youth Department of the German Athletics Club, and 10 years later he became a member of its Adult Department.

In 1890 Alfred passed the examination required to qualify as teacher of athletics, and at 21, he was the youngest person to hold that position in Germany at the time. Flatow served as a volunteer soldier in the 66th Infantry Regiment in Magdeburg in 1893 and 1894.

The following year, Flatow was a member of the gymnast delegation from the German Athletic Union that participated in the Italian Athletic Federation Festival in Rome. Flatow came in second in the general competition.

In 1896, Flatow was one of the 10 Germans chosen to represent his country in athletics at the Athens Olympics. He did well, but not nearly as well as some present-day records indicate. He is listed as having won the equivalent of three gold medals in that competition and a silver one, but by his own testimony, he won first place in the parallel bars and placed second in the horizontal bars. Another member of the delegation, Gustav Felix Flatow, has often been described as Alfred's brother, but they were not related.

At about this time Alfred began writing articles for the *Berliner Zeitung*. He gained a reputation as a gifted writer, and continued to write for the same newspaper for 40 years.

In 1898, at the Ninth Athletic Festival of German Athletes in Hamburg, Flatow won the Twelve Rounds competition, a series of gymnastic events. He considered this victory as important as his Olympics accomplishment.

Flatow was also a champion in 1899 at the Markisch Kreis Athletic Festival in Guben, Germany. The next two years he supervised athletic activities in Berlin.

He belonged to the elite of German gymnasts, and became an honorary member of the Deutsche Turnerschaft, the Union of German Gymnasts. Until World War I erupted in 1914, Flatow was active in athletics and even at the age of 50 he was still working out on the parallel bars. To earn a living he ran a bicycle shop in Berlin.

Three years after Hitler came to power, Flatow was the subject of a sympathetic newspaper article in the *Berliner Tageblatt* (April 18, 1936). The article read in part: "We met Alfred Flatow at his home in the first floor of an old house on Alexandrinen Street. The door led directly into a large room which served both as a storeroom for bicycle parts and an office. Flatow has lived here for over three decades. The 66-year-old man invited the guests into his semi-office. Numerous

diplomas, some framed, others in glass cases, decorated the walls. Among these are some precious pieces."

When Hitler came to power, he moved against the Berlin Gymnasts Club, whose most famous member was Alfred Flatow. The Jewish club members were politely asked to resign. They were bitter but no one dared protest. Rupert Naumann, chairman of the Berlin Gymnasts Club, had expressed support for Flatow. But Flatow was unable to resist Hitler and wrote to Naumann: "After receiving your letter of October 18, 1936, I reported my announcement of resignation from the organization of German gymnasts to Adolf Sengebusch [secretary of the German Turnenschaft]. For your expressions of your private feelings, I thank you very much. Concerning my own feelings and thoughts I prefer to keep silent." The letter was written October 20, 1936.

Flatow was sent to the Theresienstadt concentration camp. He died either there or in some other death camp during World War II. No record of the precise date or cause of his death has been preserved.

Alfred Flatow is a member of the Jewish Sports Hall of Fame in Israel.

NAT FLEISCHER

Founder and Editor of *Ring* Magazine

FLEISCHER, NATHANIEL STANLEY "NAT" (born November 3, 1887, in New York City; died June 25, 1972) American boxing promoter and editor. One of the major pioneers of modern boxing, Nat Fleischer became its outstanding promoter and authority. Founder and editor of the influential boxing magazine, *Ring.*

Nat Fleischer grew up on the lower East Side of New York. The exact date of his birth is unknown. (When he was 21, he selected November 3 as his birthday because he wanted to vote in that year's election.) While at P.S. 15 in New York City, he became interested in journalism and became editor of the school's monthly newspaper.

Nat's interest in boxing was first sparked when his father gave him photographs of fighters which came with packages of cigarettes. Nat watched his first world championship fight at the age of 12 in Tuckahoe, New York, when Terrible Terry McGovern knocked out Pedlar Palmer for the bantamweight title. The photographs and the title fight hooked Fleischer on boxing, a passion which never left him.

Two weeks after Nat watched that title fight, he took up boxing and became, in time, captain of the boxing team as well as president of the Oregon Athletic Club in New York City. He also played first base and catcher on the Oregon AC baseball team.

Nat desperately wanted to be a prizefighter, but, at age 15, and weighing in at 122 pounds, he was flattened in the first round of an amateur match at the Boys Club of New York. It was his first important bout, and it turned out to be the last time he put on boxing gloves.

Nat did better at sprinting. He became the Public School Athletic League 220-yard sprint champion. After graduating from Townsend Harris High School in New York, he entered City College of New York (CCNY) in the fall of 1904. He and Dan Daniel, who went on to become a famous New York sportswriter, founded the first CCNY intercollegiate basketball team. It was at CCNY that Nat got his first taste of serious writing, becoming the campus correspondent for two New York dailies and working on the sports desk of the *New York Press*.

In 1908, Nat graduated from CCNY with a bachelor of science degree in botany and chemistry. While working on the *Press* at night, he passed the teachers' examination, and began teaching sixth-grade girls' botany at New York City's P.S. 7. His new vocation did not agree with him too well.

He decided next to take a graduate course in commercial chemistry at New York University. But in a few months his course of study came to an abrupt end. Arriving at the lab one day, sleepy following a long, hectic night at the *Press*, Nat mixed the wrong solutions and blew up part of the lab. He was promptly dismissed from the course.

Fleischer followed this scholastic experience with a new one at Yale University where he enrolled in a forestry course. This too did not last long, and he decided to become a full-time journalist, investing all of his energies in his work at the *Press*. He went on to become sports editor of the *Press*. When the *Press* later merged with the *Morning Sun*, Fleischer became an assistant to the new sports editor.

In 1914, Nat became sports editor of the *Sun Press*. Over the next 13 years, he was sports editor of the *Morning Herald*, the *Mail-Telegram*, and the *Evening Telegram*. Then, in 1927, Scripps-Howard bought the *Telegram* and Fleischer was fired. He decided to devote all of his time to *Ring* magazine, which he and three associates had founded five years earlier, in 1922. Several years later, Nat acquired full ownership of the magazine. The magazine provided the only

comprehensive coverage of boxing in the world. Its ratings of fighters were accepted as authoritative.

Fleischer was a small man (5 feet, 2 inches) who frequently wore a brown hat with the brim curled up at the sides. While serving as editor, sportswriter, and referee, he could not help but notice that boxing was plagued with questionable promoters who had foisted much impropriety on fans and participants. Nat vowed to free boxing of these promoters. Fleischer wanted to protect boxers against mismatches and give the fans the quality fight they had paid to see.

Nat's influence on boxing is unmatched. As a promoter, he insisted on rigorous physical examinations for boxers before a fight was staged, and better care for those seriously hurt during a fight. He also protected spectators from questionable promotional gimmicks. In addition, he advocated closed-circuit television coverage and home viewing of fights, to encourage and maintain public interest in boxing. Despite threats on his life by vested interests who were being hurt by his progressiveness, he persevered.

Fleischer initiated boxing's rating system, and awarded handsome belts to world boxing champions. He also helped to establish boxing commissions around the world.

Nat refereed and judged more than 1,000 fights. His career as a boxing official, however, was not without its brushes with danger. In 1939, he was to referee a bout between the American fighter Joey Archibald, the featherweight champion, and Simon Chavez, in Caracas, Venezuela. The night before the fight, two men entered Nat's room while he sat in his pajamas. Throwing a good deal of money on his bed and brandishing a gun, they informed him tersely that they had bet heavily on Chavez and "you know what you're going to do." Brushing the money to the floor, Nat barked orders to the men: "Put that gun away. I am going to call police headquarters the moment you leave the room." The men, obviously surprised by his reaction, promptly left the room.

The fight went on under heavy guard, and Chavez won. Before the fight, Fleischer had asked Joey Archibald to make a special effort to win on a knockout, but the high altitude had sapped his strength. After the match, Nat explained to the defeated fighter why he had encouraged him so much. "Gee, Nat," said Archibald, "I just thought you wanted me to put the U.S. on top of the heap."

Another time, when Nat was refereeing the Harry Jeffra-Spider Armstrong featherweight title bout in Baltimore on July 29, 1940, Fleischer had to put up with 102-degree heat at ringside. After the eleventh round, he took off his tie; after the twelfth, he unbuttoned his shirt; after the thirteenth, he pulled the shirt off; came the fourteenth round, and off came Nat's undershirt; came the fifteenth, he held up Jeffra's hand and slumped against the ropes, unable to move.

Just then, a lady, who obviously had taken Fleischer's preaching of morality in boxing (as espoused in *Ring* magazine) seriously, approached him and said: "So you're the Nat Fleischer who preaches morals in *Ring*. You should be ashamed of yourself, taking off your underwear in public!"

Nat Fleischer wrote 60 books on boxing. His first, *Training for Boxers,* came at the prompting of his wife. It was written immediately after the bank in which he had deposited his money collapsed in 1929. The book sold almost a million copies at $1 each. In 1942 he published the first edition of the annual *Ring Record Book,* still considered the authoritative source book in the sport.

A nonstop author, Nat once wrote a 30-chapter biography of the famous Jim Corbett in 36 hours shortly after the boxer had died in 1933. One estimate has it that Nat wrote 40 million words in his life.

"Mr. Boxing," as Nat Fleischer came to be called, gave boxing a respectability it did not possess before his time.

SIDNEY FRANKLIN

The First Jewish Bullfighter

FRANKLIN, SIDNEY(born June 11, 1903, in Brooklyn, New York; died April 26, 1976) American bullfighter. Not the first American to step into the ring, but most certainly the first Jew to take up the sport.

He became one of Spain's leading matadors, reaching the zenith of his career in the early 1930s.

His real surname was Frumkin, but he took the name Franklin out of admiration for Ben Franklin. Sidney's parents were Russian Jewish immigrants and he was the fifth of their 10 children. His father was a policeman. The future bullfighter, intimidated by other children, shied away from them. At age 13, he won a first prize offered by Wanamaker's Department Store for beaded embroidery.

Franklin's ambition was to become an actor. For a while he appeared in the Peter Rabbit Annual Shows at the Globe Theatre and was a member of a theatrical stock company.

After three years at Brooklyn's Commercial High School, Sidney studied Spanish at Columbia University's Extension Department. In 1922 after an argument with his father, he sailed for Mexico and told friends that he was making the journey to study Mayan art.

Once there, he began a poster business which featured artwork for bullfight impressarios. To check whether the sketches he was selling were accurate, he attended a bullfight and got caught up in the excitement.

Some Mexican acquaintances argued that no American, including Sidney Franklin, could learn the sport. Franklin took up the challenge. He had watched bullfights carefully and had been overwhelmed by the precision and grace with which the matadors handled the cape. The slim, sandyhaired Franklin sought out Rodolfo Gaona, the great Mexican matador, and asked for instruction.

After several weeks of strenuous training, Sidney Franklin entered the ring for the first time on September 20, 1923. He lost his balance twice but killed his bull. "If you've got guts," he once said, "you can do anything." In fact, Franklin's debut that autumn day was made possible by a local promoter who believed that the spectacle of a "gringo" pursued around the ring by a fighting bull would be a superb amusement for the crowd. He never bargained on Franklin becoming a great star.

After some years in Mexico, Franklin went to Spain in 1939 and became the first American to engage in bullfighting there. He became a drawing card not only throughout Spain, but also in Portugal, Mexico, and other parts of South America, earning as much as $100,000 a year. In a March 1930 fight in Madrid, he was gored so badly that he could not fight for a number of years. About the risk of being injured in the ring, Franklin once said, "It is part of the game and makes no difference to any of us."

Sidney Franklin's performances in the ring were impressive. His costume and highly decorative cape cost $1,000—an extravagant sum for those years. The costume weighed 50 pounds and it took him an hour to dress for the fight. The actual working cape cost only $50.

Naturally righthanded, Sidney taught himself to be ambidextrous so that he could handle the seven-pound sword with either hand. He was highly superstitious, and would never pick up a salt shaker to hand to someone. Instead, he always slid it along the table. He also knocked on iron for good luck.

In 1945, Franklin reached the pinnacle of his profession when he became the headliner in Madrid's Plaza de Toros. "I didn't have the gracefulness or art of the Spaniards," he said later, "but I was brave and that made me famous."

Ernest Hemingway, one of Sidney's close friends, described Franklin in *Death in the Afternoon:* "Sidney Franklin is brave with a cold, serene, and intelligent valor. No history of bullfighting that is ever written can be complete unless it gives him the space he is entitled to."

Franklin had hoped to introduce bullfighting in the United States, but his plan to hold a bloodless bull-dodging contest in Newark, New Jersey, was barred in 1930. His only opportunity to show his prowess to his former Brooklyn neighbors occurred during the 1939 New York World's Fair when he put on a series of bull-dodging exhibitions with the approval of the Society for the Prevention of Cruelty to Animals.

Sidney managed a cafe in Seville, Spain, in the 1950s, and also had the cafeteria concession at the American Strategic Air Command base at nearby Moro de la Frontera at the same time. He wrote his autobiography in 1952, *The Bullfighter from Brooklyn.* After that he fought only intermittently, devoting most of his time to running a school for bullfighters at Alcaia de Guerdaira, near Seville.

In 1957, Franklin was fined and jailed for illegally keeping an automobile in Spain. After serving nine months of his 25-month sentence, he was pardoned, and returned to the U.S.

Franklin tried to make a comeback in June 1958, but did not do well. In May 1959, in Juarez, Mexico, he suffered a serious injury which ended his career.

In the years that followed, his love for the sport did not wane. "The pleasurable thing about bullfighting," he said once, "is the thrill of matching one's agility and wits against those of an active opponent who can kill you if he catches you."

He became an authority on the history of bullfighting. The article on the subject in the *Encyclopedia Britannica* was written by Franklin.

Franklin died in 1976 while residing at the Village Nursing Home in New York where he had lived since 1970. His obituary in *The New York Times* included this terse statement: "Sidney Franklin was the only matador ever born at 14 Jackson Place in the Park Slope section of Brooklyn."

BENNY FRIEDMAN

The Quarterback Who Never Made a Mistake

FRIEDMAN, BENNY(born March 18, 1905, in Cleveland, Ohio; died November 23, 1982) American football player. Football's first great passer, and one of the greatest Jewish football players in history. A true popularizer of the game, he added imagination to football and was once described by coach Fielding Yost as "the quarterback who never makes a mistake." Red Grange, the legendary runner, called Friedman the best quarterback he had ever seen.

Friedman was an all-around athlete in high school. Upon enrolling in the

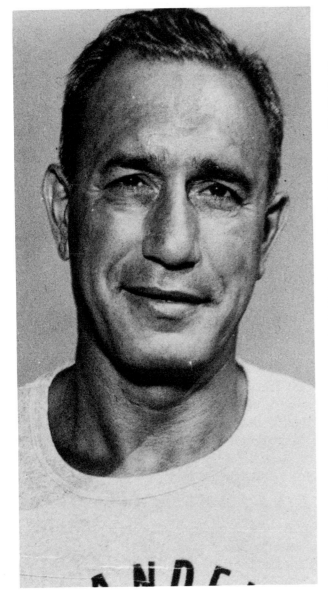

University of Michigan in 1923, he immediately made the freshman football team. The next year he was invited to try out for the varsity and made it.

For the first half of the season Benny was a benchwarmer, and he felt that the coach was not favorably inclined toward Jews. Later that season, when Friedman was given a chance to play toward the end of one game, he performed so well that from then on he was a starter.

In 1925, Benny Friedman became Michigan's starting quarterback, enjoying a great year and becoming a first-team All-American choice. He passed for 11 touchdowns and did all the place kicking. The Wolverines were 7-1 that year, winning the Western Conference Championship. Largely because of Benny Friedman, Michigan's 1925 team was one of football's greatest. The Wolverines scored a total of 227 points while allowing their opposition only three. Friedman's most spectacular performance that season was in the game against Indiana: he ran 55 yards to score one touchdown, threw another five touchdown passes, and kicked eight extra points. Friedman was personally responsible for 44 of Michigan's 63 points that day. Final score: Michigan 63, Indiana 0.

In 1926 Friedman was Michigan's captain and he enjoyed another marvelous season. The team again was 7-1 and again he was a first-team All-America selection. He was also chosen Most Valuable Player in the Western Conference.

Friedman was one of the pioneers who helped change football from a contest of brawn to one of intelligence. Fiercely competitive, he was one of the first quarterbacks to dare to pass from behind his own goal line. Friedman had a toughness and durability that helped him avoid injury through 10 years of rugged football. In those days, good players like Benny Friedman played 60 minutes each game.

Benny encountered little anti-Jewish feeling in his college days. In fact, as a superstar on campus, he was, for the most part, immune from whatever anti-Semitism might have lain under the surface. He wrote: "There were times when I thought the grade was made harder for me on account of racial prejudice. I soon found out that was bunk. The fact that I was a Jew didn't preclude social recognition for me on the campus."

In a letter to the author (written December 23, 1981), Friedman provided this illustration of his family's Jewish faith as it related to his football career: "We had an Orthodox home and on the kitchen wall was a *pushke* (charity box). I noticed when I was a high school player mother would go over to the box after serving me brunch and drop some coins in the box. I would see her lips moving as though she was saying a prayer. I asked what she was doing and she said she was protecting me by putting 18 cents in the *pushke.* I asked why. She told me that 18 in Hebrew stands for *chai* which means life.

"Mother would come out to the game and watch. In the course of a game on occasion someone would be hurt or laid out. She never worried that it was I, because she had taken care of me through her faith. I never was hurt and throughout my high school and college career mother continued her vigil. I never questioned her whether it was my ability that kept me aloof from injury; I let it go that it was *chai* working for me."

When the 5-foot, 8-inch Friedman began playing pro football, he seemed somewhat concerned about the large size of the pros facing him. Once, in a game, from nowhere, he heard someone say in Yiddish, "Keep your chin up, Benny. It's a nice, friendly game." Wondering who this fellow-Jew was, Benny looked over at the rival team's line and saw a hefty tackle grinning from ear to ear. "What's your name and where are you from?" asked Friedman. The large-framed tackle replied with the same grin, "O'Donnell of Notre Dame."

Friedman joined the pros in 1927 and played for the next seven years, making All-Pro each of his first four years. He played first with the Cleveland Bulldogs. In 1928 he was with the Detroit Wolverines, and from 1929 to 1931 with the New York Giants. He concluded his pro career by playing with the Brooklyn Dodgers football team between 1932 and 1934.

Until Friedman arrived on the scene, the pass had been used on third down as a weapon of desperation in long yardage situations—or when the team was far behind. The Chicago Bears' owner, George Halas, called Friedman the first pro quarterback "to exploit the strategic possibilities of the pass." Halas noted that "Benny demonstrated that the pass could be mixed with the running plays as an integral part of the offense."

Because of Benny Friedman's innovative use of the forward pass, the professional rules committee slenderized the football, one more major step in the evolution of pro football from a purely straightforward running game into the passing-and-running game it eventually became.

Friedman retired from football in 1934, not without a measure of bitterness at having become a pro football player rather than the stockbroker he had desired to be. "For the past six years," he wrote later, "I've made $10,000 a year at pro football. It's been fun, hard-earned fun. But where has it got me?" Still, he was not prepared to advise others against pursuing a pro football career.

In 1934 Friedman returned to collegiate football as head coach of the City College of New York, a job he held until 1941. In that year he joined the U.S. Navy and became a naval officer assigned to aircraft carriers. Between 1949 and 1963 he served as head football coach and athletic director at Brandeis University, the Jewish-supported and sponsored school in Waltham, Massachusetts. He also ran a summer camp for boys and at the end of the summer a special camp for quarterbacks, both in Kohut, Maine.

In April 1963, Friedman resigned as athletic director at Brandeis, citing the growing responsibilities heaped upon him by his outside business interests and his summer camp in Maine. Another factor in his decision was the university's new athletic policy which dropped intercollegiate football as an activity.

In February 1976, Friedman wrote a letter of protest to the sports editor of the *New York Times*. He felt that he had been denied the ultimate recognition due him. He recounted his exploits, calling himself "the highest-priced and yet the least-expensive player of the game." By least-expensive he explained that he had always played 60 minutes, never had to be taken out of a game due to injuries, and always was ready for the next game: "I not only ran the ball and passed, but also did all the place kicking." What grieved Friedman was that while he is a member of the Citizens Savings Hall of Fame and the National Football Foundation Hall of Fame, as well as the Jewish Sports Hall of Fame, he had been skipped over by the Pro Football Hall of Fame in Canton, Ohio.

Friedman died on November 23, 1982 in his East Side apartment in New York City of what the police described as a self-inflicted gunshot wound. At the time of his death, he had still not been inducted into the Pro Football Hall of Fame.

MAX FRIEDMAN

A Pioneer of Basketball

FRIEDMAN, MAX "MARTY" (born July 12, 1889, in New York City-) American basketball player. Considered a great defensive star and team leader, he was a pioneer of basketball. One of the "Heavenly Twins," he was chosen on Nat Holman's All-Time Pro Team in 1922 and named to an All-Time Pro Second Team in 1941.

Friedman attended the Hebrew Technical Institute, a vocational high school in New York, graduating in 1908. At the same time, he was playing with the University Settlement House team on New York's lower East Side. He turned pro in 1910 when the Hudson River League of New York was formed.

In 1914 he played on the Utica, New York, basketball team in the Hudson River League. The following year Friedman played with Carbondale in the Pennsylvania-Intercounty League, where his team set a record of 45 straight wins. Carbondale beat the competing Penn State League winners that year.

From 1915 to 1917, Friedman played with the Philadelphia Jaspers of the Eastern League. The team reached the championship finals in 1917. Max then enlisted in the army, went to Officers Training School, and qualified as a pilot. He was sent to France but never saw combat.

While overseas, Friedman organized an athletic program for troops who stayed in Europe, and he organized and captained the basketball team that took the American Expeditionary Forces title. In 1919, he captained the team that beat the French and Italians for the championship in the Interallied Games.

On his return to the U.S., Friedman joined the championship Albany, New York, team which won the New York State League in 1920. That year he began playing for one of the greatest pro teams ever, the New York Whirlwinds. His teammates were Barney Sedran and Nat Holman. Marty Friedman and Barney Sedran became known as the "Heavenly Twins," an indication of how well the two of them played together.

Friedman was part of two championship teams in 1921: Albany and Easthampton of the Interstate League. He played for two teams in 1922: Albany and the Brooklyn Dodgers of the Metropolitan League.

An injured knee and shoulder kept Friedman out of action for most of the next year. He then joined the Cleveland Rosenblums and captained them from 1925 to 1927. In 1927 the team lost the American League title to the New York Celtics.

After the 1927 season, Friedman retired from playing, but in 1939 he was back in basketball as coach of the American League's Troy Haymakers. Then he went into the garage business with his playing partner, Barney Sedran, and stayed in the business until retiring in 1958.

SIDNEY GILLMAN

One of Pro Football's Great Innovators

GILLMAN, SIDNEY (born October 26, 1911, in Minneapolis, Minnesota-) American football player and coach. He played for Ohio State in the early 1930s and was an All-American honorable mention end in 1932 and 1933. But Gillman is best known as the coach of the Los Angeles Rams between 1955 and 1959 and then of the Los Angeles and San Diego Chargers, of the fledgling American Football League, between 1960 and 1971.

Gillman grew up in Minneapolis. He attended Ohio State from 1931 to 1933 and was co-captain of the 1932 team. In the 1933 game against Northwestern he recovered a fumble and ran 54 yards for a touchdown.

Sid intended to pursue a law career, but coaching was his real love. He began his career in 1934 as assistant coach at his alma mater, Ohio State. He had his heart set on winning the job of Ohio State head football coach, but the offer never came.

From 1935 to 1937 he was assistant coach at Denison University in Granville, Ohio, and returned to Ohio State as assistant coach from 1938 to 1940. In 1941 he went back to Denison as assistant coach. In 1942 and 1943 he was assistant coach at Miami of Ohio (located in Oxford), and head coach from 1944 until 1947.

In his first season in 1944 at Miami's helm, Gillman's team was 8-1-0, and from that year on his college teams never failed to post a winning season. After an 8-0-1 mark in the 1947 season, his Miami team won the Sun Bowl against Texas Tech. His overall four year record at Miami was 30-6-1. In 1948 he became an assistant coach at West Point. Red Blaik, Army's coach, observed that "there are few brilliant thinkers left in football. Sid is one of them."

From 1949 to 1954, Gillman was head coach at the University of Cincinnati where he succeeded in establishing a career record of 49-12-1.

In 20 seasons of coaching in the Midwest, Gillman never saw his teams win fewer than seven games in a season. Despite his impressive record, he failed to obtain that coveted job of head coach at Ohio State. Sid always suspected that his being Jewish was a factor, so he went to the pros.

In 1955, he became head coach of the National Football League Los Angeles Rams and in his very first year he led the team to a Western Division title. (The Ram team that year had Bob Waterfield, Norm Van Brocklin, Tank Younger, Elroy Hirsch, and Tom Fears.) The Rams lost the 1955 NFL championship to the Cleveland Browns, 38-14. Gillman's overall Ram record between 1955 and 1959 was 38-35-1.

Sid was considered one of football's great innovators. He was a strong advocate of frequent use of the forward pass and was responsible for its wide usage in the NFL. He was the first to put the names of players on their jerseys. He is credited with being one of those who introduced the two-platoon system. And, in

1956, he was the first to begin filming practice sessions, and the first to cut game films and organize them according to plays.

Gillman sometimes watched films for 18 hours a day. The whole exercise came naturally to him: "I had the advantage of my family being in the movie business (in Minneapolis in the '20s and '30s). I used to be able to get newsreels in the old days, when we had Paramount News and Fox News. I'd clip the football parts off." He was once asked how he had been able to do so well in pro football, to which he replied: "The movie projector. You've gotta get your butt behind a movie projector, constantly test your theories, examine your ideas to see where they hold up, to get better ideas."

When the American Football League was founded in 1960, Sid accepted the dual post of head coach and general manager of the Los Angeles Chargers. He led the club to the Western Division title, but lost the playoff to Houston. The Chargers moved from Los Angeles to San Diego in 1961, and Gillman, general manager and head coach, organized their move.

In 1963, when San Diego won the AFL title, Gillman advocated a revolutionary idea, a "super bowl" between the AFL and the NFL title winner, the Chicago Bears. Bears owner George Halas and NFL Commissioner Pete Rozelle would hear nothing of the idea. At the time of Pope John XXIII's Ecumenical Council in the early '60s, Gillman wired Rozelle: "Pope John was a great man because he recognized the other league." Rozelle wired back: "Yes, but it took a thousand years."

Gillman's Chargers that year were regarded by some observers as the greatest offensive team in pro football history. They averaged an incredible 29 points per game, had an 11-3 record, and crushed the Boston Patriots in the AFL title game, 51-10. Sid himself called the team the best ever produced in the AFL.

In 1964, Gillman's team won the Western Division but lost the title game to Buffalo, 20-7. In all, he won five division titles: 1960, 1961, 1963, 1964, and 1965. His overall record with the Chargers: 86-53-9.

Gillman's teams won because they used the forward pass: "We had to throw the ball. Nobody had any great defenses. I thought that the AFL, from that standpoint, had a slight advantage. You start something new, people want to see the

ball. They don't care where it goes, as long as you put it in the air." His teams always did just that.

A duodenal ulcer and hiatal hernia forced his premature retirement in November 1969. But he returned to guide the Chargers in 1971. Sid and millionaire owner Gene Klein did not get along. Bitter disputes ensued; some said over money, some said over Klein's desire to dictate which players to use. Klein dismissed Gillman in midseason.

Between November 1971, when he left the Chargers, and 1973, Gillman enjoyed a brief retirement. For a time he served as an aide to Dallas Cowboy coach Tom Landry. Then the opportunity arose to take over the Houston Oilers.

In 1973 he was hired as executive vice president and general manager with orders to rebuild the Oilers. They had not had a winning season since 1967. In 1972, the year before Gillman joined the organization, the Oilers had been 1-13. Five games into Gillman's first season (1973), Oiler coach Bill Peterson had led the club to a dismal 0-5 record. Gillman decided to become his own head coach; he put jobs on the line, imposed curfews, fines, and bed checks, and added hours of hard work to the training schedule. By the end of 1973, the Oilers were still losing (they wound up 1-13), but they had become competitive. The dramatic change came in 1974, when Houston finished 7-7. "It was like winning the Super Bowl," recalled Sid.

Gillman had problems with Oiler owner J. C. (Bud) Adams, who felt Sid was extravagant. "I'm a believer that you have to have an edge to win," observed Gillman, "and that takes money. You have to try things the other teams aren't trying. Adams didn't want to hear any of that." He fired Gillman. Soon thereafter, Sid was named Coach of the Year for 1974.

Since then Gillman has written a column for a syndicated newspaper supplement called *Inside Football Report,* and beginning in 1977, he spent a year as offensive coordinator for the Chicago Bears. The Bears made the playoffs that season for the first time in 14 years. But, eventually he felt his ideas were not getting through to anyone, so, in disgust, he quit.

For 18 months (1978-79) Gillman was athletic director at the United States International University in San Diego, California, near his home in La Costa. He hoped to upgrade football there, but when he got a call from Philadelphia Eagle head coach Dick Vermeil in April 1979, asking him to join the Eagles as an assistant, he quickly agreed. "Pro football is my life," Sid explained.

In July of that year, Sid had a six-way bypass heart operation and he recovered well from it. His title for the Eagles was special assistant in charge of research and quality control. Gillman's major contribution was turning Eagle quarterback Ron Jaworski into a first-class quarterback. "He's the guy who turned us around offensively, as far as being innovative," said Ron of "Coach Sid." Sid taught the Eagles how to use the entire 53 1/3 yard-width of the football field on their passing plays.

At the close of the 1980 season, Gillman retired to his La Costa, California, home, with its football-shaped swimming pool. His home is alongside the first fairway of the La Costa Country Club golf course near San Diego. But he could not bow out of football completely. He lectured the Green Bay Packer coaching staff on passing offense and then ran a camp for 10-to-15-year-olds in La Jolla.

When the 1981 season rolled around, Gillman was again in retirement in

California. He missed the action: "You wouldn't believe how badly," he admitted. So he came back to the Eagles in March 1982, in his old job of assistant coach in charge of quarterbacks. He is a member of the Ohio State University Hall of Fame, the University of Cincinnati Hall of Fame, and the Jewish Sports Hall of Fame in Israel.

In February 1983, he was elected to the Pro Football Hall of Fame.

SHLOMO GLICKSTEIN

The Greatest Israeli Tennis Player

GLICKSTEIN, SHLOMO (born January 6, 1958, in Rehovot, Israel–) Israeli tennis player. In November 1982, he was ranked twenty-second in the world, his highest ever. He concluded the 1981 pro circuit with a ranking of thirty-third in the world, compared with his standing of 57 at the end of 1980, and 153 at the end of 1979. In 1981, he was thirty-fifth on the list of money-winners among the pros, earning $93,112. Glickstein is the greatest tennis player Israel has ever produced. He has defeated many of the top stars, including Australian Peter McNamara, ranked eighth in the world. Glickstein's best tournament win to date was the South Orange, New Jersey, $75,000 Grand Prix, held in August 1981. Glickstein's 1982 world rank was thirty-three.

Shlomo began playing the game when he was 10. He played at a small club near his home in Ashkelon about twice a week until the age of 16. An excellent athlete, Shlomo played basketball and soccer as a child, but at age 16, he gave them up to concentrate on tennis. One major problem he faced was the lack of courts in Israel. "We had to move from one club to another to practice on different days every week," recalled Glickstein. "It was really tough." No club would accept the national team (of which Shlomo was a member) and allow them to practice because members wanted to use the courts for themselves.

By age 12, Shlomo had made enough progress to catch the eye of national coach Ron Steele. "Shlomo was undoubtedly the best tennis prospect in Israel," recalled Steele. "I used to go down to Ashkelon on Saturdays especially to train him." During the 1975 and 1976 seasons, Shlomo competed in a number of international tournaments, doing rather well in general. "By the time he finished the juniors," noted Steele, "Shlomo was one of the top ten juniors in the world."

But an obstacle awaited him: the Israel Defense Forces. Like all Israeli males, Shlomo Glickstein had to serve three years in the Israeli army, beginning at age 18. Though the army gave him special consideration (he was based close to the Israel Tennis Center in Ramat Hasharon outside Tel Aviv), there is no denying that military service took three years out of his life at the most productive time in a

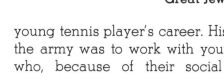

young tennis player's career. His job in the army was to work with youngsters who, because of their social backgrounds, had little motivation to take the army seriously. Shlomo did manage to play on Israel's Davis Cup team from 1976 to 1980, despite his army service.

For a time, Glickstein wavered in his committent to tennis. Then in 1978, his father, Moshe, a former chairman of the Israel Tennis Association's Youth committee, died. Shlomo told Ron Steele at the time, "I've made my decision: I'm going to be a tennis player. I want to honor my father's name in tennis." From then on he dedicated himself completely to the game.

Glickstein joined the professional tour in May 1979, shortly after his release from the army. That year he won his third straight Israeli national championship. Then came a turning point in his career. At the Tel Aviv Grand Prix that October he reached the quarterfinals, but more importantly, coach Ron Steele, arguing that he was still not aggressive enough, advised him to play in Sweden and in Australia. "Shlomo was instructed to attack, attack, attack," said Steele.

In November 1979, Glickstein managed to stretch John McEnroe to three sets in the first round of the Stockholm Grand Prix after losing the first set 6–0 in five minutes. "Shlomo realized," noted Steele, "that the giants of the game were only human." Glickstein learned that aggressiveness pays off.

In January 1980, Glickstein won the Australian Hard Courts Championship in Hobart, a victory which brought him $8,750 and enabled him to advance a full 200 places in the ATP rankings within three months. His second major success was also won below the equator as he climbed to the quarterfinals of the Sigma Open in Johannesburg, South Africa. Returning to the American circuit, Glickstein defeated Bill Scanlon to reach the semifinals at the Stowe Grand Prix in Vermont.

But, it was a first-round upset win at Wimbledon in 1980 that won Glickstein instant international recognition. He defeated Raul Ramirez (then ranked 35). Britain's mass circulation *Daily Express* carried a banner headline which read: "Shlo-motion." The subhead announced: "Ramirez Rocked by Israeli Hero." Israeli journalists, noting that Glickstein had grown up in Ashkelon, compared him with the Biblical Samson, another native of that seacoast town.

In the second round at Wimbledon, Shlomo faced Bjorn Borg. The Swede triumphed on his way to his fifth Wimbledon championship, but the loss was tempered by Borg's kind words for Shlomo: "He has been doing very well. After all, he's been on the circuit only one year." Glickstein won the Wimbledon Plate, the consolation tournament, that year.

Then Shlomo defeated the world's No. 11 player, Brian Gottfried, at the Stockholm Open, and made it to the quarterfinals there. He also got into the finals of the British Hardcourt championships in Bournemouth. His biggest financial reward that year came in December when he earned $20,000 in prize money at the World Championship of Tennis Challenge Cup in Montreal, coming in fifth in the eight-participant tournament which included some major figures in international tennis.

In 1981 Glickstein continued to improve, and he won the South Orange, New Jersey, Grand Prix, the first time an Israeli has won a tennis grand prix. He reached the semifinals of the South African and Canadian Opens and the quarters of the Australian Championship. He also reached the quarterfinals in another five Grand Prix meets. During that year Glickstein defeated Harold Solomon and Eliot Teltscher, ranked 9 and 10 on the ATP computer. In doubles, he was runner-up at South Orange, with his Davis Cup teammate Dave Schneider and he reached the semifinals in two other Grand Prix tournaments with different partners. And, in the Grand Prix standings, he was ranked twenty-fourth at the end of 1981: he had been thirty-eighth at the end of 1980.

Ivan Lendl, the Czech tennis star, commented on Shlomo in the summer of 1981: "He has great anticipation. He always waits for the ball where the ball is coming. He looks as if he's going to move very slow, but he is really very fast. He always does the right thing. He has great shots, especially passing shots on the backhand down the line. He has great touch."

On his own performance in 1981, Glickstein noted, "My game is now steadier and I am not making so many unforced errors. I believe I am capable of beating any player on the circuit, except perhaps the top six."

He has one gripe: the media. "They quote me and that makes me nervous. They write all sorts of things about my personal life outside tennis."

In May, 1982, Glickstein achieved one of his most impressive wins, taking the eight-man Tennis Classic in Tulsa, Oklahoma. He picked up $25,000 for the triumph, but, unfortunately for him, no ATP points to improve his ranking, since the tournament was outside the Grand Prix circuit. The following August, he reached the semifinals of the South Orange, New Jersey, Grand Prix tournament, the one he had won the previous year.

MARSHALL GOLDBERG

All-Pro Defensive Football Player

GOLDBERG, MARSHALL "BIGGIE," "MAD MARSHALL" (born October 24, 1917, in Elkins, West Virginia-) American football player. One of football's most powerful runners. He played for the University of Pittsburgh from 1936 to 1938 in the backfield. Twice chosen All-American. Played for the Chicago Cardinals from 1939 to 1943 and from 1946 to 1948. At Pittsburgh, in 29 games, he gained 2,231 yards and scored 18 touchdowns. An excellent defensive player in the pros, he led the National Football League in interceptions (7) in 1941. He was on the All-Pro defensive team in 1946, 1947, and 1948.

Marshall and his family were heroes in Elkins, West Virginia, a small town of 7,500. Marshall's father, Sol, a Russian immigrant, gained prominence in the town because three of his five sons were football stars with the local Davis-Elkins High School team. Marshall was chosen as the student "most likely to succeed." In 1934 and 1935 he was on the All-State basketball team and he captained the State Championship basketball team in 1935. He was All-State in football in 1934 and a member and captain of the track and basketball teams as well during his senior (1935) year of high school.

Marshall earned the nickname "Biggie" because he could play football with boys much older than he. He was 5 foot, 11 inches tall and weighed 183 pounds when he entered the University of Pittsburgh in 1935. Marshall's effectiveness in college was hampered because he never did learn how to pass well; nevertheless, his college career was studded with marvelous feats of running.

Goldberg broke into the Pitt varsity lineup as a sophomore in 1936 and contributed significantly to the team's being chosen to play in that year's Rose Bowl. He scored two touchdowns in the first game of the 1936 season. In the fifth game against Notre Dame, he carried the ball 22 times for 117 yards, scored a touchdown, passed for another, and set up a third. He was a national hero. New York reporters, impressed with his speed, called him "Glittering Goldberg." He was also described by sportswriters as "the finest ball carrier since Red Grange." Pitt was 7–1–1 in 1936; the team went on to beat Washington in the Rose Bowl 21–0. Goldberg had scored six touchdowns that season. He received an honorable mention for the All-American team.

The story is told of Marshall's father breaking the tension before the Pitt-Washington game on New Year's Day, 1937. With all the excitement surrounding the Rose Bowl, the Pitt team had a bad case of jitters before the game. In the dressing room, the coach, Doc Sutherland, read a telegram from Marshall's father:

"Dear doctor, Bring home the bacon. And you know how I hate pork!"

Laughter erupted, and the team went on to beat Washington 21–0. When Sol Goldberg was not watching the team from the Pitt bench, he was back home running his movie theater. When a competing movie theater showed Marshall Goldberg playing in the Rose Bowl, Sol wrote to Fox Movietone's News Department: "When you have any more Goldberg pictures, for God's sake, send them to Goldberg!"

Marshall Goldberg's first great year was 1937 when he made the All-America first team, picking up 701 yards in 10 games and scoring five touchdowns. He was fifth in rushing in the nation. Pitt was undefeated, 9–0–1 and college national champion. In selecting Marshall Goldberg All-American in 1937, the Associated Press wrote: "Coaches say that he is the fastest man they have observed in years.

But Biggie is not only a hard-driving, deceptive runner, especially dangerous off the tackles or around the ends. He is a good blocker, hard-hitting on the defensive, and plays the safety spot."

In 1938 he was switched from halfback to fullback. He scored seven touchdowns and picked up 375 yards as the Pittsburgh Panthers were 8–2. Again, he was an All-American selection, one of the few players to become an All-American twice and in two different positions. After Goldberg helped Pitt destroy Temple, 38–6, one sports reporter wrote: "Goldberg had to be seen to be believed. He slashed at the tackles, swept the ends, ripped on reverses, pummeled the middle."

In 1939, Goldberg began his pro career, playing with the Chicago Cardinals. He was less impressive than in college because the pros relied more on passing than running, the latter being Marshall's real talent. In addition, the Cardinals were, quite simply, a poor team. From 1939 to 1946 (with two years out for navy service) Goldberg played on teams which compiled a 15–47–3 record.

Besides leading the NFL in interceptions with seven for 54 yards in 1941, he was also NFL kickoff return leader with a 24.2 yard average, 12 for 290 yards. In 1942 his kickoff return average jumped to 26.2, with 15 for 393 yards.

In 1947, the Cardinals finally had a championship team, but Goldberg hurt his knee in the ninth game of the season and he finished the year playing only defense. After Chicago won the title game, Goldberg wanted to retire but decided to try one more season. In 1948, he limited himself to defense, helping the Cardinals win a second straight Western Conference title. (They lost to the Philadelphia Eagles in the title game, 7–0.) At the time, Goldberg was considered the league's best defensive back.

"Football," Goldberg once noted, "taught me to look for and expect only victory. It also taught me singleness of purpose, poise, competitiveness, the ability to get along with others and the ability to sacrifice."

After retirement he became head of one of the largest used machine tool companies in the nation with headquarters in Elk Grove, Illinois. In 1974 he sold that firm to a West German company. Four years later, in 1978, Goldberg formed a new firm dealing with the acquisition and disposal of used machinery. He is currently president of that company, located in Chicago.

Goldberg is a member of the Jewish Sports Hall of Fame in Israel.

SIDNEY GORDON

A Talented and Well-Liked Baseball Player

GORDON, SIDNEY (born August 13, 1918, in Brooklyn, New York; died June 16, 1975) American baseball player. One of the most popular New York Giants. He played 13 years in the major leagues. In 1,475 games, he had 1,415 hits, 202 home runs, 805 runs batted in, and a career batting average of .283. A power hitter, he hit two homers in one inning in 1949, and four with the bases loaded in 1950.

Sid Gordon was a typical Jewish kid from Brooklyn whose ambition was to become a major league baseball player when he grew up. At Samuel Tilden High School, Gordon developed into a fine hitter, but since the school team played only twice a week, Sid had time to play semipro ball for the Bushwicks and the Brooklyn Pirates. In the summertime, he drove his father's coal truck and hauled coal which helped develop his muscles.

In 1936, Gordon almost had his first break in baseball after his high school graduation. Casey Stengel, the Brooklyn Dodgers' manager, had an eye on him and told the youngster that he would have a place in the Dodger farm system at the first opportunity. But Stengel was fired, and Gordon missed his chance.

The following year, Gordon was playing with the Queens Alliance League when he was spotted by a New York Giant scout. The scout offered Gordon a tryout with a Giant farm club in Milford, Delaware, on condition that Sid pay his own way. He would be reimbursed for the trip if he made the team. As he was getting ready to leave for the Milford tryout, his father died. Gordon believed he should stay home to run the family coal business, but his mother insisted that her son travel to Milford. She gave him $32.00 for the trip and the gamble paid off.

Earning $17.32 a week playing for Milford (a minor league team in the Eastern Shore League), Sid won the league batting title in 1938 with a .352 average in 112 games. He played third base, hit 25 homers and led the league in total hits with 145. He was promoted to Clinton in the Three-I League, and by the end of the 1938 season, was moved farther up—to the Jersey City Giants. Two seasons later (by this time he was married to Mary Goldberg), he had done well enough for a crack at the majors. In the 1941 season, he got his chance.

Gordon was switched to the outfield. In his first game, he caught eight fly balls and hit a triple and a single. He finished that first season with a .304 batting average. That season the Giants had four Jewish players on the squad: Gordon and Morrie Arnovich playing the outfield, Harry Feldman pitching, and Harry Danning catching. In 1942, Gordon started at third base for the Giants, but he was sent back to Jersey City in the minor leagues where he hit .300 for the rest of the year. Gordon returned to the Giants in 1943 and remained with them through the 1940s except for 1944 and 1945 when he served in the armed forces.

Gordon's best seasons were after World War II. In 1947, he hit .272 with 13 home runs, a big improvement over the mere five he had hit the year before. In 1948, Giants' coach Red Kress advised Sid to change his batting stance so that Gordon could take advantage of the short leftfield wall at the Polo Grounds. The advice worked. That year Gordon reached his peak: he belted 30 home runs, hit .299, and drove in 107 runs.

In 1949, Gordon played the outfield, first base, and third base, hitting .284, with 26 home runs. During the winter of 1949 he was traded to the Boston Braves, and the next year—one of his best—Sid hit .304, with 27 homers, and 103 runs batted in. He also tied a major league record for most home runs (four) with the bases loaded in one season.

Even though the Braves slumped in 1951 and 1952, Gordon still did well, hitting .287 in 1951 and .289 in 1952. In 1953 his batting average was .274, with 19 homers and 75 RBIs. Sid ended his career with the Pittsburgh Pirates, playing for them in 1954 and 1955.

Gordon was one of the most respected and well-liked ball players. When some of the St. Louis Cardinals made derogatory anti-Semitic comments to him from the bench during a June 1949 game, New York's newspapers rushed to his defense. Sid refused public comment.

He always played well in Ebbets Field, home of the Brooklyn Dodgers, during his career. He had a simple explanation: "If 30,000 fans were in the park, I knew 25,000 of them."

In 1956, he became a player-coach for the Miami Marlin team, then the newest entry in the International League (minor league). After his connection with baseball ended, he was employed as a life insurance underwriter with Mutual of New York.

BRIAN GOTTFRIED

One of the World's Best Male Tennis Players

GOTTFRIED, BRIAN (born January 27, 1952, in Baltimore, Maryland-) American tennis player. Semifinalist at Wimbledon in 1980. Best year on the circuit was 1977, when he won five tournaments and reached the finals in 15. In 1982 he was ranked fifteenth best tennis player in the world.

Brian, the son of a land development construction executive, began hitting balls across the net as an undersized seven-year-old in North Miami, Florida. When he was nine, his family hosted some Japanese youngsters who were participating in the junior circuit's prestigious Orange Bowl tennis tournament. The visitors provided the inspiration for his taking the game seriously. A year later, he was playing well enough to get an occasional free racquet from the local Wilson racquet agent.

Then a stroke of luck befell Brian in the person of Nick Bollettieri, a veteran teaching pro. Bollettieri spotted Gottfried practicing one day, liked what he saw, and agreed to take him on as a pupil. For the next six summers, Brian was on the court by seven o'clock every morning for intense drills. "It constructed the entire foundation of my game," Gottfried recalled.

Brian won the national 12-and-under doubles championship (with partner Jimmy Connors) in 1962. The following year, Brian and Dick Stockton won the doubles title, and in 1964 Brian won the under-12 singles. For this last performance, *Sports Illustrated* focused on him in its "Face in the Crowd" section, suggesting he was a young tennis player with a bright future.

Brian spent the last two years of high school at the Baylor School, a military academy in Chattanooga, Tennessee. He went there because of the school's excellent tennis complex (where tennis could be played all year round), and because of the tennis coach, Jerry Evert (tennis star Chris's uncle). One of Brian's classmates was Roscoe Tanner, another tennis star. Gottfried and Tanner soon became close friends and later rivals on the court. In Brian's junior year, Baylor placed second in the National Interscholastics and in his senior year, first.

But life at Baylor had difficult aspects for Brian. He recoiled at Baylor's strict military regimen. "My whole life had been spent in a warm, liberal-thinking, closely-knit Jewish family pattern where nothing was especially structured and an atmosphere of relaxed enjoyment prevailed. Now, suddenly, here's all this Mickey Mouse stuff coming at me. I found it hard to cope."

When Brian was 16, he discovered the opposite sex. Before that he had never dated. "How could I? I was always on a tennis court." He also developed a fondness for liquor, particularly rum and cokes.

He entered Trinity University in San Antonio, Texas, with a full tennis scholarship, but on academic probation due to his high school antics. Brian admitted to having little interest in academic life. "Truthfully, ever since my younger years in Florida, my Bar Mitzvah and all that—I'd lost interest in academics." His choice of college was based on the opportunities offered to improve his tennis.

Troubled by Gottfried's drinking, Trinity tennis coach Clarence Mabry minced no words when lecturing Gottfried in his office one day. Mabry told Brian that he could easily fritter away his talent on the court by too much carousing. "The choice is simple," said the coach. "Either play around or learn to play this game half decently." After that, Gottfried never took another drink.

The results were impressive. As an 18-year-old freshman, he won the 1970 National Junior Outdoors title (beating Jimmy Connors in the final). Gottfried was ranked as Trinity's No. 2 player after Dick Stockton. Together, they led the university to the NCAA title. While in school, Brian had won 14 national junior titles. In 1972, he was runner-up in both the singles and the doubles in the NCAA championships. Gottfried left college after three years; the lure of the profits in professional tennis was too tempting.

In 1973, his first full year as a pro, Brian won $90,000 and was named rookie of the year by *Tennis Magazine*. He won the distinction largely because he was the only newcomer to win a major international tournament, namely the Alan King Classic held at Caesar's Palace in Las Vegas, Nevada. That triumph earned him $30,000 and a $6,000 car, making the Classic the most rewarding tennis tournament in history. The undersized kid had become a 6 foot, 170 pound champion. Brian's response to his victory was restrained, which caused his wife, Windy, to scream: "Get happy, will you!" *Sports Illustrated* concurred when it wrote of Brian, "He has eyes about the color of har-tru, his scraggly hair reminiscent of a net, his expression revealing all the emotion of a baseline."

Sandy Mayer, a tennis colleague who has played with Gottfried since they were nine years old, explained Brian's passive reaction: "Brian just always wanted to be a purist. He could put the ball where he wanted to anytime, anywhere, and it really didn't matter so much to him whether he won or lost." Purist and perfectionist.

From 1976 to 1978, Gottfried was a member of the U.S. Davis Cup team. Until 1977, he was regarded largely as a great doubles player, teaming up with his close friend and partner, Raul Ramirez. But his singles record is excellent as well. In 1976, he ranked sixth in the U.S. and tenth in the ATP rankings. A crucial turning point in his career was the U.S. Open in 1976. He was leading Bjorn Borg two sets to none in the quarterfinals when he came apart and the match eventually went to the Swede. "I could have beaten him," Brian said afterward, remorsefully. "I found out today that I can play those top guys and I can win. I'm sure of it."

He was right. In April 1977, *Newsweek* called him "simply the best male tennis player in the world at the moment." That year he won four tournaments and almost $100,000, and lost only three matches. He was a runner-up at the French Open in 1977, reached the quarters of the U.S. Open in 1978, and was a semifinalist at Wimbeldon in 1980.

Gottfried thrives on practice and puts an unusual amount of time into it. On his wedding day, he managed to practice for a few hours in the morning, and then took the afternoon off to get married. To atone for those missed hours, he put in double sessions the next day. Says Brian: "I wouldn't like to believe I lost a match because I wasn't in shape or well prepared."

EDDIE GOTTLIEB

Founder of the National Basketball Association

GOTTLIEB, EDDIE (born September 15, 1898, in Kiev, Ukraine; died December 7, 1979) American basketball coach and basketball administrator. One of the founders of the National Basketball Association, and one of the pioneers who held pro basketball together during its early decades. He coached the Philadelphia Warriors from 1947 to 1956, piloting the team to its first NBA championship in 1947. Gottlieb's 263–318 coaching record with the Warriors belies his true ability as a coach.

Eddie's family lived in New York when he was a youngster. There, he would hitch rides on the back of ice trucks to get to the Polo Grounds to watch the New York Giants play baseball. Baseball was his first love. As a player he was quite

average. "Two things were wrong with me as a catcher," he said, "I couldn't hit very well, and I couldn't throw very well. But I was an A-1 receiver."

When he was nine, his family moved to Philadelphia. He graduated from South Philadelphia High School in 1916, and two years later from the Philadelphia School of Pedagogy. In 1918, he organized and coached the Philadelphia SPHAs (South Philadelphia Hebrew Association) basketball team.

In those days basketball was so underdeveloped that it was only a prelude to dances. On Saturday nights, one could enter the Grand Ballroom of the Broadwood Hotel in Philadelphia (65 cents for men, 35 cents for women), dance, and watch the SPHAs play. "After such a game," Gottlieb recalled, "one of the players named Gil Fitch would get out of his uniform, shower, get into a suit, climb onto the stage and lead his band as the dancing began. In those days many of the Jewish people wouldn't let their daughters go to an ordinary dance except when the SPHAs were in action before the dance."

The team reached its peak in the 1925–26 season when it defeated the Original Celtics and the New York Rens in a special series. In the 1930s the SPHAs dominated the Eastern and American leagues with 11 championships. Eddie managed the quintet to American Basketball League titles in 1934, 1936, 1940, and 1945.

In 1946, Gottlieb assisted in organizing the Basketball Association of America which later became the NBA. He coached the Philadelphia Warriors from 1947 to 1955 until illness forced him to resign. His two greatest players were Joe Fulks and Wilt Chamberlain.

In 1952, Eddie purchased the Warriors for $25,000, thus keeping a pro basketball team in Philadelphia. The club went on to win its second NBA championship in 1956. In 1962, Eddie sold the Warriors for the then record-price of $850,000 and stayed on as general manager when the team moved to San Francisco. In 1964, after serving in that role for only two years, he returned to Philadelphia.

Gottlieb was involved in another sports activity: he made up the season schedules for teams. He once said that he felt as though he had been making schedules "since I was born." From 1952 until 1970 it was Eddie who drew up the schedules of all NBA teams.

Gottlieb was called the "mogul" because, as *The New York Times* wrote upon his death, "his mental powers were extraordinary and his memory almost fault-less. He remembered the scores of games, the gate receipts, the attendance, and even the weather. His only difficulty was often pinpointing the exact year." Gottlieb, when told that he was like a mogul, agreed, saying, "a mogul is a top banana."

Gottlieb is a member of the Basketball Hall of Fame and the Jewish Sports Hall of Fame in Israel.

HENRY "HANK" GREENBERG

The Baseball Hero John McGraw Refused to Hire

GREENBERG, HENRY BENJAMIN (born January 1, 1911, in New York City-) American baseball player. One of baseball's greatest right-handed hitters. In baseball's first century (1839–1939), Greenberg is generally regarded as the best Jewish player. He played for the Detroit Tigers from 1933 to 1947 and the Pittsburgh Pirates in 1947. His career batting average was .313 in 1,394 games. He had 1,628 hits in 5,193 at bats, with 331 home runs (including 11 grand-slam homers) and 1,276 runs batted in.

Greenberg was the first National Leaguer to earn $100,000 a year. He was Most Valuable Player in 1935 and 1940, and was selected to the All-Star teams from 1937 to 1940. He led the American League in home runs and in runs batted in, four times.

Hank Greenberg is the son of Orthodox Jewish parents from Romania. He attended James Monroe High School in the Bronx and won letters in four sports. He began playing baseball for the Bay Parkways in New York. One day, Paul Kirchell, the New York Yankee scout, was present when Greenberg hit three homers in one game. The youngster was offered $1,000 down and $500 a year while he attended college, but he did not accept it. Instead, he entered New York University on an athletic scholarship.

In July 1929, while playing baseball with a team in East Douglas, Massachusetts, a mill town, Hank was noticed by Washington Senators scout Joe Engel, who offered him a $10,000 bonus plus a salary of $800 a month if he would agree to play immediately in the Washington chain. Greenberg again refused. Detroit made a more attractive offer: a bonus of $9,000—$3,000 immediately and the rest after he graduated from NYU. The Detroit offer allowed him to stay in college and guaranteed him a job in baseball afterward. Hank agreed. But Hank became restless as spring training was nearing. After one semester at NYU, Hank wired the Tigers that he wanted to join them at once. He was given the remaining $6,000 of his bonus, and began receiving $500 a month to play with the Tigers' minor league farm team in Raleigh, North Carolina. That year, 1931, Greenberg hit .314.

At that very time, John McGraw, the famous New York Giants manager, wanted to buy or develop a great Jewish player. But McGraw overlooked Hank. Later, Greenberg enjoyed recounting how his father had once spent three hours waiting to see John McGraw to convince him to add Hank to the Giants' roster. When McGraw finally met with the elder Greenberg, the manager told him that his scouts had reported adversely on Hank and had concluded that he would never make the major leagues.

In 1932, playing with Beaumont in the Texas League, Greenberg drove in 131 runs, hit 39 homers, and was voted the league's most valuable player. In 1933 he joined the Detroit Tigers. He had problems that first season and was moved to third base, because the Tigers already had a first baseman (Harry Davis, who had cost the club $50,000). Not an outstanding third baseman, Hank looked ahead and practiced in the mornings to improve his glovework at first base. Meanwhile, he hit .301 in 117 games, had 12 homers, and 87 RBIs. By 1934, the Tigers sold Davis and moved Greenberg to first base. That year he batted .339 and led the league in doubles (63) and homers (26), and batted in 139 runs.

As the season neared its autumn finale, Detroit was in a tight pennant race. The concern among fans grew that if Hank did not play on Yom Kippur, the Jewish Day of Atonement, the team's chances of winning the pennant might be hurt. To compound matters, the Tigers infield, of which Greenberg was a part, had played all season without a substitution. When Yom Kippur came, Hank refused to play and the Tigers did indeed lose that game. But Hank had won the city's respect. The Tigers went on to win the pennant (but lost the World Series).

Edgar Guest, America's most popular poet at the time, wrote a poem in homage to Greenberg:

Come Yom Kippur—holy fast day worldwide over to the Jew—and Hank Greenberg to his teaching and the old tradition true, spent the day among his people and he didn't come to play. Said Murphy to Mulrooney, "We shall lose the game today! We shall miss him in the infield and shall miss him at the bat. But he's true to his religion—and I honor him for that!"

In 1935, Greenberg was voted Most Valuable Player in the American League after hitting .328, leading the league with homers (36), and batting in 170 runs. He also collected more than 200 hits. In 1936, when the season was only 12 games old, Greenberg broke his wrist in a collision near first base, and was unable to return to play that year. But he returned in 1937 and drove in 183 runs, second highest in the history of the American League at the time, and batted .337. From then on, Greenberg was considered one of the the best right-handed sluggers in the game.

In 1938 he set the major league season record for the most games in which a player hit two home runs in one game— 11. He also tied two major league records that year, for most home runs by a right-handed hitter (58) and for home runs in consecutive appearances in two games (four).

When Greenberg hit his fifty-eighth home run, with five games left in the season, his mother offered to make him 61 baseball-shaped gefilte fish portions if he would break Babe Ruth's 1927 record of 60 homers in one season. The gefilte fish never was served because Greenberg didn't hit another home run that season.

Greenberg spent the All-Star break that season trying to improve his hitting: he paid semipro pitchers $10 and $20 to pitch to him all day long. He refused to attend the All-Star game, because the year before he had traveled all night on a Detroit–Washington train only to sit on the bench the entire game. After hitting four consecutive home runs on July 26 and 27, giving him 33, he realized that he was ahead of Ruth's pace, so he began aiming for the fences.

In the final game of the season, with a slim chance to break Ruth's record, he hit three singles before the game was called due to darkness in the seventh inning. "It's just as well," Greenberg said much later. "There was no way I could have eaten all that gefilte fish."

In 1940 Hank moved to the outfield to allow the slower Rudy York to take over at first base. The move was not easy since Greenberg had been an All-Star first baseman. In 1941, he was earning $55,000 a year, a huge sum in those days. But with America's approaching involvement in World War II, Greenberg was drafted into the army after the nineteenth game of the season. Because he was nearing the age limit for military service, he was released from the service in December, two days before Pearl Harbor, only seven months after he had been inducted.

When war was declared against Japan, he immediately reenlisted, became an officer, and was sent to the China-Burma-India Theater where he was in charge of a B-29 squadron of the 20th Bomber Command. In July 1945, he was discharged as an air force captain. He returned to baseball to help the Tigers win the pennant and the World Series that year. Although he played only half a season, and was somewhat out of practice, he still hit 13 home runs and ended the season with a .311 average.

Hank was traded to the Pittsburgh Pirates on January 18, 1947. So loyal to the Tigers was Greenberg that he considered retiring, but he did play for Pittsburgh for one season.

In 1948, Bill Veeck, Cleveland Indian owner, hired Greenberg to work on the administrative side of the ball club. He traveled around the country studying Cleveland farm teams to improve their overall organization, and was paid $15,000. His suggestion to establish a central training camp was accepted by Veeck.

Shortly thereafter he became general manager of the Cleveland Indians, and in 1955, became a part owner. In 1956 Greenberg became the first Jewish major leaguer to be elected to the Baseball Hall of Fame. (He and Sandy Koufax are the only two Jewish major league players who have received that honor.)

Greenberg joined the Chicago White Sox in late 1958 as a part owner and moved to New York the following year. In 1959, the White Sox won their first pennant in 40 years (but Chicago lost to the Los Angeles Dodgers in the World Series, four games to two). Hank sold his interest in the club in 1961 and devoted himself full-time to the management of his personal investments.

He had married department store heiress Carol Gimbel in 1946 and they had three children. Greenberg divorced her in 1958 and, in 1966, married actress Mary Jo Tarola.

In 1974, he moved to Beverly Hills where he still takes an active interest in managing his personal investments. He is also an avid tennis player.

Greenberg is a member of the Jewish Sports Hall of Fame in Israel.

RANDY GROSSMAN

The Football Player Who Was Called "Rabbi"

GROSSMAN, RANDY (born September 20, 1952, in Philadelphia, Pennsylvania-   ) American football player. All-American in his senior year at Temple University; later an outstanding receiver for the Pittsburgh Steelers of the National Football League. His best year as a pro was 1978 when he caught more passes (37) than any Steeler tight end since 1966.

Randy Grossman began his football career at Haverford High School in Philadelphia during the late 1960s. He was also a member of the high school wrestling team. Two schools recruited him: Temple, and Xavier, a Roman Catholic university in Cincinnati, Ohio. Xavier's interest in him was puzzling; "Maybe," said Grossman jokingly, "they figured I was a prime prospect for conversion." The school had not been known for recruiting Jewish football players.

At Temple, Randy Grossman vindicated the University's interest in him, doing well on a team that didn't pass that often. During the three years he played (1971–74), Randy had a career record of 89 pass receptions for 1,505 yards and 10 touchdowns. In his senior year Randy was named All-East, All-Pennsylvania, and All-American. Said Wayne Hardin, Temple's football coach: "He can catch anything in nine countries. He's a really super player—quick as a cat, super-quick, tough, durable."

Randy has acknowledged that he owed his chance to play both college and professional football to Steve Joachim, the quarterback who passed to him in high school and college. College scouts, watching films of Joachim in their high school games, spotted Grossman by chance. The same thing happened when pro scouts watched films of Joachim in their college games: they noticed Randy!

Grossman was one of 14 rookies to make the Pittsburgh Steelers in 1974. He was signed as a free agent, making the team only because a players' strike prompted the league to increase rosters to 47 players. The Steelers decided to keep three tight ends, including Grossman.

Randy managed to make a few razzle-dazzle plays in his early years as a Steeler. He helped the team win the Super Bowl in that first season. In 1975, he caught four passes in the American Football Conference championship contest and scored the team's first touchdown in the Super Bowl against Dallas. Still, he was seldom a starter or a star.

In the sixth game of the 1978 season, Bennie Cunningham hurt his knee and Grossman replaced him. That was Grossman's best year. He started the final 10 regular season games and three post-season games. He caught a total of 37 passes during the season and added three more in the playoffs, including three in the Super Bowl victory over the Dallas Cowboys. By the end of the 1979 season, Grossman had pulled in nearly 100 passes for more than 1,000 yards gained. Noted for his quickness, he enjoyed the reputation of being able to pluck out a bullet-speed pass in midair. But what gave him his greatest thrill as a Steeler was seeing his picture on a bubble-gum card for the first time.

After the 1978 season, Grossman played somewhat fewer games because of Cunningham's recovery. In 1980 he started 15 games and caught 23 passes (12.7 yards per catch). In the 1981 season his playing time was limited to short yardage situations as a tight end and to the punt and kickoff return teams.

Grossman was nicknamed "The Rabbi" by the other Steelers. But, laughed Randy, "They didn't come to me for spiritual advice." When he grew a beard, he admitted that he "looked like a Hassidic Rabbi." A reporter once asked him at a Super Bowl, what a nice Jewish boy was doing in a place like this. Grossman replied: "They called me some pretty bad names when I was on the high school wrestling team. Here they just call me Rabbi." He was once asked if he practiced on Rosh Hashanah, the Jewish New Year: "Why yes," he said, "the gentiles have to practice on their new year, so I practice on mine."

When he is not on the football field, Grossman works as an insurance executive with a firm in the Pittsburgh area. One of his hobbies is flying an airplane. Grossman obtained an airplane pilot's license and has done macrame on airplane trips. "I do a lot of things," joked Grossman, "but I'm the master of none."

ERNIE GRUNFELD

Romanian-born American Basketball Star

GRUNFELD, ERNEST (born April 24, 1955, in Satu-Mare, Romania–   ) American basketball player. He played for the University of Tennessee from 1973 to 1977, averaging 22.3 points per game and making the *Sporting News* All-America second team in 1977. He began playing pro basketball in 1977 with the Milwaukee Bucks. Grunfeld was traded to the Kansas City Kings in 1979 and signed to play with the New York Knickerbockers in 1982.

Until he was nine years old, Ernie lived in Satu-Mare, his birthplace behind the Iron Curtain. His father, Alex, had been torn between table tennis and soccer as a youngster. By 1952, the elder Grunfeld was ranked sixteenth in the world in table tennis.

But Ernie, as a child, concentrated on soccer, playing goalie fairly well. It was the only game he knew. His parents, sensing that Jews were not able to get fair opportunities in Romania, decided to emigrate. At first they considered moving to Israel. But in 1964 Alex Grunfeld decided to take his family to New York, where he opened a fabric shop similar to the one he had.

Ernie grew up in Forest Hills, New York, learning basketball in the schoolyard and playground courts. There he developed a competitive streak that he carried into college and professional ball. On the courts at Russell Sage Junior High School in Forest Hills, the team that lost had to stop playing and wait before it got to play again. The winning team kept on playing. The rule had an important effect on Ernie: he hated to lose!

From Russell Sage he went on to a record-breaking career at Forest Hills High School. Ernie was All-American and All-City in his senior year, averaging 25.4 points and 16.6 rebounds per game. He was 6 feet, 6 inches and weighed 215 pounds. In addition, he was selected as the outstanding student-athlete in New York City.

In the summer of 1973, Grunfeld earned one of his greatest honors: He was selected to play on the American team for the Maccabiah Games, the only high school student on the starting five. He led the team in scoring with a 20-point average, but unfortunately Israel defeated the U.S. in the final, 86–80.

Some 200 colleges pursued him. He rejected such major basketball powers as Marquette and Notre Dame, and picked the University of Tennessee because he liked the facilities, the schedule, and the chance it afforded him to become a college star.

In his first season's opening game at Knoxville, Tennessee, Ernie scored 28 points, leading his school to a victory over North Texas State. His best offensive move was the drive from the wing, either down the baseline or up the foul lane. He was especially strong on the offensive boards. Grunfeld was unusual for a freshman. De Paul's veteran coach Ray Meyer noted that Ernie was "like a bull in a china shop, but slick along with it."

Teamed with center Bernard King, Grunfeld helped Tennessee achieve success. (They were later to call it "The Bernie and Ernie Show.") As a freshman he averaged 17.4 points per game. But the following year, Ernie broke his wrist in a preseason scrimmage against Western Kentucky and was forced to miss six games. Still, he managed to average 23.8 points per game that season. Pro scouts rated him equal—or perhaps superior—to King because he was so rugged.

The elder Grunfeld insisted that his son not work during the college's summer vacation periods so that he could refine his basketball skills. Ernie repaid his father's interest with diligence. In high school, he was a 58 percent free-throw shooter; as a Tennessee freshman, he increased it to 73 percent. Then, in his sophomore year, he hit 81 percent, 80 percent in his junior year, and 79 percent in his senior year. Ernie wore out countless nets to achieve these results.

Grunfeld played for America's gold medal-winning team in the Pan American Games in the fall of 1975. But his biggest moment in sports came in the summer of 1976 when he helped the U.S. team win the gold medal in the Olympic Games at Montreal. In July of that year Ernie obtained his American citizenship.

His performance at Tennessee was impressive enough to warrant the careful scrutiny of the professional teams. In his sophomore year he had averaged 23.8

points per game; in his junior year, 25.3,; and in his senior year, 23.8.

Grunfeld turned pro with the Milwaukee Bucks in 1977. His shooting average dropped considerably, but he has been a steady ballplayer and has held his own in the NBA. He averaged 6.9 points in 1977–78, and 10.3 points per game in 1978–79, with Milwaukee. In 1979–80, playing with Kansas City, he had a 5.9 point per game average; and in 1980–81, a 7.5 point per game average. In the 1980–81 playoffs he averaged 16.8 points per game.

Playing for Kansas City, Ernie was put in the guard position, an unusual choice for a 6 foot, 6 inch, 215-pound player with his build. His coach, Cotton Fitzsimmons, recognized that the move seemed improbable. He acknowledged that Ernie looked like the "first Clydesdale pulling the Budweiser wagon." But the coach was confident that Grunfeld would do well, and he was proven right.

ALFRED HAJOS-GUTTMANN

Recipient of Olympic Medal
for Swimming and Architecture

HAJOS-GUTTMANN, ALFRED (born February 1, 1878, in Budapest, Hungary; died November 12, 1955) Hungarian swimmer. The first Olympic swimming champion and the first Hungarian Olympic gold medal winner. Winner of the medal for architecture at the 1924 Olympics.

Born Alfred Guttmann, he took the name "Hajos" for his sports career because it was an Hungarian name. Alfred began swimming at the age of four. His father entrusted him to a swimming teacher who in a few short weeks had the child swimming better than his friends or his father.

Despite his swimming ability, Alfred remained a thin, weak boy. He was unable to climb a pole in one physical education class and was therefore excluded from the exercise in the future. As a result he began doing physical exercises to strengthen himself.

In school, Alfred paid little attention to geometry or drawing at first. His gym teacher reproached him for not taking these subjects seriously. Alfred became more serious about his studies, and one day when he showed the geometry teacher his homework, the teacher was so convinced that a professional draftsman had done the work for him that he was severely reprimanded. Later, realizing his mistake, the teacher predicted that Alfred would succeed as an architect.

Alfred was first noticed during the Hungarian Swimming Association's first international meet in 1895 in Siofok, Hungary. He won the 100-meter freestyle, and desperately wanted to travel to Vienna to enter the European Championships, but his mother would not permit him to go unless he was accompanied by an adult. In addition, he could not afford the trip since he would have to cover his own expenses. He tried to convince his family that the potential victory in Vienna would bring them fame and help his future career, but to no avail. Despite their opposition, he went on his own, hoping that some Vienna sports enthusiasts would give him room and board.

Alfred's faith in himself was justified as he became European champion, winning the 100-meter freestyle in Vienna. In 1896 he again was European champion in the 100-meter freestyle.

When the first modern Olympic Games were to convene in Athens in 1896, Alfred Hajos was a first-year student of architecture at the Budapest Polytechnical University. He was one of Budapest's best known swimmers. Hajos asked the dean of his faculty, Lajos Llosvay, a chemistry professor, for permission to take a four-week leave of absence to allow him to train for the Olympics. The dean responded very coolly: "Only frivolous people practice sport instead of studying. It can't lead to an honest path." In the end, however, the dean grudgingly permitted Hajos to take the leave of absence.

Training for the Olympics was difficult. Hajos practiced at a pool 23 meters long, six of which were too shallow for swimming. He had to walk four kilometers to the pool each day, pay the equivalent of a 20 cent entrance fee and $10 for 50 training sessions. Alfred had no money, and he persuaded the pool director, Istvan Sad, to let him train without paying the fees.

At the first Games held in Athens, Hajos won the 100-meter and 1200-meter freestyle swimming events. He swam 100 meters in 1:22.2, a time far below the 61.4 of England's Jack Typers when he won the 100-yard title in England that same year. But Typers did not compete in Athens. However, the Hungarian's 18:22.2 time for 1200 meters was definitely superior to the performance of contemporary English distance swimmers.

Alfred joined the other Olympic prize winners at a festive dinner with the King of Greece. The King asked Hajos where he had learned to swim so well. Alfred replied wryly, "In the water."

The Greek newspaper *Akropolis* nicknamed Hajos the "Hungarian Dolphin."

On his return to Budapest, Alfred proudly went to see the dean, Professor Llosvay, who was indifferent to his student's medals. "I am just impatient to hear your reply to your next exam." Two months later, Hajos took the exams and he was concerned that he would not do well. Hajos was questioned orally by the dean himself. Afterwards, when Alfred passed the exams, Llosvay congratulated him on winning at Athens. He wished his student the same success in architecture as he had achieved in sports.

Hajos excelled in other sports as well as swimming. In 1898 he became Hungary's junior champion in the 100-meter sprint and national champion in the 400-meter hurdles as well as the discus. Hajos was also a pioneer in Hungarian football (soccer). In 1901, 1902, and 1903 he played on several national cham-

pionship teams in the position of forward. For the next few years he worked in football administration. At one stage he was managing director of the Hungarian Football Union. Between 1902 and 1904 he edited a sports newspaper called *Sport Vilag* (The World of Sport), and also wrote a sports column for Budapest's important daily newspaper *Pesti Naplo*.

In 1899 Hajos completed his studies and received his degree in architecture from the Budapest Polytechnical University.

In modern times, fields of endeavor other than sport were included in the Olympics competition. At the 1924 Paris Olympics, a quarter of a century after he completed his degree, Hajos entered the arts competition with a design for a stadium, drawn in collaboration with Dezso Lauber, an equally famous Hungarian athlete. Hajos defeated 13 other entrants for the silver medal. Hajos did not get the gold medal (it was not given to anyone that year) because the French did not want to give it to a non-Frenchman, and especially not to a Hungarian since Franco-Hungarian relations had been cool since World War I.

In 1929, Hajos won the Hungarian architects and engineers Grand Prix with a swimming pool study. The next year he created his masterpiece, the Margaret Island National Sports Hall, in Budapest, with a 3,000-seat capacity. That same year (1930) the Hungarian Architects Federation awarded him the title of Master for his "extraordinary creations."

In 50 years of work. Alfred Hajos-Guttmann created a variety of sports facilities as well as hotels, banks, factories, churches, and theaters. When he was 75, the International Olympic Committee awarded him the Olympic diploma of merit. Hajos had achieved the same success in architecture that he had in swimming.

He wrote a short book, *How I Became an Olympic Champion*, in his later years. But he died at the age of 78, a poor man, a few days after delivering the manuscript to the publisher. The book appeared a year after his death (in 1956) on the 60th anniversary of his first winning an Olympic gold medal.

SIGMUND HARRIS

Quarterback on Knute Rockne's All-Time Jewish Team

HARRIS, SIGMUND (born July 2, 1883, in Dubuque, Iowa; died November 8, 1964) American football player. One of the great quarterbacks of his day. Selected quarterback on Knute Rockne's All-Time Jewish Football Team. In 1903, Harris was first team Fielding Yost All-America, and in 1904, third team Camp All-America.

Sig's father was Polish, his mother a Chicagoan. When Sig was a boy, the family moved from Dubuque to Minneapolis, Minnesota. His parents raised him to feel a strong tie with Judaism, and he was sent to *cheder* (Hebrew school).

Harris made the Minneapolis Central High School football team in 1899. The following year, playing an exhibition game against Minnesota University at the start of the football season, he helped to hold the Gophers to a scoreless tie.

In 1901, Harris enrolled at the Minnesota College of Engineering and Mechanical Arts and became second-string varsity quarterback in his freshman year. When the regular quarterback left the next year, Harris took over. He was 5 feet, 5½ inches, and weighed only 140 pounds. During the 1902 season, Sig led Minnesota to a 10–2–1 record. The Minnesota *Alumni Weekly* of December 1, 1902, noted: "Harris has played a wonderful and consistent game all the season, and deserves credit for his work."

The following year (1903), Minnesota was undefeated (14-0-1) and scored 656 points while its opponents managed to score only 12 points. The 1903 Minnesota backfield, with Sig Harris at quarterback, has been rated one of the best in history. In 1904 the Gophers again had a dazzling season record: they were undefeated in 13 games and they scored 725 points while holding their opponents to a meager 12.

After his graduation in 1904, Harris served as assistant football coach at Minnesota, a post he held until 1920. For the next six years he worked in a Minneapolis machine business. In 1926, he returned to fill the job as assistant coach, but left again to return to his business. After three years, he was back as assistant head coach at Minnesota, and this time remained until 1941.

From 1941 until his death he was engaged in his machinery business. Aware that it was odd that he had never been offered a head coaching job, Harris refused to attribute it to anti-Semitism: "I never felt any anti-Semitism in my long contact with college football," he observed.

JULIE HELDMAN

One of America's Best Tennis Players

HELDMAN, JULIE (born December 8, 1945, in Berkeley, California-) American tennis player. One of the finest American women tennis players in the United States in the late 1960s and early 1970s. She was ranked No. 2 in the U.S. in both 1968 and 1969. She was also ranked No. 5 in the world in 1969, her highest world ranking.

Julie came from a family steeped in tennis. Her father, Julius Heldman, had won the National Junior Championships in 1936. Her mother, Gladys, was Texas State champion in the early 1950s and founder of *World Tennis* magazine in the summer of 1953.

From Berkeley, where Julie was born, the family moved to Long Beach, California, in the late 1940s for a short time and then (also in the late 1940s) to Houston because Julie's father was working for the Shell Oil Company there. He was transferred to New York in the summer of 1953, and the family moved again.

Julie began playing tennis in the summer of 1954 when, as an eight year old, she was sent to the United States' first tennis camp, the Hoxie Tennis Camp in Hamtramck, Michigan (located in the Greater Detroit area). At Hoxie the emphasis was on being competitive. Winning was all that mattered. Julie attended Hoxie for the next seven summers.

By her third summer she was winning some local tournaments. Julie's first major victory was the Canadian Junior Championships (for age 18 and under) in Ottawa in August 1958, and her next major achievement was winning the U.S. National tournament in the summer of 1960 in Ohio (for ages 15 and under).

Julie attended private schools from eighth through twelfth grades, first at the Walt Whitman School and later at the Dalton School, both in New York City. She had skipped two grades while in grammar school and as a result graduated from high school at age 16.

To get far away from home and in order to play tennis, she enrolled in Stanford (California) in September 1962. (At the time, Stanford had no woman's tennis team.)

In August 1963, at the end of her first college year, she won the National Junior (18 and under) tournament, held that year in Philadelphia. To win this tournament was a "life's goal" because she wanted to match her father's achievement in 1936.

She spent part of her third college-year studying in Tours, France, as part of a Stanford program. When the spring season ended in March 1965, Heldman played in a number of European tournaments, reaching the semifinals in the Italian Open in May, her greatest achievement until then. Later that year she played in her first Wimbledon, and got to the final 16 before bowing out.

In May 1966, she played for the American team in the Federation Cup competition, a woman's team championship held in Turin, Italy. Playing No. 2 for

the U.S., she swept all five of her matches in the five-nation tournament won by the U.S.

The pressures of the tennis circuit grew more and more burdensome until they became overwhelming. Heldman graduated from Stanford as a history major in December 1966, quit tennis, and went off to live in a hippie commune in Woodside, California, near Stanford. Within a few months she tired of the unstructured commune life and early in 1967, left for New York City where she found work in the art department of an advertising agency. That job lasted three months. She then returned to California where she obtained a job teaching at a summer tennis camp at the Berkeley Tennis Club.

Toward the end of the summer, Heldman returned to the tennis circuit and she played in several California tournaments, reaching the quarterfinals in one and defeating Billy Jean King in the opening round of another. Heldman realized that playing tennis could be a passport to the good life in a way that working for an advertising agency could not.

In 1968, playing in tennis tournaments in Guadalajara, Mexico, she won the mixed doubles (with Herb Fitsgibbon), came in second in the doubles (with "Peaches" Bartkowicz) and third in the singles. Two weeks later, she won a mixed doubles tournament (also with Fitsgibbon) in Buenos Aires, Argentina. She was ranked No. 2 in the U.S. that year, and No. 11 in the world.

In May 1969, Julie won the Italian Open. Then in August she traveled to Israel where she won the singles, doubles (with Marilyn Aschner) and mixed (with Ed Rubinoff) in the Maccabiah Games. That same month she played No. 1 for the U.S. in the Wightman Cup competition held then in Cleveland, Ohio, winning two singles and a doubles match. She was named the outstanding player in the tournament. In 1969 she was ranked No. 2 in the U.S., and No. 5 in the world, her highest world ranking.

Heldman never experienced any blatant anti-Semitism on the tennis tour, although she did acknowledge feeling uncomfortable when playing tournaments at East Coast tennis clubs that excluded Jews and blacks from membership.

Julie was forced to quit tennis for six months in the summer of 1970, when she injured her elbow. In the fall of 1970, her mother, Gladys, was the key organizer of the Virginia Slims Tennis Circuit, the first all-women's tennis circuit. Gladys wanted Billy Jean King and other women tennis players who helped form the new circuit to separate women's professional tennis from the men's, to achieve parallel status for the women. Julie served as a liaison between her mother and the players.

Julie returned to active tennis in early 1971, but didn't play well. She hurt her knee in August of that year, while playing in the Wightman Cup in Cleveland. In March 1972, she underwent surgery in London for torn cartilage in her knee.

Toward the end of 1973, Heldman came under the tutelage of Angela Buxton, the great woman tennis star of the 1950s, and Jimmy Jones, Buxton's teaching partner. Heldman lost most of her good strokes because she tended to favor her injured knee, but Buxton and Jones helped restore her game. The next year, 1974, was Julie's second best of her career. (Her best year was 1969.) In 1974, she reached the semifinals of the U.S. Open in Forest Hills (losing to Billy Jean King), and she reached the finals of a Virginia Slims tournament in Sarasota, Florida.

Fellow-players consider Julie Heldman one of the toughest competitors the game has known. She was a hard and accurate hitter from the baseline, and her serves were soft, carefully-placed slices. She rarely went to the net. Heldman would usually win, not because of raw talent, but because of tactical superiority. Her strokes were never perfectly smooth, but she hit the right shots at the right time. Mixing up forehands and backhands with off-speed drop shots and lobs, Heldman used the tennis court like a large chess board. She also had an unorthodox forehand—a snappy undercut delivered with an oddly-cocked elbow. Although Heldman admitted that her stroke looked odd, it helped her get better topspin control. Her trademark was a floppy brimmed cap.

During Julie's tennis career, which ended in 1975 because of a shoulder injury, she carried on an active second career in writing, radio, and television. She wrote tennis articles for her mother's *World Tennis* magazine and provided commentary for matches broadcast on TV. Between 1973 and 1975 she covered the U.S. Open on CBS-TV. Between 1975 and 1977 she helped cover Wimbledon for NBC. In 1976 she was the first woman to comment on a men's tennis tournament—the Avis Challenge Cup in Hawaii.

In August 1978, she entered UCLA Law School and graduated in May 1981. That same month she married Bernard Weiss, a businessman. He has two sons from a previous marriage.

Heldman began clerking for William A. Norris, a circuit court judge of the U.S. Court of Appeals, Ninth Circuit, Los Angeles, for one year. In the fall of 1982, she entered the Los Angeles law firm of Johnson, Manfredi, and Thorpe.

VICTOR HERSHKOWITZ

A Legendary American Handball Player

HERSHKOWITZ, VICTOR (born October 5, 1918, in Brooklyn, New York-) American handball player. The *United States Handball Association Magazine* rated him best all-around handball player in history. Few athletes have won as many championships as he did. Beginning in 1942, he accumulated 43 titles, including nine straight three-wall championships from 1950 to 1958, which no other player has repeated. "I don't know why," Vic said in 1974, "but people considered me a legend."

Victor Hershkowitz, born in the Williamsburg section of Brooklyn, was the youngest of seven children of an immigrant baker from Hungary. He went to Alexander Hamilton and Eastern District high schools. He was captain of the sixth-year high school intramural team in baseball, for whom he played outfield and catcher, but could never make the high school handball team. One of the high school handball team's members was Red Auerbach, the great basketball coach of the Boston Celtics.

It is quite likely that, had he wished, Vic could have carved out a career for himself in pro baseball. Vic explained it this way: "The late Sid Gordon of the New York Giants and Carl Erskine of the Brooklyn Dodgers used to tell me that. But I started playing handball. And anyone who plays handball gets addicted. It's like a disease—once you're exposed to it, it's got you."

Out of school in the depression year of 1936, Vic took whatever jobs were available, mostly in the shipping departments at various stores. He started playing handball in 1936 at the Lafayette and Marcy playground in Brooklyn. Compact and powerfully built, Vic entered his first tournament at the Washington Baths in Coney Island that same year and won. He entered his first national tournament two years later, losing in the finals of the one-wall tournament. But he continued to practice and improve his game. "I got to be good at handball and played it more than other sports," he said. "The fact is," he admitted, "I was unemployed and that's why I was playing ball."

He married in June 1941, and the couple had two boys and a girl. By 1942 he teamed with Moe Ornstein to capture the National One-Wall Championship. He then entered the service (in 1944) and did not play handball again until 1946. He was released from the armed forces in November 1945, and became a postman in 1947, remaining one for the next three years, and playing handball in his spare time.

His handball record was impressive. He won national titles each year from 1947 to 1967, except for 1959. "That's a tough record to beat in any sport," Hershkowitz wrote in 1982. In National AAU competition, he won the one-wall doubles in 1942, 1948, and 1956. He was one-wall champion in 1947, 1948, 1950, 1952, and 1953, and singles champ in 1949 and 1952. Hershkowitz was international three-wall champion every year from 1950 to 1955; he won the National YMCA singles title in 1953. In 1954, he won the National American Handball Association singles crown and the doubles in 1961. During this time he represented the Brooklyn, New York, YMCA in his handball career.

Until 1947, he was strictly a one-wall player but then he defeated Angelo Trulio, the defending national four-wall champion, in a New York state tournament (which Vic went on to lose, by the way). In 1949 Hershkowitz won the national four-wall and one-wall tournaments.

Hershkowitz was one of the few players who played all year round, four-wall in the winter, one-wall at the beaches in the summer.

In April 1950, he became a fireman and remained one until July 1973. He had no special duties as he explained: "I just put out the fires." He liked his new profession because his work schedule fit in well with his playing: He worked two days from 9 a.m. to 6 p.m., then two nights from 6 p.m. to 9 p.m., and he was off for 72 hours. Thus, he was able to play at least three times a week. He usually played doubles when not participating in actual tournaments.

Harold Rosenthal, writing of Hershkowitz in *The New York Times* in 1948, said: "The report is that the Brooklyn champion has no obvious weakness. He can kill off either hand, is as tireless as an eight-day clock. He can pick the little black ball off the back wall with an almost unbelievable deftness."

In 1952 he gave his greatest performance on the courts, winning the four-wall, three-wall, and one-wall titles. At the time he was the only player who could accomplish that feat. Vic was nominated for the Hickok Belt as the Athlete of the Year but, as Hershkowitz recalled, "Handball being such a minor sport, I didn't get enough votes. But that doesn't bother me. When you talk about handball to someone who knows about handball, just mention my name. Everyone has heard of me. And that's a nice thing, you know?"

In 1953, he tied Sam Atchinson's national record of 14 championships by adding the YMCA laurels to his collection. The following year he won his fifteenth, making handball history.

His strong points were his service and being able to hit hard with both hands: "I've got a good opposite (left) hand," he said. The secret of his success was putting pressure on when it was needed: "You force the other guy by speeding up the tempo. If you go for a kill, you hit a kill, and don't go for a foot above it to make sure you don't miss. You see an opening, you go for it. You don't lose your confidence. Will to win is the difference."

Hershkowitz contended that handball is "the toughest sport there is. There's no rest—you've got to go all the way. It's timing, accuracy, stamina, and no coasting."

His Judaism matters to him. "I always felt that being a Jew made me play and try harder to defeat my adversaries. My Jewishness had to show the nation in this sport that I was proud of being a Jew."

"Vic," observed Sid Belinsky, a handball aficionado, "is the Babe Ruth of the sport. He has that certain something that is far above an ordinary player. He is colorful, graceful, has legs like springs, and he hooks with either hand. He would be a terrific athlete in any game." Because he adapted himself to four-wall and three-wall games after starting with one-wall, Hershkowitz got Belinsky's vote as the greatest handball player of all time. The others were outstanding in four-wall play only. Vic's achievements earned him a spot in the Helms Athletic Hall of Fame in 1957.

In addition to being a fireman, Hershkowitz has been a salesman of business forms.

Vic was asked on March 8, 1969, what, as a sports star, was the height of his ambition. His answer: "To live as long as the old biblical characters lived, well beyond 100. My pop is 95. My mom 90. With parents like that, I stand a pretty good chance of realizing my ambition. That's about all. I have everything else I want in life."

Vic Hershkowitz moved to Florida upon his retirement as a fireman in July 1973. In March 1974, he said that he continued to play handball once or twice a week, but other than that, "I do nothing. I'm retired. I'm supposed to do nothing."

ART HEYMAN

College Basketball Hero of 1963

HEYMAN, ART (born June 24, 1942, in Rockville Centre, New York-) American basketball player. A three-time All-American (1961, 1962, and 1963) at Duke University, he was their highest scorer, averaging 25.1 points per game, with 1,984 total points. Art later played four years in the NBA and three in the ABA. In 147 NBA games he averaged 10.3 points per game. In the ABA he averaged

15.4 points in 163 games. He was voted 1963 college baketball player of the year by the Associated Press and *The Sporting News.*

Heyman had always been interested in playing basketball. At age 10, growing up in Rockville Centre on Long Island, he would constantly dribble a basketball in the playgrounds, as well as in the school corridors.

Once, at age 12, he put tape over the lock on the gym door of his elementary school so that he could slip inside on Sundays to practice. Sometimes he would shoot alone, but more often, being tall for his age, he would be invited by older boys to play in a pickup game. He thus learned to be aggressive at an early age. He said that the most important thing he learned was not to shy away from the basket.

In his three years at Oceanside High School (Oceanside, Long Island), from 1957 to 1959, Heyman scored more than 1,500 points, setting a Long Island record for most points scored in a high school basketball career, a record which still stood in the spring of 1982. As a senior in high school, he averaged over 30 points a game as well as 15 rebounds. The team won the Nassau County championship in Art's final year (1958–59) and Oceanside coach Frank Januszewski complimented his star by noting that "Artie was the team."

Art was also an outstanding soccer goalie on Oceanside High School's un-defeated team, and received scholarship offers for both soccer and basketball. He preferred basketball.

In all, Heyman was offered nearly 100 scholarships. Adolph Rupp, Kentucky's great basketball coach, even showed up at Art's house one day to urge the basketball star's mother to send her son to the best basketball school in the nation and be coached by the best basketball coach in the nation.

Meanwhile, Vic Bubas, the new coach of Duke University, sat in the Playbill Restaurant of New York's Manhattan Hotel to discourage Art from following other New York basketball players to the rival University of North Carolina, then a basketball powerhouse. In the end, Art chose Duke, because his father was for it and because Art thought it was academically superior.

The summer after his high school graduation, 1959, Heyman played summer league basketball, often with some of the best college basketball players. Some of those he played with were eventually involved in the college game-fixing scandals in 1961 in the New York area. But the fixers, Art suspected, never approached him because he was too affluent; they probably figured he did not need the money. When he arrived at Duke in the fall of 1959, Art had already played more basketball, against faster competition, than any Duke senior.

Heyman made a brilliant start. He was soon scoring 30 points a game for Duke in his freshman year. The Duke–North Carolina rivalry flared bitterly during one game that year. When a North Carolina player became angry during a scuffle, Heyman was knocked cold by a roundhouse right to the jaw. He needed five stitches.

In his sophomore year, he joined a team made up entirely of seniors. In the first 10 seconds of his first home game against Louisiana State University, he took a rebound and dribbled the entire length of the court, evading four opponents and driving over a fifth for a basket. That year, his 629 points—eighth best in the nation—led Duke to a 22-6 record. Duke was ranked tenth in the country.

In his junior year, Heyman scored 608 points and helped Duke finish with a 20-5 record and a national ranking of tenth again. In his senior year, he scored 747 points for an average of 25 per game and led Duke to a 28-2 record, and a national ranking of second. He was All-American in his sophomore, junior, and senior years. Duke had a 69-14 record during Heyman's three years.

Art's coach Vic Bubas said that aggressiveness and strength were what set Heyman apart from other players. He was a great driver. Beyond that, he was fast for his size. He was so strong that it was impossible to take the ball from him.

Heyman was not overly modest about his prowess. He once said, "I was the biggest thing that ever happened to Duke." He was certainly one of the most controversial. Heyman was involved in violent incidents both on and off court. Once, after he and a premed student were exchanging insults in the TEP fraternity house, Heyman hit the student and damaged his retina. (Heyman insists that the student began the fracas.) The student lost the lawsuit he brought against Heyman. During Art's sophomore year, he was accused of assaulting a male cheerleader from North Carolina. The charges were dismissed, but Heyman was suspended for involvement in a fight later in that game.

At Duke, a Methodist university that did not admit blacks until 1966, no one was particularly aware of Heyman's Jewishness. Many thought Heyman was a Protestant from Connecticut. Heyman discovered that southerners with whom he came into contact could not compre-hend a Jew being a great athlete. He received letters of praise from organiza-tions like The Fellowship of Christian Athletes. A man in Alabama named Horace Shelton regularly sent Heyman telegrams urging him to continue to up-hold the principles of white Christian supremacy. Once, Shelton, head of the Ku Klux Klan, offered Art membership in the Klan. Heyman ignored the invitation.

A hero at Duke, Heyman became less heroic after joining the pros. He was the number one draft choice in the NBA and was picked by the New York Knicks in May 1963. He received a large bonus (sum undisclosed) for signing with the team. He played for the Knicks for two years—in 1963-64 and 1964-65—averaging 15.4 points per game that first year, the highest rookie average for a Knick until that time. In his second year, he fell to 5.7 points per game. In 1965, Heyman was traded to the San Francisco Warriors for cash and one player.

In all, Heyman played six seasons of pro basketball (1963 to 1970) with seven teams in the NBA and the ABA. In 1967–68 he played for the New Jersey Nets and the Pittsburgh Pipers in the ABA, averaging 18.5 points per game. In 1968–69, he joined the Minnesota ABA team, averaging 14.4 points per game. In his final year, 1969–70, he was traded to the Miami Floridians of the ABA with whom he averaged 7.4 points per game.

He played a total of 310 games in the NBA and ABA and scored 4,030 points for a 13.0 average per game.

During that last 1970 season, he suffered from a bad back, and he would need a spinal fusion if he hoped to continue playing basketball. Heyman decided to quit and went into the restaurant business. He owned several restaurants in New York from 1968 to 1981. He also had investments in real estate and other fields. In 1968 he married a professional model. They were divorced in 1974.

Art was inducted into the Helms Hall of Fame in 1974.

MARSHALL HOLMAN

A Bowler Who Earned More Than $100,000 in One Year

HOLMAN, MARSHALL (born September 29, 1954, in San Francisco, California–) American bowler. Winner of 14 National Tour championships, including the 1976 Firestone Tournament of Champions and the 1981 Bowling Proprietors' Association of America U.S. Open. The $550,000 he earned in eight years makes Marshall one of the top ten on the PBA's all-time money-winners list. Elected to *Bowling Magazine*'s All-America first-team in 1977, 1978, and 1979.

Marshall Holman's family moved from San Francisco to Medford, Oregon, where Marshall's father, Phillip, was a disk jockey for radio station KFHA. After Phil did a show from the top of a flagpole in the early 1950s, he was known as "Holman the Poleman." Marshall contended that he inherited a tendency to be a "ham" (his own phrase) from his father.

Marshall took up bowling at age 12 and was only fair at the beginning. In his first year he averaged only 99. In 1971, at age 17, he joined a pro bowling tour, but succeeded in winning only $500. For the next few years he bowled nearly every day, playing at least twenty practice games.

In 1974, Holman felt his game had improved considerably and he joined a summer tour. In his fourth tournament, in Tucson, Arizona, he predicted that he would win the whole thing, but instead finished fifth. In the championship round telecast on cable television, Holman rolled a lowly 149. His earnings for the year totaled only $4,845.

Marshall Holman's first PBA tournament victory came in Fresno, California, in 1975, during his second year on tour. He also won a tournament that year in Hawaii, and his yearly earnings climbed to $27,543. The next year he had one of his biggest tournament triumphs, the Firestone Tournament of Champions in Akron, Ohio. He was the youngest bowler ever to win this highly-prestigious tournament. That year, Holman won $48,630. His yearly winnings climbed to $71,350 in 1977, thanks in part to victories in the Brunswick World Open in Chicago and in the PBA Doubles Classic in San Jose, California, in which he was teamed with Mark Roth.

Despite winning only the Ford Open, in Alameda, California, and a tournament in Cleveland in 1978, he still earned $70,160 for the year. However, the following year Holman won the Quaker State Open, the Columbia-PBA Doubles Classic with Mark Roth, the Seattle Open, and the Brunswick Memorial World Open in Chicago. It was his most successful year; he earned $107,255 and thereby became only the third player to win over $100,000 in one year.

Holman has become famous—and controversial—for his mannerisms on the bowling alley. He wiggles, squirms, and leaps after almost every bowling toss. He talks, swears, and shouts at the pins. "It's not that I'm in another world," he says by way of defense, "but I get pumped up in big matches and most of what I do is the natural outlet for that extra energy." At times, his gestures have been called obscene, though he denies any such intention.

After a 1979 Seattle tournament he was put on probation for six months for kicking a chair and a ball rack, and then throwing pencils when the match was going against him. Then in 1980 at the Showboat Tournament in Las Vegas,

Nevada, there was another outburst. Holman needed a tenth frame strike to put him and his partner in a position to win the tournament. When Marshall failed to make that particular score, he kicked a protruding foul light on a lane. He was fined $2,500 and received the longest suspension in PBA history: ten tournaments.

Holman managed to make a successful comeback after the incident. Although he earned only $46,035 in 1980, the year of the suspension, the next year, 1981, he enjoyed his best season. He won the Quaker State Open, the BPAA U.S. Open, and the King Louis Open, with winnings of $122,880 for the year.

NAT HOLMAN

The American Coach Who Taught
Israelis How to Play Basketball

HOLMAN, NAT (born October 18, 1896, in New York City-)
American basketball player and coach. A master teacher and inno-
vator, and the brains behind the Original Celtics. Holman is considered one of the greatest basketball players of all time. He coached
City College of New York from 1920 to 1953, and again in 1955-56,
1957-58, and 1959-60. His career coaching record: 422-188.

Nat Holman learned to play basketball in the parks, playgrounds, and settlement houses of New York's lower East Side. An all-around athlete at Commerce
High School, he played four sports there.

Nat, 5 feet, 11 inches tall, chose a career as a pro basketball player in 1916
while attending the Savage School of Physical Education at New York University.
He turned down an offer to play baseball with the Cincinnati Reds.

Having graduated from the Savage School, Nat was appointed instructor of
hygiene at the City College of New York in 1917, with extra duties that included
coaching soccer and freshman basketball. After serving a one-year hitch in the
U.S. Navy during World War I, he returned to CCNY and was named head
basketball coach for the 1919-20 season. At 23, Holman was the youngest
college coach in the country. Asked how he managed to get so far at so young an
age, he joked: "I think my older brother, Morris, put in a good word for me."

While continuing to coach at CCNY, Holman played pro basketball weekends
with the New York Whirlwinds in 1920 and early in 1921. He joined the Original
Celtics toward the end of the 1921 season and remained with them until 1929.
The Celtics rarely lost with Holman. They were 193-11 in 1922-23; 204-11 in
1923-24; and 134-6 in 1924-25. In 1926-27, the Celtics joined the American
Basketball League where they were nearly unbeatable and no team could put up
a decent fight against them. After a few seasons the team decided that it made no
sense for the players to remain together, a move that strikes any observer of
professional basketball of the 1970s and 1980s, with its high salaries for the
players, as quite odd. Still, in 1929, the Original Celtics disbanded. In 1933, Nat
retired as an active player.

Holman was regarded as the finest ball handler, playmaker, and set-shot artist
of his day. While with the Celtics, he devised the pivot play, one of the most
important plays in the game. It revolutionized basketball, and college coaches
flocked to watch Holman feint an opponent out of position and run him into the
pivot or post. He would then cut by him, receive a short give-and-go pass, and lay
up an easy basket.

At CCNY, he was slender and dapper, appearing at games with neatly
combed hair and freshly shined shoes. The winning teams he turned out at CCNY
were unique because his players were not there on athletic scholarships. "They
were all boys who entered CCNY," said Holman, "because of their academic

Nat Holman, at blackboard, going over play with his CCNY squad on November 3, 1954.

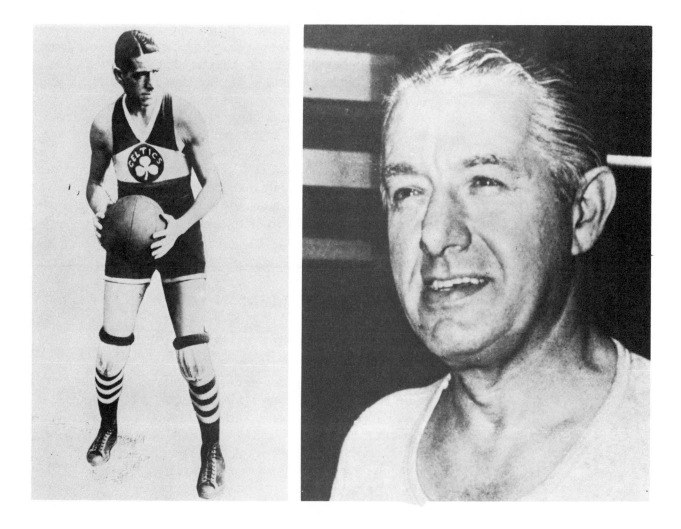

achievements. Yet they, too, found in basketball the things that spurred me on. They, too, brought to the game a dedication and skill that enabled CCNY to rise to basketball prominence during the years I was there." He believed that winning required a positive mental approach as well as finely-honed skills. Once, after a team loss that he could not figure out, he said to his players, "You need a psychiatrist, not a coach."

Nat Holman's most successful season was 1949–50, when his CCNY Beavers won the "grand slam" of college basketball: the National Invitation Tournament and the NCAA playoffs. No other coach had accomplished that feat. Sadly, however, most of the players who won that "grand slam" were part of a point-fixing scandal the next year (though there had been no reported evidence that the team's players had point-fixed during the year of the "grand slam"). Nat himself was suspended from the physical education department of CCNY, but was eventually (after two years) cleared of all wrongdoing and reinstated as coach.

Holman has always been a proud Jew: "Some of what I heard and learned sitting next to my father in the synagogue rubbed off on me," he once said. He was a member of the committee that helped send the first American team to the Maccabiah Games in Palestine in 1932. And, he was the first American coach to go to Israel in 1949 to teach Israelis to play basketball.

Asked about his relationship with non-Jews, he observed, "I experienced no anti-Semitism from my opponents during my pro career. Occasionally, there would be some nasty remarks from the sidelines. But on the whole I had very little of it." There was one highly publicized incident in 1946 in Madison Square Garden: CCNY was playing Wyoming. When CCNY took a quick lead, Wyoming's coach directed some anti-Semitic remarks against Holman's players. Leaping from the bench, Holman had to be held back from going after the coach, who eventually apologized.

In 1967, Holman was elected to the Basketball Hall of Fame. In 1973 he became the president of the American Committee for Sport in Israel.

Three years later Nat was named the greatest New York City athlete in basketball by the Boys' Athletic League. In 1977, CCNY's new gym was named after him and the following year the Wingate Institute in Israel dedicated the Nat Holman School for Coaches and Instructors. He was inducted into the Jewish Sports Hall of Fame in Israel in July of 1981.

KEN HOLTZMAN

An Outstanding American League Pitcher

HOLTZMAN, KENNETH (born November 3, 1945, in St. Louis, Missouri–) American baseball player. Major league pitcher from 1966 to 1979 with a career won-lost record of 174–150. He helped the Oakland Athletics win three straight World Series between 1972 and 1974. In 1973, Holtzman was named *The Sporting News* left-handed pitcher of the year in the American League.

Ken attended the University of Illinois and was awarded a Bachelor of Arts degree in Business Administration in 1965. That same year he was signed to a bonus contract by the Chicago Cubs. The major highlight of his first major league season (1966) was his triumph over his boyhood idol, Sandy Koufax. Ironically, the two Jewish pitchers played against one another because of Yom Kippur. Holtzman was to pitch on the day after Yom Kippur while the Dodger southpaw was scheduled to pitch on the holy day itself but asked to skip his turn. So the following day the two men faced each other at Wrigley Field in Chicago.

For seven innings Holtzman preserved a no-hitter and allowed only two hits in the end. Koufax allowed only four hits, but lost the game 2-1. It was Sandy's last loss in regular-season play as he retired the next year. Holtzman had been regarded as another Sandy Koufax: he threw hard like Sandy, was left-handed like Sandy and was Jewish.

With the Chicago Cubs between 1966 and 1971, Holtzman pitched two no-hitters, one in 1969, the other in 1971. He had a 74-69 won-lost record for those years. After the 1971 season, he asked to be traded, and was sent to Oakland.

Holtzman won two American League playoff games and had four World Series wins for Oakland. In 1973 he won 21 games, lost 13, and was chosen best

left-hander of the year in the league. In all, he recorded 67 victories between 1972 and 1975, years when the Athletics finished in first place.

Ken went to Baltimore in 1976 where he won five games while losing four in 13 starts. He next played for the New York Yankees from 1976 to 1978 but did not get along with Yankees' manager Billy Martin. The problem began when Holtzman was kept on the bench during the 1976 playoffs and World Series. Martin, it seemed, had a low opinion of Holtzman's pitching, and Ken didn't pitch often while with the Yankees. In 1977 he was 2-3; in 1978, 1-0. Holtzman pitched only 90 innings altogether in those two seasons.

Holtzman was the New York Yankee player representative—the ball player who represented the Major League Players' Association, the ball players' union, on the team. Each team has one such player representative. Holtzman was eventually traded (on June 11, 1978) back to the Chicago Cubs. He had been 0-1 with the Yankees up until that point in 1978, and was 0-3 with the Cubs for the duration of the season.

In 1979 Ken pitched 118 innings and was 6-9. He decided to quit after the 1979 season.

Holtzman had talents and interests outside of baseball. He could speed-read an entire paperback while sitting in an airport terminal waiting for a flight. Holtzman was a member of a national telephone chess league and an excellent duplicate bridge player.

Ken has always been proud of his Jewish heritage. He has publicly stated that he believed in Jewish values and religion. He tries to observe Jewish customs as much as life on the road would allow. At home he observes Jewish dietary laws and he never pitched on a Jewish holiday.

He has made his home in Lincolnshire, Illinois, a suburb of Chicago. He is in the insurance business.

WILLIAM "RED" HOLZMAN

The Basketball Coach Who Was a Great Communicator

HOLZMAN, WILLIAM "RED" (born August 10, 1920, in New York City-   ) American basketball player and coach. During the 1960s and 1970s he was highly successful as coach of the New York Knickerbockers of the National Basketball Association. He compiled a better record than any other active coach in pro basketball: up to the 1981–82 season he had 696 victories in regular season play.

Holzman, an All-City guard in high school, was an All-American when he played for City College of New York in 1942. After service in the U.S. Navy during World War II, he joined the Rochester Royals of the NBA in 1945. An All-League player, he was part of the Royals' 1950–51 championship team. Red acquired his nickname from the color of his hair—red!

The Milwaukee Hawks hired Holzman as player-coach in 1954. In 1958, he became chief scout for the New York Knicks, a post he held for the next decade. In December 1967, he succeeded Dick McGuire as New York's head coach. When he took over, the club was 15-22 but ended the season with a record of 43-39.

In Holzman's first full season at the helm of the Knicks, the team won 54 games, a club record at the time. A year later, in 1969-70, he skippered the club to its first world title with 60 victories, including 18 straight, then an NBA record. Holzman was chosen NBA coach of the year in 1970.

The 1971-72 Knicks reached the NBA championship finals, and in 1972-73 the team recaptured the world title which it held three years earlier. In that six-year period—known as the Knicks' Golden Era—Holzman's team compiled 320 victories in 492 games, for a winning record of 65 percent. In nine of the 13 seasons that he coached the Knicks, the team made the playoffs.

Red retired as the Knick coach upon completion of the 1976-77 campaign, turning the reins over to Willis Reed, who had been the team's captain. Holzman was named consultant to the team. Reed coached the Knicks in 1977–78 to what was considered a disappointing second-place finish with a 43–39 record. Red Holzman was summoned back as Knick coach on November 10, 1978, after the club had played only 14 games of the 1978–79 season.

That year and the next were problematic: the team wound up 31–51 in 1978–79, and 39–43 in 1979–80, neither time qualifying for the NBA playoffs. But the Knicks finished the 1980–81 season with a 50–32 record, enabling the team to make the playoffs. The Knicks, however, lost two games straight to the Chicago Bulls, thus being eliminated early in the playoffs.

Holzman explained in March 1981 how he has managed to survive 28 years of living out of a suitcase. "The answer is so simple, you won't believe it. I'm just one of those people who likes to travel, who likes to the movies, and who reads a lot—mostly bestsellers that my married daughter picks out for me. But in the off season, my wife and I never leave our house unless it's to go to the beach."

Bill Bradley, who was elected a United States Senator from New Jersey in November 1980 and who was one of Holzman's stars in the 1960s and early 1970s, wrote of his former coach: "Other men Holzman's age who became coaches in the NBA have difficulty communicating with black players. Holzman

never makes racial mistakes. Everyone is subject to the same treatment. It seems natural that he senses the right course, for he grew up in a non-Jewish world where discrimination was a very real part of his own life. He understands the dividing line between paranoia and reality."

His eye is still as sharp as it was as a youngster. Once, Marvin Webster, the Knicks' center, bet Holzman $10 that he could outshoot him from the top of the free-throw circle. Webster went first, hitting nine out of ten. He was extending his hand to collect his winnings when Holzman scored nine out of ten as well.

As of 1982, Holzman was one of only six coaches in NBA history with 500 or more victories. The others are Red Auerbach, former coach of the Boston Celtics;

Jack Ramsey of the Portland Trail Blazers; Gene Shue of the Washington Bullets; Dick Motta of the Dallas Mavericks; and Al Attles of the Golden State Warriors.

Holzman retired as Knick coach in May 1982, following a 33-49 season. In the last few years of his career, his teams had not fared well: the Knicks had made the playoffs only once in the last four seasons before Holzman's retirement. His 696 career victories (as against 604 losses) made him second in NBA to Red Auerbach of the Boston Celtics who, at retirement, had 938 wins.

Red Holzman continues his relationship with the New York Knicks as a consultant.

HIRSCH JACOBS

The Trainer of More
Thoroughbred Winners Than Anyone Else

JACOBS, HIRSCH (born April 8, 1904, in New York City; died February 13, 1970) American race-horse trainer. He saddled more winners (3,569) than anyone else in thoroughbred racing. Between 1946 and 1969, Jacobs bred such winners as Hail to Reason, Affectionately, Straight Deal, and Regal Gleam. By turning unlikely prospects into winners, he earned more than $12 million in purses.

Unlike the other great horse trainers, Hirsch Jacobs did not come from the south. He was born on New York City's East 62nd Street, one of 10 children. Soon after Hirsch's birth, his father, an immigrant tailor, moved his family to the East New York section of Brooklyn.

A popular avocation of the residents of this new neighborhood was the raising of pigeons. Young Jacobs loved this activity and by age 12 had learned to identify 100 pigeons by sight. This training of his memory was a great help to him in his future training of horses.

At age 13, Hirsch learned to install and repair steampipes. He got a job as a steamfitter and learned horse racing from Charlie Ferraro, brother of his boss.

In 1924, Charlie bought a horse for $1,500 and asked Hirsch Jacobs to train the animal. Four years later, on December 29, 1929, Jacobs saddled his first winner, a horse named Reveillon, at Pompano, Florida.

Hirsch's unusual ability consisted of taking horses that would not run for anyone else and winning with them. "You just got to use common sense," the short, chunky, red-haired trainer would say. "When a horse feels like running, he'll run. They're like humans. You got to baby them and humor them along; kid them along."

Unlike other great trainers, Hirsch Jacobs bred and trained horses he personally owned. Whereas his rivals tended to concentrate on a few promising horses,

grooming them for a handful of high-stake races, Jacobs sent his thoroughbreds to the gate in wholesale fashion. As a result, only infrequently would he train a truly famous horse, but he managed to amass a staggering total in purses through the years.

Jacobs was always sensitive to the disappointments in his work. "This business," he said at one point, "is full of heartaches. You get a horse worth $50,000 one morning; by afternoon you can't get $10,000 for him. The biggest menace is sore shins. Anyone can train a horse. But to win, you've got to have a horse that's in shape. That's the only secret there is."

In 1931, Jacobs entered into a life-long partnership with Isidor (Beebee) Bieber.

In 1936, he had his finest year when he saddled 177 winners. The 84 horses in his stable ran 632 times that year. A $2 bet on each of his horses that started that season would have netted over $142 per horse for the year. That was the year Jacobs started to run his horses in the salmon-pink and emerald-green silks which became known as the identifying marks of some of the best thoroughbred race horses.

Stymie, a failure of a race horse Hirsch Jacobs found in 1943, revealed Jacobs' intuition at its best. The two year old had hardly been able to gallop in earlier races, but Jacobs told his partner Bieber, "I've got a feeling about that colt. I like the way he walks." Hirsch bought the horse for $1,500. By the end of his career, Stymie was the world's leading money winner, earning $918,485 in purses.

Jacobs turned another extremely slow horse around in 1955, a filly named Searching. "The walls of Searching's hooves were very thin," Jacobs recalled. "She wouldn't try because she thought her shoes were too tight. So we got her a new pair of shoes, and she started winning." Searching won a total of $327,000.

Jacobs married the former Ethel Dushock in 1933. Her father owned a boarding house near the old Empire City track in Yonkers and it was there that she and Hirsch met. Occasionally, Mrs. Jacobs would try to convert her husband to her own faith, Catholicism. But he always had the same reply: "If they go to the moon and a Catholic greets them, that's the day I'll become a convert." He retained his Jewish faith, but permitted his children to be brought up as Roman Catholics.

Jacobs neither smoked nor drank, but was superstitious. He always wore the same suit for weeks during a winning streak—and he only drove green Cadillacs. He suffered a stroke in 1966, but remained partially active as a trainer until a month before his death in 1970. He died of a cerebral hemorrhage at the Miami Heart Institute in Miami Beach, Florida.

Hirsch Jacobs is a member of the Jewish Sports Hall of Fame in Israel.

JAMES JACOBS

One of the World's Great Handball Players

JACOBS, JAMES (born 1931, in St. Louis, Missouri–   ) American handball player. One of the world's greatest. Ranked as one of the top three four-wall handball players of all time. Despite injuries in his prime years, he won 15 national titles. In 1966 *Sports Illustrated* suggested that he might have been the greatest athlete of his time in any sport. By 1972, Jacobs had won the American Handball Association four-wall singles title six times, the four-wall doubles six times, and the three-wall singles three times.

Jim moved from St. Louis to Los Angeles with his parents when he was five years old. Shortly, thereafter, his parents divorced and he was raised by his mother.

As a boy, Jim Jacobs was in love with comic books. He bought and read hundreds of them. He loved to pretend that he was Dick Grayson, alias Robin, Batman's comic-strip sidekick, and he found that identifying with Robin was a tremendous help to him in sports. He would think of what Robin would do in a stressful situation, and would gain strength by pretending to be this other emotionally unaffected character. Over the years Jacobs amassed an impressive comic-book collection.

As a teen-ager, Jacobs played football, baseball, and basketball, and was good enough in basketball to be invited for an Olympic tryout. He ran the 100-yard dash in 9.8 seconds; he was also a skeet shot of championship rank.

At Los Angeles High School, Jacobs was rarely eligible for sports due to his poor grades, especially in English. His mother recalled that Jim was happy only at sports. He played halfback in football, shortstop in baseball, and forward in basketball for the George Gershwin chapter of the AZA (American Zionist Association), a branch of the B'nai B'rith. Because youngsters of all faiths could play, competition was keen. With Jacobs on the team, the Gershwin chapter won the AZA title three years in a row. One year it won all three major team championships.

At the Hollywood YMCA, Jacobs often played handball against Art Linkletter, the TV master of ceremonies. Jim Jacobs lost at first. But then he began spending time practicing whenever he could. He spent hours in front of a mirror, practicing left-hand returns, although he was right-handed. When he passed the May Company department store, he would halt for five minutes to check his handball form in the reflection of a large window to the surprise of passersby. Within a few months he could whip Linkletter and anyone else in Los Angeles.

Believing that they had a prodigy on their hands, Linkletter and a few others financed Jacobs' trip to the handball Junior Nationals in Bremerton, Washington. There he won the singles title. At that time Jim was also playing American Athletic Union basketball on a team sponsored by a printing company. He was invited to try out for the Olympic team but declined so he could concentrate on handball.

In 1950 Jacobs met Robert Kendler, a multimillionaire Chicago home remodeler, who was obsessed with handball and had already taken the dozen or so best players in the country and employed them in his own business. Kendler built the Town Club of Chicago so these players would have a place to practice. Gus Lewis, a former national handball champion, played Jacobs, and then reported to Kendler: "I've just played a kid who doesn't know what he's doing, and for a kid who doesn't know what he's doing, he's a hell of a handball player."

Kendler hired Jacobs as a home remodeling salesman and invited him to practice at the club during off-hours. This group provided Jacobs with his education. After 18 months there, he was drafted. He served as a rifleman with the First Cavalry Division in Japan and Korea, and after his discharge, Jacobs returned to Los Angeles where he worked as a salesman for a business machine company.

Jacobs worked hard at the Los Angeles Athletic Club, and in 1953, he competed in his first national tournament and finished fifth. In 1954 he was third and in 1955, playing on his home court in Los Angeles, he won the singles, defeating another great handball star, Victor Hershkowitz. Until then, handball had been mostly a power game of "kills," but Jacobs, having mastered the art of ceiling shots, was able to force Hershkowitz to the rear of the court where he could not make his slam-bang kills. Jacobs had thus revolutionized handball. In fairness, Hershkowitz at that time was past his prime.

In 1956, Jacobs again won the national singles. He repeated the feat in 1957, beating Hershkowitz for the third time in the finals. In 1958, Jacobs forfeited the finals due to an injury caused by a collision in a doubles match. He did not play in 1959 because of a heart condition. In 1960 he again took the national singles title, but had to withdraw the following year because of a torn tendon. In 1962 and 1963 he passed up the singles to win the doubles. In 1964 he took the singles title easily.

While engaged in handball, Jacobs was developing a second profession:

collecting fight films. While traveling extensively to compete at handball, Jacobs searched for films of important historic boxing matches. By 1961, he had accumulated several thousand prints and had become the world's foremost private collector.

"The more I got into athletics myself," he said, "the more I admired boxers. Theirs is the ultimate individual sport, the one where emotional and psychological factors play the largest roles. A fighter has to deal with fear and its counterforce, courage, in a way no other athlete does. It's what makes fighting and fighters so fascinating to me."

Collecting the fight films was not simple. In response to the race riots that had accompanied the victories of Jack Johnson, the first black heavyweight champion, the Federal Government had enacted a law banning the interstate shipment of fight films. The law was in force between 1912 and 1940. Thus, many films had been stored away and were forgotten. Many films deteriorated and later had to be reproduced at considerable cost. The oldest film shows an 1894 James Corbett fight.

In 1961, Jimmy went into partnership with Bill Cayton, producer of the original Greatest Fight television series which was aired between 1949 and 1955 after the Friday night fight program. Jacobs' library of fight films was merged with Cayton's collection. Greatest Fights now owns some 16,000 fight movies, many times more than anyone else.

Jacobs makes his living by splicing these films together in entertaining ways. His and Cayton's best customer is foreign television. However, many of the old fight clips are also shown on domestic TV news and sports shows. The business grosses some $10 million a year, and Greatest Fights has been nominated for two Academy Awards in the documentary films category.

Jacobs believes that modern fighters are far better than the older ones who appear in his films. "Comparing them with the old-timers," he notes, "is like comparing a modern tank to the World War I models. Fighters today are faster, stronger and know more."

In 1979, Jacobs was inducted into the Jewish Sports Hall of Fame in Israel.

IRVING JAFFEE

A Speed Skater Who Won
Two Olympic Gold Medals

JAFFEE, IRVING (born September 15, 1906, in New York City; died March 20, 1981) American speed skater. Winner of two gold Olympic medals in the 1932 winter games in the 5,000- and 10,000-meter races. He was stripped of a third gold medal at the St. Moritz Winter Olympics in 1928 through no fault of his own.

Four Olympic gold medal winners gather at a dinner in their honor at the 1932 Lake Placid (New York) Winter Olympic Games. (From left) Irving Jaffee, Karl Schaeffer of Germany (men's figure skating gold medal winner), and Jack Shea of Lake Placid (500- and 1500-meter gold medal winner for speed skating).

Irving Jaffee was the second of three children of parents who had come from Russia in 1898. His family arrived in New York impoverished, and his father found employment operating a push-cart.

Irving wanted to be a baseball star. The Yorkville section of New York City in which he grew up had spawned Hank Greenberg and Al Schacht, two other baseball heroes. But when Jaffee could not make the baseball team at DeWitt Clinton High School, he was so upset that he left school.

He took up boxing, hoping to follow in the footsteps of Jewish boxing star Benny Leonard, but in his first fight he was knocked out, ending his career ig-nominiously.

One evening, some friends asked Irving Jaffee to go to the Ice Palace in New

York City. A schoolmate, Myer Steinglass, recalls that first skating attempt on ice: "He was a grotesque figure that night, somewhat abashed at his gauche posture in his frantic efforts to maintain his balance." From then on, Jaffee always carried a pair of skates under his arm.

Frequently he would skate at the Gay Blades (which later became the Roseland Dance Hall). Admission to the rink was 75 cents, but as Jaffee recalled, "I got in free by getting a job scraping the ice off the rink. I must have scraped tons of it in my lifetime." His sister gave him his first pair of ice skates but they were three sizes too large, and he was forced to wear nine pairs of socks to skate. Even with the extra socks, he often wobbled and fell.

Jaffee was reluctant to enter special skating competitions because he felt that ice skating, a Nordic sport, was not for Jews. But his friends convinced him to compete, sensing that he had great hidden talent and could become a good speed skater.

He began actual skating competition on Monday nights at Iceland in New York. Using the skates his sister had given him, he lost the first nine of ten races he entered. Then, Norval Bapte, one of the great skaters of the time, advised him that his skates were too large. Bapte bought him a pair of secondhand skates for $6 and he took third place in his next race. Jaffee began to develop good endurance and speed, which he credited to a newspaper route which he worked on roller skates on Saturdays and Sundays.

Irving Jaffee's first major competition was the Silver Skates Derby of 1924. He fared poorly that year and again in 1925; but in 1926 he won the Silver Skates two-mile senior championship. Then, the following year he won the five-mile national championship at Saranac Lake, breaking the world record and making him eligible for the 1928 Winter Olympics—or at least so it appeared.

He was not sure he would be going to St. Moritz, Switzerland, site of the 1928 Winter Olympics, until two days before the boat sailed. The authorities felt that he would be no match for the Scandinavian skaters. In the end, the U.S. Olympic Committee decided that he could go, but the boat had to be delayed so he could secure his visa and passport.

His fourth-place finish in the 5,000-meter race at the Olympics that year was the best ever run by an American. In the 10,000-meter race, seven time-trials were held, but then the ice began to melt, and an official of the International Skating Federation called the rest of the race off. Consequently, three skaters did not compete. The Executive Commission of the International Olympic Committee recognized Irving Jaffee, with the fastest time among those who had raced, as the winner. However, the International Skating Federation overturned the Commission's decision, ruling that the race had to be rerun to allow everyone to participate. Since most of the skaters had left St. Moritz by the time of the Federation's decision, the race was canceled. Jaffee's gold medal was, in effect, snatched from him just before he was to receive it as the official winner of the race. Nevertheless, many in the American press as well as a few of Jaffee's racing colleagues considered him the winner.

After the 1928 Olympic Games, Jaffee took a job on Wall Street in New York as a broker's clerk. Friends at the office took an interest in his career and sent him to Lake Placid to train. However, his training had to stop when his mother became ill, and he was forced to devote all of his time to taking care of her.

As a result, Jaffee had trained too little for the 1932 Winter Olympics, held at Lake Placid, and did not expect to do well. When the Olympic trials were held at Lake Placid, he failed to qualify in the 500- and 1,500-meter races, but still had a chance in the 5,000- and 10,000-meter races.

Irving's teammates at the trials made life unbearable for him, and he suspected there was some anti-Jewish bias involved. They stole his mattress, started a fistfight with him, and shone a light in his eyes at night so he could not get sufficient sleep. Just before the 5,000-meter race, he slept away from the Olympic Village to be sure that he would get enough rest. He went on to win both the 5,000- and 10,000-meter races. His time in the 5,000 was 9:40.8 and in the 10,000, 19:13.6. Before Jaffee came along the Europeans had dominated the skating races in the Olympics, but with his great performances Irving became an American hero.

With the Depression in full swing, Jaffee needed money more than glory. In 1932, in order to help pay the food bills at home, he sold his Olympic medals plus 400 others to a Harlem pawnshop for $2,000. "They were all gold," he said, "some with diamonds, worth thousands of dollars. Because I didn't redeem them in a year, I never saw them again. I got hundreds of letters from people wanting to buy me some duplicate medals. I refused. It was my doing. I have to pay the consequences." Just prior to the 1976 Olympics in Montreal, the American Broadcasting Company presented a report on Jaffee in an attempt to describe the problems and sacrifices of certain athletes. A nationwide search was made for his medals, but they did not turn up.

In 1940, Jaffee was elected to the United States Skating Hall of Fame. Six years later he was teaching youngsters speed skating at the Newburgh, New York, Recreation Park. He had also been appointed coach of the Delano-Hitch Speed Skating Club.

In the 1950s he became associated with Grossingers, the famous resort in the Catskills, in upstate New York. In 1951, he began the promotion of the world barrel-jumping championships and it became an annual event. In his later years he assisted in the training of 10 Olympic speed skaters. Though he considered himself on "permanent vacation," as he put it, in the 1970s he was quite busy. He lectured often, and produced an annual show on barrel jumping for ABC television. Golfing was also part of his daily regimen. Irving Jaffee died in a San Diego, California, hospital in 1981.

Jaffee is a member of the Jewish Sports Hall of Fame in Israel.

LOUIS "KID" KAPLAN

World Featherweight Champ From 1925 to 1927

KAPLAN, LOUIS "KID" (born December 4, 1902, in Kiev, Russia; died October 26, 1970). American boxer. Ranked by Nat Fleischer as the tenth best featherweight of all time. He was world featherweight champion from 1925 to 1927. His record: 131 bouts of which he won 101 (17 by knockout), drew 10, and lost 13. Seven were no contests.

Born Gershon Mendeloff, Louis Kaplan came to the United States at the age of five and settled with his parents in Meriden, Connecticut, where his father had set up a junk business. Louis' first job was working as a helper to a fruit peddler. He began fighting as an amateur at age 13, and six years later he turned pro. He fought his first bout under the name of Benny Miller.

When Johnny Dundee vacated the featherweight title in 1925 because he could not make the weight, an elimination tournament was held in which Kid Kaplan took part. On January 2, 1925, Kaplan won the tournament, defeating Danny Kramer in a ninth-round knockout. Kid Kaplan thus became the feather-weight champion. Nat Fleischer called the Kaplan-Kramer fight "the tenth best of the first half of the twentieth century."

Kaplan defended his title three times before outgrowing the division. His main adversary at the time was Babe Herman of California, against whom Kaplan fought six times. Before they fought for the title on August 25, 1925, in Waterbury, Connecticut, Herman and Kaplan had fought four times, with Herman winning once and holding Kaplan to a draw the other three times. But when they fought for the title, the match ended in a draw, and Kaplan retained his title. The match attracted 20,000 fans and grossed $59,180, both all-time Connecticut records at the time.

The two men fought again on December 18, 1925, in New York's Madison Square Garden and Kaplan won—this time on a decision after 15 rounds.

Kid Kaplan vacated the title in 1927, when he was over the 126-pound weight limit. That year he was approached by racketeers and was offered $50,000 to throw a title fight. Although the opportunity to leave the ring a wealthy man was appealing, Kaplan responded courageously: "I can use the money. But every time I box, my pals bet their hard-earned money on me. I would never be able to face them again, not for a million dollars."

Kaplan was called the "Uncrowned Lightweight Champion," an honor given him after such lightweight fighters of the time as Tony Canzoneri, Al Singer, and Al Mandell would not fight him. They feared his twisting left hook.

Finally, in 1933, Kid Kaplan retired from the ring. In his last fight—against Cocoa Kid in February of that year—he had been thrashed solidly. He quit boxing when an eye doctor told him he had lost sight in one eye, and it would not return.

After retiring from the ring, Kaplan acquired a half interest in a Hartford, Connecticut, restaurant, which he retained for the next 15 years. He died in 1970 after suffering paralysis on his left side.

ELIAS KATZ

The Finnish Long-Distance Olympic Star

KATZ, ELIAS (born 1901, in Abo, Finland; died December 25, 1947) Finnish track star. He won a gold medal in the 1924 Olympics as a member of Finland's victorious team in the 3,000-meter, team cross-country race. His teammate was the famous Finnish runner, Paavo Nurmi. Katz also won an Olympic silver medal in the 3,000-meter steeplechase in the 1924 Games with a 9:44.0 time.

At age 19, he joined the newly-established Jewish Maccabi Sports Club in Turku, Finland, where he had grown up. That summer, the club sponsored a decathlon event. Katz ran in the 1,500-meter race, his first time on such a long track, and won easily. Friends, sensing that he had a special talent for medium-distance races, urged him to continue training. A few weeks later, another Finnish sports club arranged a 1,000-meter race for beginners, and Katz won that one as well.

More races followed, with Katz doing well, coming in second more often than winning. In 1922 he moved to Helsinki, the Finnish capital, where he became a member of the Jewish Athletic Club, Stjarnan (The Star)—later Makkabi.

In 1923, he blossomed into a great track star. He ran his best time for the steeplechase that year, 9:40.9. He also won a 1,500-meter race in 4:14, an excellent time then.

He qualified for the 1924 Paris Olympics. In the 3,000-meter steeplechase, he won his heat easily, setting an Olympic record at 9:43.8, fastest time ever posted until then. But in the finals Katz stumbled and received only the silver medal (his time: 9:44). He won a gold medal in the 3,000-meter cross-country race.

In 1925, Bar Kochba of Berlin, the first Jewish national sports club in Germany and Central Europe (founded in 1898) learned that Katz was Jewish and invited him to come live in Germany and represent the club. Katz responded positively to the invitation.

He worked in Berlin as a packer in a department house and as a trainer at Bar

Kochba. His presence encouraged many outstanding German Jewish athletes to leave other athletic clubs in favor of Bar Kochba. As a result, the club gained stature in both Jewish and gentile eyes; it grew to 5,000 members and flourished until the 1930s when the Nazis forced it to disband.

Katz participated in all the European Maccabiah Games in the late 1920s, and was quite successful in medium-distance running. On July 12, 1926, he ran the second leg for a Finnish club team which set a world record of 16:26.2 for the 4 × 1,500-meter relay.

In 1927, the Sports Association of Finland appealed to Elias Katz to return to train for the 1928 Olympics. Katz, still a Finnish citizen, returned to Turku. He trained hard. Once, practicing on the outskirts of Turku, he encountered a horse-drawn cart and decided to challenge the horse to a race. Katz won by a wide margin. Later that year, Elias developed a foot injury which required surgery. He was unable to run anymore and missed the chance to be in the 1928 Olympics in Amsterdam.

Returning to Germany, Katz came upon growing anti-Semitism, and left for Palestine in 1933. There he worked as a common laborer, sometimes as a bricklayer. He married and lived in Rehovot with his wife and a daughter who was born in 1942. He was also a trainer and sports manager for the Maccabi organization in Tel Aviv.

Katz was selected to coach the first Jewish team for the 1948 Olympics in London. But he never got to England.

In December 1947, Katz was employed as a film operator at the Al Mugahzi camp, 15 kilometers south of Gaza. Immediately after the evening film showing, he, the only Jew in the camp, was killed by three Arabs. A Jewish soldier was wounded in the attack. Katz was buried in Ramat Gan, outside Tel Aviv.

Elias Katz is a member of the Jewish Sports Hall of Fame in Israel.

BENNY KAUFF

A Great Batting Star During World War I

KAUFF, BENJAMIN MICHAEL (born January 5, 1891, in Pomeroy, Ohio; died November 17, 1961) American baseball player. He played between 1912 and 1920 and was best known for his superb hitting. Kauff's career batting average in 859 games in the major leagues was .311, with 961 hits and 454 runs batted in.

Scouts for the New York Yankees noticed Kauff, a left-handed hitter and outfielder, in 1910, while he was playing with the minor league team in Parkersburg, West Virginia. The Yankees signed Kauff in 1911, but sent him to the minor leagues where he remained for the next five years.

Kauff did get to play five games for the Yankees in 1912, but he spent the bulk of the season with the minor league team in Hartford, Connecticut, where he had a remarkable .395 batting average. The Yankees came under some fire from

baseball enthusiasts for not giving Kauff his chance. In 1914 when the new Federal League came into existence, Benny moved over to that league and became one of its greatest hitting stars.

In 1914, playing for Indianapolis, he led the Federal League in hitting with .370, collecting 211 hits and stealing 75 bases. The following year, playing for the Brooklyn Feds, Kauff again won the batting title, hitting .342; he also stole 55 bases. He was suitably nicknamed "the Ty Cobb of the Feds."

Impressed by Benny Kauff's drawing power, John McGraw, the manager of the New York Giants, virtually kidnapped Kauff, hoping thereby to put the Federal League out of business. Until then the Feds had been raiding the player ranks of the National and American leagues.

One day in 1915, McGraw produced Kauff dramatically at New York's Polo Grounds for a game between the Giants and the Phillies. But Phillies' owner William F. Banker refused to let his team take the field as long as Kauff was scheduled to be in the Giant lineup. The game was delayed for more than an hour until National League president John K. Tener was reached by telephone and ordered McGraw to return Kauff to the Brooklyn Feds.

Then, in 1916, the Federal League collapsed and Kauff had his chance after all to play with the Giants. The Giants purchased Kauff for $30,000 from Harry Sinclair, Brooklyn Feds' owner. Benny demanded a share of the $30,000 and when Sinclair rejected his demand, Kauff refused to report to the Giants. Finally, the matter was settled as McGraw and Sinclair agreed to pay Benny $5,000 each.

With that money Benny bought himself some fancy clothes, and when he showed up at Giant spring training in one such outfit, he caused quite a stir. Along with a loud striped shirt, an expensive blue suit, patent-leather shoes, a fur-collared overcoat, and a derby hat, he had on a huge diamond ring and a gold watch encrusted with diamonds. Still, he had come to play baseball, and very soon after arriving, he boasted that he would hit .300 "blindfolded."

He was slightly inaccurate. In 1916, he managed to hit only .264, but even so he proved valuable to the Giants. In both 1916 and 1917 (when he hit .308), he helped them win pennants. He hit two home runs in the 1917 World Series, both in one game, against the Chicago White Sox. Chicago, however, won the Series.

During the 1918 season, Benny was drafted into the U.S. Army. He returned to the Giants when the war was over, and played three more seasons, hitting .314 in 1918, .277 in 1919, and .294 in 1920.

In 1920, he was charged with being a member of an automobile theft ring in New York. He was tried and acquitted, but baseball commissioner Kenesaw Landis ordered him barred from baseball for life because the testimony at the trial showed that Kauff had associated with thieves.

AGNES KELETI

The Hungarian Gymnast Who Won Five Olympic Gold Medals

KELETI, AGNES (born January 9, 1921, in Budapest, Hungary-   ) Hungarian gymnast. She won five Olympic gold medals and a total of 11 Olympic medals during the 1940s and 1950s.

At age 15, Agnes developed an interest in gymnastics, joining the famous VAC (Fencing and Athletic) Sports Club, the only Jewish club in Hungary. When the Nazis moved into Hungary in March 1944, however, her gymnastics career came to an abrupt halt.

In 1944, her father and other close relatives were sent to Auschwitz where they died. Only she, her mother, and sister survived. Her mother and sister were saved when the Swedish diplomat Raoul Wallenberg, well-known for having helped many Jews escape the grip of the Nazis in Hungary, obtained refuge for them in a "Swedish house" in Budapest. Agnes eluded the Nazis by buying Christian documents which enabled her to leave Budapest.

After World War II, she returned to gymnastics, winning her first Hungarian title in 1946 in the uneven bars competition. In 1947, she was the star of the Central European Gymnastics Championships. From that year until 1956, she won the all-around Hungarian Championships 10 times. At the same time she continued studying and received the equivalent of a Masters degree in physical education in 1950.

Agnes won many medals in Olympic competition. In London in 1948, she was awarded a silver medal for team-combined competition, although she did not participate because of an injury late in training. (The medal was awarded to Agnes because, though injured during the Olympics, she was still considered a member of the team.) In the 1952 Helsinki Olympics, she won a gold medal in the free-standing exercise, a silver medal in the combined team competition, and two bronze medals in hand apparatus-team and uneven parallel bars.

Keleti became the 1954 world champion in uneven bars and was a team member that year of the squad which won the team exercises with portable apparatus.

In the 1956 Melbourne Olympics, Agnes Keleti won gold medals in the free-standing exercise, beam exercises, parallel bars, and combined exercise-team (portable apparatus). She also won silver medals in the combined exercise and combined exercise-team (nine exercises).

"Hungary," she recalled, "gave me everything. The Communists were very interested in sports for political reasons. It gave them, they thought, much prestige. They could win the population over. It didn't bother them that I was Jewish. There was no discrimination by the regime. I worked so hard so I could see the world. Sport was the best way to achieve that."

It was during the October 1956 Hungarian revolt that Agnes Keleti decided not to return to her native Budapest. Two weeks after the revolt, she and the rest of the Hungarian team left for the Melbourne Olympics. Once there, she defected to the West. A number of her Hungarian colleagues in the Olympic delegation, as well as other Eastern bloc sportsmen in Melbourne, did the same. For some time after the Olympics, Agnes stayed in Australia because her sister lived there. Later, their mother joined them. In June 1957, Agnes settled in Israel,

Though she arrived in time for the 1957 Maccabiah Games, she did not compete because at that time gymnastics was not yet a competitive sport in Israel. Instead, she gave two special performances demonstrating her skills. She was then 36 years old which is old for a gymnast.

She then became an instructor in physical education in a Tel Aviv college which later became the Wingate Institute for Sport in Netanya, where she developed a number of national gymnastic teams. She also taught coaches and was instrumental in creating a gymnastics school at Wingate.

In 1959, she married a fellow Hungarian who also taught physical education. They have two sons in their late teens.

Agnes Keleti is a member of the Jewish Sports Hall of Fame in Israel.

IRENA KIRSZENSTEIN-SZEWINSKA

The Greatest Woman Track
and Field Star in the World

KIRSZENSTEIN-SZEWINSKA, IRENA (born May 24, 1946, in Leningrad, Russia–) Polish track and field star. Considered the greatest woman track and field athlete of all time: she won medals in each of the first four Olympics in which she competed—a feat never accomplished before by any runner, male or female. She is recognized as one of Poland's greatest athletes and was named the greatest woman athlete in the world by the Soviets.

Born to Polish parents who had fled to Russia during World War II, Irena and her parents eventually settled in Warsaw. When Irena's athletic ability became obvious at school, her mother pressed her to join a local sports club, and the youngster became a sprinter and long jumper.

When Irena was 18, she surprised everyone at the 1964 Tokyo Olympics by winning silver medals in the 200-meter run and the long jump and a gold medal in the 400-meter relay. In the long jump she established a national record of 21 feet, 7½ inches and in the 200 meters she set a European record of 23.1 seconds. Irena ran on Poland's winning and world-record breaking 400-meters relay team.

The next year Irena became a favorite of the Poles. She studied economics at Warsaw University and pursued her athletic career. She began the season by tying the world record for 100 meters with an 11.1 time. In a meet in Warsaw against the United States that same year (1965), she defeated two American Olympic champions in the 100- and 200-meter races. She also raced a leg on the winning 400-meter relay team, and took the long jump. In the 200-meter race, she broke the world record with a 22.7 second race.

Her triumphs that year won her recognition as a national heroine in her native Poland. Tens of thousands stood to applaud her. Songs in honor of her achievements were sung. All Poland followed her career. She was stopped on Warsaw streets, stared at in awe, and her autograph was in great demand. Some anti-Semitic Poles found it convenient to forget her Jewish origin.

She was named Poland's Athlete of the Year in 1965. Tass, the official Russian news agency, also voted her the outstanding woman athlete in the world. After she won three gold medals (in the 200-meter race, long jump, and 400-meter relay) and a silver medal in the 100-meter race in the European Championships in Budapest in 1966, the British magazine, *World Sport,* chose her as Sportswoman of the Year.

Irena became Mrs. Szewinska in 1967. Her husband Junusz, a photographer who was once a runner and also her coach, is not Jewish. In 1968, in Mexico City, Irena won a gold medal in the 200-meter Olympics race, setting a new world record at 22.5 seconds. She also won a bronze medal in the 100-meter race.

Her son Andrzej was born in February 1970. Irena believed having a child helped her performance in sport. After 1968 she was tired, and was content to spend a year uninvolved in competitive sport. The rest was beneficial both physically and mentally. She felt better, trained better, and enjoyed running more. And her performance improved. She devoted all her time outside her family to her passion, track. Because she never tired of the sport she was still able to beat younger rivals.

Between 1971 and 1973 Irena was still an outstanding sprinter, although not number one in the world. She earned two more bronze medals after the baby's birth: in the 200-meter event at the 1971 European Championships and at the 1972 Munich Olympics.

Until 1972 Irena's principal events were the 100-meter and 200-meter sprint, but after Munich she concentrated on the 400-meter race. She followed the advice of her husband and coach, and as a result, in 1974 she became the first woman to break 50 seconds at that distance, running it in 49.9 seconds.

She made a great comeback in 1974 after her place at the top had been captured by the younger sprinter, Renate Stecher, of East Germany. In that year Irena chopped a tenth of a second from her 200-meter world mark by running that distance in 22.0 seconds. And she recorded the second fastest ever time for a woman in the 100-meters: a 10.9 second sprint. She set a world record in the 200-meters by running it in 22.21 seconds. Finally, she won the European 100-meter and 200-meter races, beating Olympic champ Stecher in both events. Irena clocked 11.13 in the 100, the third fastest electronic time ever for a woman. She had an undefeated season at each distance. And she even ran a remarkable 48.5 anchor for Poland's team in the 1,600-meter relay at Rome in the European Championships.

For her achievements United Press International voted her Sportswoman of 1974. *Track and Field News* named her woman athlete of the year. At the 1976 Montreal Olympics, she won the 400-meter race, setting a world record at 49.29, and lowering her own world record by almost a half second. For her, it was her most exciting victory. It garnered her a seventh Olympic medal. When asked if her victory was a triumph for the Communist system, she replied: "I know the people from Poland were very happy to see the Polish flag flying highest. But I run because it gives me great pleasure and satisfaction. I run for me."

Her total of seven Olympic (three of them gold) and 10 European (five gold) medals is a record that has no rival in the history of women's track and field. But Irena still maintained that no title gave her as much joy as the birth of her son. Irena contended she kept competing for many years because she enjoyed the training and the competition, especially the important meets like the Olympics. She did not relish those easy meets where she knew she would win without difficulty. Her best achievements came in the major competitions where she had to fight to win.

The year 1977 was one of her most successful. She won the 400-meter race in the Düsseldorf World Championships, establishing a new world record of 49.0. In 1978 and 1979, Szewinska worked toward the goal of trying to be the first person to win eight gold medals in the Olympic Games, bettering the record seven that Mark Spitz won in Munich in 1972. Age finally caught up with her at the 1980 Moscow Games, and she came home without a single medal.

A graduate of Warsaw University, Irena is now an economist, working in the Transportation Research Center in Warsaw.

Irena Kirszenstein-Szewinska is a member of the Jewish Sports Hall of Fame in Israel.

JOHN KLING

The Guiding Spirit of the Chicago Cubs Championship Teams

KLING, JOHN G. (born November 13, 1875, in Kansas City, Missouri; died January 31, 1947) American baseball player. Ranked as one of the greatest catchers of all time. The guiding spirit of the famous Chicago Cubs teams of the early twentieth century, teams which won four pennants and two World Series. In 1,260 games, Kling had 1,161 hits, 531 runs batted in, and a .271 career batting average.

When Johnny was a youngster in Kansas City, Missouri, he began playing baseball as a pitcher, but one day the catcher failed to appear and Johnny took his place. In the 1890s John played semipro ball starring for Houston in 1899 and for St. Joseph of the Western League in 1900.

John remained with St. Joseph until 1901 when he joined the Chicago Cubs and alternated as catcher with Frank Chance. When Hall-of-Famer Chance (of Evers-to-Tinker-to-Chance double-play fame) switched to first base, Kling became the regular catcher.

John's real name was Kline, and he used it in the minors, but as a Cub he was known as Johnny Kling, probably to sound less Jewish. At the time, catchers remained at a distance from batters unless the hitter had two strikes. Kling was the first major league catcher to stand right behind the batter at all times. His throwing arm was so strong that he became the first catcher to throw out base runners from a crouching position.

In 1906, Kling had his best season, hitting .321. Chicago that year recorded 116 victories and won the pennant, but they lost the World Series to the Chicago White Sox. In 1907 and 1908 the Cubs took the pennant and the World Series.

The following year (1909) Kling refused to play for the Cubs. Some said he was holding out for more pay, others suggested that he preferred to devote all his time to the billiard business he had established the previous year. While holding out, he was busy organizing a team in an independent baseball league and, at the same time, capturing the

world's professional pocket billiard championship. Without him that year the Chicago Cubs came in second in the pennant race.

Unable to stay away from baseball, Kling rejoined the Cubs in 1910 and led them to a pennant. The team, however, lost the World Series to the Philadelphia Athletics. In the middle of the 1911 season John was traded to the perennial last-place Boston Braves. The following year, Kling became the Braves manager, and again the team wound up in the cellar. In 1913, Kling played with Cincinnati, his last major league year.

Twenty years later, Kling returned to baseball. He bought a minor league team, the Kansas City Blues. Four years later, in 1937, he sold the team to the New York Yankees for a large profit.

In the years before his death, Kling operated the Dixon Hotel in Kansas City, Missouri, and was a partner in the Kling and Allen bowling alley and billiard parlor. In 1947 he died of a cerebral hemorrhage in Kansas City.

SANDY KOUFAX

The Youngest Player Ever Admitted to the Baseball Hall of Fame

KOUFAX, SANDY (born December 30, 1935, in Brooklyn, New York–   ) American baseball player. One of the greatest pitchers of all time. The first pitcher in the major leagues to pitch four no-hit games. He won the Cy Young Award three times in four seasons and in 1972 was the youngest player ever admitted to the Hall of Fame. He was the *Sporting News'* Pitcher of the Year each year from 1963 to 1966. He struck out 2,396 batters, pitched 40 shutouts, and established numerous major league records, including the most seasons (three) with 300 or more strikeouts.

Sandy (Sanford) was born in the Borough Park section of Brooklyn, the son of Jack and Evelyn (Lichtenstein) Braun. His name at birth was Sanford Braun. At age three, his parents divorced. Sandy and his mother lived with her parents for some time. When Sandy was nine, his mother remarried. Sandy always considered Evelyn's second husband, Irving Koufax, an attorney, his real father.

Sandy Koufax entered Brooklyn's Lafayette High School in the fall of 1949, and played on its basketball and baseball teams. He played first base on the school baseball team. Most of the pitching was done by Fred Wilpon, a future president of the New York Mets.

After high school graduation, Sandy was awarded an athletic scholarship to the University of Cincinnati on the strength of his basketball record. He enrolled in the school in the fall of 1953 and majored in architecture.

Koufax became a member of the baseball team and in the first two games he pitched for the university, he struck out 34 batters. A sportswriter named Jimmy Murphy took note of Koufax's performances and informed the Brooklyn Dodgers of Koufax's pitching talents. The Dodgers offered him a $14,000 bonus plus an annual salary of $6,000, a respectable sum in those days. On December 14, 1954, two weeks before his nineteenth birthday, he signed with the Dodgers.

His first spring training (in 1955) was less than satisfactory. He had come too far, too fast. "I was so nervous and tense," he recalled. "I couldn't throw the ball for 10 days. When I finally started pitching, I felt I should throw as hard as I could. I wound up with an arm so sore that I had to rest for another week." Because he had received the $6,000 bonus, he was required to spend at least two years with the Dodgers, thus forgoing a chance to obtain valuable experience in the minor leagues.

His first start for the Dodgers was on July 6, 1955. He pitched just over four innings, striking out four, and walking eight. In his second start, however, he showed his potential: on August 27th, he shut out the Cincinnati Reds on two hits, striking out 14 batters, the most in one game by any National League pitcher that year. His final two appearances of the season left the Dodgers organization a bit confused, wondering whether Koufax would really be an asset to the team. In one of the two games, he lasted only one inning; in the other he shut out the Pittsburgh Pirates on five hits, striking out six.

That year the Dodgers took seven games to win their first World Series, defeating the New York Yankees. Koufax mostly sat and watched, because Buzzie Bavasi, the Dodger executive, told him, "You have one pitch—high." Koufax acknowledged later that only because he had been signed for a bonus did the Dodgers keep him. "I was a guy trying to find himself," he recalled. "You're on a team that is usually a contender, you have to show control." The Dodgers, he felt, didn't work him enough, so he didn't have an opportunity to improve his control. "If I'd have signed with the Pittsburgh Pirates, they would've been forced to use me. In those days, they were pitching anybody who was alive."

So, for the next six years, Koufax had, as he has said, "good periods, bad periods. Mostly bad." In his first six seasons, he won 36 games and lost 40. He had one day of glory in 1959, and that was the day he struck out 18 batters, tying the major league record set two decades earlier by Cleveland Indian pitcher Bob Feller.

In 1960, with the Dodgers now in Los Angeles, he was 8–13 and ready to throw in the towel. With the season over, he threw all of his baseball equipment away, doubting that he would return. He went into business, but did not like it. "Then," said Sandy, "I decided maybe I hadn't worked hard enough, so the next spring I reported to Vero Beach. Our clubhouse man, Nobe Kawano, handed me the gear and said, 'I took all your stuff out of the garbage.'"

He asked to pitch more frequently to improve his control. He got advice from Joe Becker, the pitching coach, and Norm Sherry, a catcher and Sandy's roommate. "And [Dodger pitcher] Don Newcombe taught me the value of running," recalled Koufax. "He was the hardest worker I ever saw." That season (1961) Koufax was 18–13, striking out 269 batters, breaking a league record held by the legendary Christy Mathewson. From 1961 to 1966, Sandy won 129 games and lost only 47.

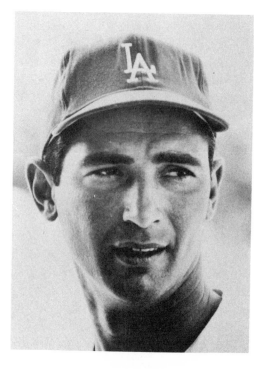

In the 1962 season, Koufax was on his way to a great season when an injury forced him to stay out of uniform at the season's midpoint. He was 14–14, with 209 strikeouts, an earned-run average of 2.06, and a no-hitter under his belt, when the index finger of his pitching hand grew numb and he was unable to produce a curve. In mid-July it was determined that he was suffering from a circulatory affliction resulting from a blood clot in the palm. Physicians thought that a finger might have to be amputated, ending Koufax's career. But an operation was not required, and the doctors successfully treated the finger with anticoagulants.

The 1963 season was Koufax's greatest! He was 13–3 by mid-July, including a no-hitter. He wound up the season at 25–5, striking out 306 batters, a figure

topped by only three others since 1900. His 11 shutouts was a major league record for a left-hander in one season; and his 311 innings pitched were the most by a National League left-hander since 1921. Koufax's earned-run average of 1.88 was the major league's best the second year running. In the World Series against the New York Yankees, his two victories were crucial in helping the Dodgers take the entire event. Koufax was named Cy Young Award winner unanimously as the best pitcher in the majors that year, as well as the National League's Most Valuable Player.

In 1964, Koufax posted a 19–5 record with an earned-run average of 1.74 before an arm ailment sidelined him at the end of August. On June 4th of that year he pitched his third no-hitter, tying the major league record at that point.

In 1965 he was hampered by arthritis in his elbow, but despite the ailment won 26 games and struck out 382 to break Bob Feller's major league record of 348. On September 9th he pitched a perfect game against the Chicago Cubs, the fourth no-hitter of his career. (In September 1981, Nolan Ryan pitched the fifth no-hitter of his career, breaking the record Koufax held for 16 years.) In 1965, Sandy again won the Cy Young Award.

A host of stories, many of them simply not true, have developed surrounding Sandy Koufax's relationship to his Jewish faith. One which appears true has it that the Dodgers took the Jewish High Holy Days into consideration so that Koufax could pitch as much as possible during September or October. Another that Sandy himself denies has it that because of Koufax, the Dodger clubhouse was stocked with bagels, lox, and chopped chicken liver, all traditional Jewish foods.

One incident which Koufax confirmed took place in October 1965, when the Dodgers and Minnesota Twins were playing in the World Series. The opening game fell on Yom Kippur, holiest day of the Jewish year, and Sandy was not at the ball park. Don Drysdale pitched in his place instead and the Dodgers lost 8–2. The following morning, the *St. Paul Pioneer Press* carried a sports column entitled, "An Open Letter to Sandy Koufax." It contained a number of veiled and uncomplimentary references. The column concluded: "The Twins love matza balls on Thursdays." (The Yom Kippur game was played on a Thursday.) Later, Sandy commented, "I couldn't believe it. I thought that kind of thing went out with dialect comics." He pitched the second game later that day and lost 5–1. But he won the seventh and deciding game, and the Dodgers won the World Series. After that, Sandy said, "I clipped the column so that I could send it back to him (the writer of the column) after we defeated the Twins with a friendly little notation that I hoped his words were as easy to eat as my matza balls. I didn't of course [send it]. We were winners."

In 1966, Koufax earned the highest salary ever paid a baseball player at that time: $135,000. That spring, he and fellow Dodger pitcher Don Drysdale had entered into a holdout alliance, threatening to tour Japan and then hinting they would leave baseball and appear in a movie in which Koufax would be an Italian waiter. The Dodgers gave in to Koufax's high demands, and he was back in uniform on opening day. His injuries remained problematic, and he made a pact with the Dodger team physician: "Let me know when I run the risk of permanent damage." The doctor, Robert Kerlan, wanted Sandy to quit at the beginning of 1966.

But Sandy persevered. He had an impressive 27–9 record, including winning the game which clinched the pennant for the Dodgers after only two days' rest. He turned in the third lowest earned-run average (1.73) of any major league pitcher ever, and won the Cy Young Award for an unprecedented third time. After the Dodgers lost four straight in the World Series to Baltimore, Koufax hired a hall in the Beverly Hills Hotel and announced his retirement: "I've had it," he declared. "I don't want to wind up with an arm I won't be able to use for the rest of my life."

He tried television, working as a commentator, but disliked it and gave it up. "People started writing that I was living the life of a hermit," he noted, "which wasn't true. All I had done was move to small towns (Ellsworth, Maine, and Templeton, California), but I continued to associate with the human race." He took a job as a manufacturer's representative, selling electrical appliances, but found that "selling wasn't my long suit." He went back to the Los Angeles Dodgers in January 1979, as a pitching instructor "to make ends meet." In the 1981 season he was a part-time pitching coach for the Albuquerque Dukes, the Dodgers top farm club.

Sandy is an accomplished do-it-yourself man and among his hobbies are building, painting, and repairing. He is married to actor Richard Widmark's daughter, Anne.

Sandy Koufax is a member of the Jewish Sports Hall of Fame in Israel.

BENNY LEONARD

The Jewish Boxing Champion Who Refused to Fight on a Jewish Holiday

LEONARD, BENNY (born April 7, 1896, in New York City; died April 18, 1947) American boxer. Considered by some to be the greatest Jewish sports figure of all time and the best Jewish boxer in history. Ranked by Nat Fleischer as the second greatest lightweight fighter ever. From 1917 to 1924, Leonard held the world lightweight title. Career record: 209 bouts, 88 wins (68 by knockout), lost 5, 1 draw, 115 no-decisions.

Benny Leonard, whose real name was Benjamin Leiner, was the son of Orthodox Jews. He grew up around Eighth Street and Second Avenue in New York City, a Jewish neighborhood, with Italians to the south, Irish to the north. The public baths were near Benny's house: to reach them, one had to walk past where he lived. "You had to fight or stay in the house when the Italian and Irish kids came through on their way to the baths," Benny recalled. When he fought on the street, it was not only with fists, but also with sticks, stones, and bottles. In part because of some of the beatings he took, Benny disliked this kind of fighting intensely.

He fought with gloves for the first time at age 11. His parents had no inkling of what he was doing, but when his mother discovered that Benny was boxing, she asked a relative to give him a job in his printing shop. Benny took the job, but it did not last long. One morning, he came to work with a black eye that he got in a fight. He was given an ultimatum: quit fighting or quit the job. He quit the job. His mother failed to understand the attraction of the ring. "A prizefighter you want to be?" she asked him weeping. "Is that a life for a respectable man? For a Jew?"

For Benny Leonard it was. His street fights included routing a group of non-Jews who had attacked an elderly Jewish woman and taking on hoodlums who were trying to deface a synagogue. He was the champion of Eighth Street.

Benny was too poor to pay for a seat to see a fight. One night, when he was 16, he sat perched on a skylight atop a small-time neighborhood boxing club, watching the fight in the ring below. Losing his balance, Benny fell onto the ring floor and an angry promoter grabbed him before he could escape. To pay for the broken glass of the skylight that shattered as he fell, Leonard offered to replace a boxer who had failed to appear for his bout that night. Benny won the match, and his career was launched.

He used the name "Benny Leonard" in his early fights so his parents would not know that he was boxing. But the secret could not be kept for long. Leonard was always concerned about his mother's feelings. He called her after every fight, carried her picture around with him, and even earned the nickname, "Mama's boy." To add to her happiness, he would never fight on a Jewish holiday.

Leonard's first big victory occurred in 1915 when he defeated Joe Mandot, a veteran pugilist. The next year he fought the lightweight champion, Freddy Welsh, to two no-decision contests. In their third meeting on May 28, 1917, Leonard knocked him out in the ninth round and became the new lightweight champ.

His most memorable fights were between 1920 and 1923. In a 1920 contest, Charlie White, a hard-hitting left-hander, belted Leonard out of the ring, but Benny still managed to knock White out in the ninth round. Jack Britton, the welterweight champ, beat Leonard on a foul in 1922. The following month, Leonard rebounded from Lew Tendler's hard hitting to win a tough decision. On January 15, 1925, Leonard retired undefeated. "My mother was so happy," he recalled. "I was 29, practically a millionaire, and without a scratch."

He might have remained in that happy circumstance had his financial position not taken an eventual plunge. From 1926 to 1931, he bought a hockey team, played in vaudeville, and taught boxing at City College in New York. But the stock market crash of 1929 wiped out all his savings, and so in 1931, at age 35, he decided to try a comeback as a welterweight. This decision has been described as the greatest mistake in his boxing career.

Jimmy McLarnin, a hard-hitting fighter of Irish descent, had developed a reputation for stopping Jewish boxers in the ring. Leonard said that a desire "to wipe out McLarnin's successful record against Jewish fighters" was one motive for his comeback. Before he took on McLarnin, Leonard fought some 20 bouts, doing well. But when he met McLarnin on October 7, 1932, the 26-year-old Jimmy had little trouble disposing of the ring-worn Leonard.

In World War II, Leonard served as a lieutenant commander in the United States Maritime Service. He was back in boxing as a referee in 1943. In 1947 he was working as a referee at New York's St. Nicholas Arena one evening when, during the seventh bout, he collapsed in the ring and died of a brain hemorrhage.

In his time, Benny Leonard was the most famous Jewish personality in America. He became a legend, due in part to the claim that no one had ever messed his slicked-down hair in over 200 fights. He would enter the ring with his hair in place, and usually leave the same way. Dan Parker, the veteran sports writer, said, "Leonard moved with the grace of a ballet dancer and wore an air of arrogance that belonged to royalty. His profile might have been chiseled by a master sculptor and there wasn't a mark of his trade upon it to mar its classic perfection."

Perhaps the greatest tribute to Benny Leonard came from Hearst editor, Arthur Brisbane: "He has done more to conquer anti-Semitism than a thousand text-books."

Benny Leonard is a member of the Jewish Sports Hall of Fame in Israel.

BATTLING LEVINSKY

World Light Heavyweight Champ During World War I

LEVINSKY, BATTLING (born June 10, 1891, in Philadelphia, Pennsylvania; died February 12, 1949) World light heavyweight champion from 1916 to 1920. Nat Fleischer ranked Levinsky as the sixth best light heavyweight ever. He fought 272 bouts, winning 66 (25 by knockout), losing 19, with 13 draws and 174 no-decisions.

Though his real name was Barney Lebrowitz, Levinsky began his boxing career in 1906 using the name Barney Williams. For the next seven years he fought, but failed to attract much attention in boxing's heartland, New York City.

But when, in 1913, the young Jewish fighter took a new manager, Dumb Dan Morgan, and fought heavyweight Dan "Porky" Flynn, Levinsky moved into the spotlight.

After watching his fighter do well against Flynn in the first round, manager Morgan convinced the ring announcer to announce that Battling Levinsky (Williams' new fight name) was ready to take on any Irishman in the country. Needless to say, Levinsky won the 10-round fight against Flynn that evening.

Battling Levinsky was indeed an appropriate name. In 1914 he battled 35 times, nine times during January of that year (he won twice by knockout that month; the other seven contests were no-decision matches). The next year, 1915, he outdid himself when, on January 1st, he fought three, 10-round, no-decision bouts—in Brooklyn, New York, in Waterbury, Connecticut, and in New York City. For his day's work Levinsky collected $400.

Levinsky fought the light heavyweight champion, Jack Dillon, nine times before he managed to capture the title in their tenth meeting. That tenth match was fought on October 24, 1916, in Boston, Massachusetts, when Levinsky finally took the title after a 12-round struggle. The two never met again.

During World War I, Levinsky became a lieutenant in the army and served as a boxing instructor. After the war, he never regained his prewar status. Jack Dempsey, soon to become heavyweight champion, knocked him out on November 6, 1918, in three rounds. That year Levinsky fought only 10 times.

After the loss to Dempsey, Levinsky's reputation suffered. On October 20, 1920, he fought the European light heavyweight champion, Georges Carpentier, in Jersey City, but Carpentier won in a fourth-round knockout. It was suggested that the fight had been fixed, but both fighters denied it.

In a fight against Gene Tunney in New York City, on January 13, 1922, Levinsky defended a new title created by his manager. It was called the American light heavyweight title (the world light heavyweight championship was fought in France). Tunney, on his way to a great career in the ring, beat Levinsky easily in 12 rounds. For the next four years Levinsky did not fight.

In 1929, Otto Van Porat, a Norwegian heavyweight, knocked Levinsky out in five rounds in Grand Rapids, Michigan. Levinsky wanted to give up the ring, but he continued because of financial problems connected with several apartment houses he owned in Philadelphia.

After his retirement from the ring in 1929, Battling Levinsky sold most of his apartment houses and purchased a meat slaughtering house in Chicago. Although he continued to live in Philadelphia, he retained ownership of the Chicago business until two years before his death in 1949.

Battling Levinsky is a member of the Jewish Sports Hall of Fame in Israel.

MARV LEVY

Head Coach of the Montreal
Alouettes and Kansas City Chiefs

LEVY, MARV (born August 3, 1928, in Chicago, Illinois-   ) American football coach. Head coach of the National Football League's Kansas City Chiefs from 1978 to 1982, compiling a 31-42 won-lost record. He was picked as an NFL coach after a successful career coaching the Montreal Alouettes in the Canadian Football League in the early 1970s. After a dismal 3-6, 11th place finish in 1982, the Chiefs dismissed Levy.

Marv Levy attended Coe College in Cedar Rapids, Iowa, where he majored in history. In 1950 he graduated with Phi Beta Kappa honors, and the following year earned a masters degree in English history from Harvard University.

While at Coe College, Levy was an outstanding back on the football team, and from 1953 to 1955 was an assistant football coach at Coe. He joined the University of New Mexico staff in 1956 and for two years served as assistant coach. In 1958 and 1959 he was New Mexico's head coach, and received Skyline Conference coach of the year honors both those seasons. He then took over at California in 1960 as head coach, coaching the Golden Bears through the 1963 season, and ending up with a rather dismal 8-29-3 overall record. One of Levy's players at the time was quarterback Craig Morton, who went on to play NFL pro football with the

Dallas Cowboys, the New York Giants, and the Denver Broncos.

Next, Levy moved to William and Mary in Williamsburg, Virginia, where he was head football coach for five years. He was named Southern Conference coach of the year in 1964 and 1965.

Levy began his pro coaching career in 1969 with the Philadelphia Eagles with whom he was assistant coach in charge of the kicking teams. In 1970, he joined George Allen's Los Angeles Rams as an assistant coach. The following year, 1971, he moved with Allen to the Washington Redskins, remaining as assistant coach through the 1972 season. Marv Levy coached the special teams for Washington's 1972 National Football Conference championship team. After defeating Dallas 26-3, the Redskins met Miami in Super Bowl VII and lost 14-7. Levy moved to Montreal in 1973 as head coach.

In Canadian football, three, not four, downs are allowed, so mounting an awesome offense is extremely difficult. Hence Levy emphasized defense. This tactic proved successful. His first Alouette squad reached the finals of the CFL's Eastern Division with a 7-6-1 record, and then went on to win the Grey Cup the following year. Levy's 1974 season record was 9-5-2. The Alouettes won the Canadian Football League Grey

Cup twice (1974 and 1977) in Levy's five years as coach. His record during those five years was 50-34-4.

Marv Levy was named head coach of the Kansas City Chiefs on December 20, 1977. His strategy was to rebuild Kansas City's defense. "Offense sells tickets," he told a news conference. "Defense wins games and kicking wins championships."

In his first year as coach the Chiefs finished 4-12 as compared with a 7-5-2 record the year before. But the record belied the team's actual strength. Levy used the rather old-fashioned wing-T offense, and despite numerous cynics in the NFL who doubted the Chiefs would move the ball easily, the team was second in the conference in rushing.

In 1979, Levy's second year, he picked up three more victories as against nine losses. He was 8-8 in 1980, and 9-7 in 1981, with a third-place finish in the Western Division of the American Football Conference of the NFL.

Marv Levy is married to the former Dorothy Prout, whom he met when both were students at Coe.

TED "KID" LEWIS

First Boxer with a Mouthpiece

LEWIS, TED "KID" (born October 24, 1894, in St. George's-in-the-East, London, England; died October 14, 1970) British boxer. He was world welterweight champion in 1915 and again from 1917 to 1919. In 260 bouts, he lost only 24. Lewis was the only British fighter to win a world title in the United States. He became Britain's youngest champion when he won the featherweight title shortly after his seventeenth birthday.

At the age of 14, he won his first professional fight, earning for himself a cup of tea and sixpence. Upon winning his next bout, the reward was greater. He received a silver cup, only to find it melted down after being left on the mantelpiece overnight. As time went on, the purses became larger and the rewards of victory more worthwhile.

Lewis won the British and European featherweight titles in 1913 and 1914. In the 1913 bout, he became the first boxer to wear a mouthpiece. In 1914, Lewis, whose real name was Gershon Mendeloff, went to Australia with his family and from there to the United States. Within a year, he had established himself as a contending welterweight. Lewis was the first Englishman to box successfully in the U.S. He was considered speedy, shrewd, and a brutal puncher.

Between 1915 and 1921, Lewis engaged Jack Britton in a series of 20-round bouts that extended over six years. These grudge matches were to decide the world welterweight title. Of the 20 fights, 12 were no-decisions, one was a draw, three went to Britton, and four were victories for Lewis. The first Lewis triumph was in 1915 in Dayton, Ohio, and with it "Kid" Lewis won the welterweight championship for the first time. He lost the title to Britton for the last time in March 1919.

Ted Lewis returned to Britain in 1921 and within a few months won the Empire and European welterweight titles and the British and European middleweight championships. In June 1922, he added the Empire middleweight title. In that same year he fought his most famous fight when he took on Georges Carpentier for the European heavyweight championship. During the first round, the referee stopped the action to speak to Lewis. Lewis dropped his guard and turned to the official to complain of a beltline smash from Carpentier. Meanwhile, the Frenchman drilled home a right to Lewis's unguarded jaw and the English boxer sagged to the canvas. The referee counted him out.

From 1925 to 1929, Lewis fought well, recording seven straight wins by knockout in 1927. In a decade of boxing, Lewis had won three division titles. In his 20 years as a boxer, he had fought in six divisions. He retired from the ring in 1929 and settled in Vienna.

The Jewish Sports Hall of Fame in Israel announced on December 1, 1982, that he had become a member of the Hall of Fame and would be inducted in the spring, 1983.

NANCY LIEBERMAN

Her Mother Bought Her Dolls—
She Wanted Basketballs

LIEBERMAN, NANCY (born July 1, 1958, in Brooklyn, New York-) American basketball player. She was a superstar at Norfolk, Virginia's Old Dominion University in the late 1970s and has since gone on to fame in women's professional basketball.

Nancy's parents divorced when she was 14 and, in her bitterness toward them, she turned to sports. "Some people have nervous breakdowns or pull out their hair," she said. "I played out all my emotion on the basketball court."

Nancy actually began with football, but one day her mother discovered what she described as "a pile of helmets and bodies but no Nancy. Then I realized my daughter was under all that. I stopped football real quick." Baseball was her sport until she was forbidden from playing in her first public school athletic league game because she was a girl. So she turned to basketball.

She began playing against boys at the Hartman YMHA in Far Rockaway, Long Island. Later, while in junior high school, she took the subway to Harlem to play on an AAU all-boys team called the New York Chuckles. The other Chuckles called the new white girl, "fire," for her style of play as well as for her red hair. Nancy said she had the best time of her life: "I had to be mean and hard-nosed." As she improved, she would be chosen over some boys to play five-on-five basketball. When arguments broke out over her being picked ahead of the boys, "I gave them lip right back," she said proudly. There were quite a number of fistfights between Nancy and the boys. She began playing with girls for the first time as a sophomore at Far Rockaway High School.

Still, her mother objected: "I'd get her dolls; she'd want balls. My kid and sports, you wouldn't believe. . . . Why don't you be a secretary? A nurse? Put on a dress? Nothing worked. She thought it was a challenge having everybody against her. She'd fight the world if she had to."

Nancy Lieberman's mind was set on basketball. She thought the game beautiful, fascinating, deceptive. She loved the split-second decisions and the way the players' bodies seemed to glide in the air. She quit piano lessons and Hebrew school. She did not have a Bat Mitzvah. Said Nancy candidly: "I was no Koufax. I'd kill myself before I'd stop playing ball on Saturday."

She was the only high school player and youngest member (at age 18) of the 1976 Olympic team which took a silver medal in Montreal, losing the gold to the Russians. Billie Moore, her Olympic coach that year, said of her: "She is quick, very smart on the court, a good shooter, excellent jumper, very, very strong rebounder, aggressive, hard-nosed, and very strong on defense. She just doesn't have a weakness. She does everything you can ask a player to do."

No woman athlete in the country had been as widely recruited for college as was Nancy Lieberman. More than 75 colleges offered her scholarships, some making illegal offers of cars, apartments, and money. She chose Old Dominion

University in Norfolk, Virginia, entering the school in the fall of 1976. She arrived on campus with a great deal of media hoopla, being the "Olympic girl," and immediately was resented by the other women on the school's basketball team. This was compounded by the unfortunate fact that her coach, Marrianne Stanely, was the woman Nancy had beaten out in 1976 for a berth on the Olympic squad.

Red-headed, fairly small at 5 feet, 10 inches, weighing 146 pounds, and nicknamed "The Lieb," she led the Lady Monarchs of ODU in her first season to a No. 14 national ranking: the team was 23-9 and she averaged 20.9 points per game.

Nancy introduced a new style of women's basketball, a more aggressive one, at Old Dominion. Only 10 years earlier women were still wearing skirted tunics on the basketball court as well as shooting underhand from between their legs.

A marketing major, Nancy had trouble with her grades, particularly in the 1978 season when the team had a 30-4 record. She acknowledged that she found it difficult to go on the road, knowing she had an important game the next night and needing to study poetry in the few hours of privacy. Often she would sit in a classroom, her mind wandering to the game that night, to the 5,000 people who would be watching her play. It was then that she focused, not on the lecturer, but on a certain offense or strategy for the game. That year she averaged 20.2 points per game and was named first team All-American.

In Nancy's junior year (1978-79), Old Dominion captured its first national championship. Nancy earned All-American honors again and was awarded the Wade Trophy for being the nation's outstanding woman basketball player. She averaged 17.4 points per game that year.

She scored less in her senior year, 15.2 points per game, but remained a leader on the floor. She again received All-American honors.

By the spring of 1980, when she was near graduation, she led Old Dominion to its second straight national title and she also captured the Margaret Wade trophy for the second time as the finest player in women's college basketball. By her senior year, Nancy was considered the finest all-around player in the game. In her four years at Old Dominion (1976-1980), she scored 2,430 points for an 18.1 point per game average.

Lieberman is a true pioneer in women's basketball. She has altered the game's techniques, quality and style, mainly because, as *Sports Illustrated* noted in December 1979: "Nancy Lieberman plays like a man. Except for a lack of dynamic jumping ability, there is not much to distinguish Lieberman from the point guard on most of the better varsity male teams." Nancy admits that such compliments please her greatly.

In her style of play, Lieberman does the one thing women had always been reluctant to do before she came along: she goes to the basket—like any male star. Still, she recognizes the difference in strength between herself and professional basketball players. She knows she could never play in the NBA and wonders if she could even have made her University's male team.

Nancy joined the 1980 Olympic squad training in Colorado Springs, but when President Jimmy Carter announced the boycott of the Moscow Olympics, she quit the team rather than take part in alternative competitions in Europe and at home. She was always a person of strong convictions and was among the first to support the boycott. Fully aware that her decision disappointed many, she felt that

competing in alternative games weakened the whole point of the boycott.

In May 1980, she was the first choice in the women's pro basketball league draft. While negotiating for her first pro contract (with the Dallas Diamonds), Nancy was conscious of the high sums other women sports stars were being paid. Although modest about comparing herself with golfer Nancy Lopez or tennis player Tracey Austin, Lieberman noted that "Tracey doesn't have to hit backhands with an elbow in her face either." Nancy was paid $100,000 a year by the Diamonds, the largest contract by far in a league where the average salary was $9,000.

In the 1980–81 season, she led the Dallas Diamonds to the league finals where they lost to the Nebraska Wranglers. She then played in the Los Angeles summer league with many of the (male) Los Angeles Lakers of the NBA. Those large-sized Lakers didn't hold back because she was a woman, and Nancy didn't hold back either.

Her aggressive play turned the Diamonds from a team with a poor 7–28 record in 1979–80 to one that closed out 1981 with a 27–9 record, tied for league best. In the process, attendance tripled to 3,300 a game.

In the middle of 1981 Nancy Lieberman made news of another sort. On August 1 she announced that she had invited women's tennis champion Martina Navratilova to live with her. Nancy contended that she was doing no more than helping a good friend get her bearings after Navratilova's breakup with lesbian activist and author Rita Mae Brown. That year Navratilova was one of the top tennis stars on the tour.

Martina reacted cautiously to Nancy's announcement. The tennis player was hesitant about moving in with Nancy and her housemate, Southern Methodist basketball star Rhonda Rompola, age 20. Martina feared implicating Nancy by association. However, when the tennis player did finally accept Nancy's invitation, the press issued reports that Rita Mae Brown complained that she had "lost" the tennis ace to Nancy Lieberman. Nancy strongly denied allegations of a romance between herself and Navratilova.

In the winter of 1981, the Women's Pro Basketball League folded after three years of inadequate financing and poor attendance. Nancy expects to settle her contract and play for a pro team in Italy.

MORTIMER LINDSEY

The Champion Newark-born Bowler

LINDSEY, MORTIMER JOEL (born December 20, 1888, in Newark, New Jersey; died May 16, 1959) American bowler. One of the top American bowlers in the early twentieth century. One of the first 11 men originally chosen for membership in the American Bowling Congress Hall of Fame in 1941. He held three American Bowling Congress titles.

As a child, Mort Lindsey was an all-around athlete: a catcher for amateur baseball teams in the Bronx; a tennis and basketball player in YMHA and YMCA leagues. He even skated for a medal in a six-day roller skating competition in a rink at 116th Street and Lenox Avenue in New York City. Mort tried boxing too at the 86th Street YMHA in New York, won a few fights, but made no further progress.

He began bowling at age 14, finishing second in his first tournament, a juvenile competition in which wooden balls were used. The locale was the 92nd Street YMHA in New York. The following year he won the event and felt confident enough to stride into wrestler George Bothner's bowling alleys at 84th Street and Third Avenue to challenge all comers. He was hardly dressed for the role of the tough guy: he wore knee-britches and ribbed stockings. George eyed him coldly. "Beat it kid," the wrestler ordered.

"But I came here to bowl," protested Mort.

"So what," retorted Bothner eyeing his short pants. "You're a kid. Get out."

Then, noticing Mort's disappointment, the wrestler relented ever so slightly: "Well, maybe I could see you roll a ball."

Mort rolled a ball, and Bothner, surprised, admitted, "That's not so bad, kid. Come back when you're in long pants." That was all Mort wanted to hear.

Getting George Bothner's approval was Mort's first major victory of his bowling career. He rushed home, badgered his parents to get him a pair of long

pants, and returned to 84th Street for some pointers, and with that his bowling career was launched. Encouraged by wrestler Bothner, he entered a juvenile tournament at Bergman's alleys at 116th Street and Lenox Avenue and beat many of the name stars in taking first prize.

Mort's mother, Minnie, tried desperately to keep her son away from those nefarious bowling alleys. "She never wanted me to be a bowler," Mort recalled somewhat sadly. "Mom thought I should grow up to be a great doctor or lawyer. In her book you couldn't become great as a bowler." Even when Mort won the 86th Street YMCA championship at age 14, he could not convince her that there was a career to be carved out of rolling a ball down a narrow alley.

It took his mother quite some time— until Mort was 27, in fact—before she appeared reconciled to Mort Lindsey the bowling champ. While bowling in the American Bowling Congress tournament in St. Paul, Minnesota, in 1915, Mort was handed a package containing a pair of tiny, gilded, five button shoes. The accompanying card read: "I am sending you these shoes for the ABC tournament because they are the first shoes you struck out in. Mom." At last, Minnie Lindsey was signaling her approval of her son's favorite pastime by showing she could recall the first time Mort had knocked down all the pins with a single ball—in bowling jargon, a strike!

As soon as Mort graduated from public school at 96th Street and Lexington Avenue, he began working for an insurance broker. At 17 he was thought good enough to write policies of any amount for the firm, the New Hampshire Fire Insurance Company. For the next seven years, he continued working, eventually changing employers and moving to Johnson and Higgins of Wall Street. In 1911, he decided to make bowling his full-time occupation.

That year, in partnership with Morris Herman, Mort Lindsey opened a five-lane, ten-pin alley behind a bar in New Haven, Connecticut, on Church Street near Crown. Lindsey was always having fun with bowling. That year he and another bowler, George Kelsey, rolled a 12-hour marathon in bathing suits in New Haven; Mort spotted his opponent 550 pins and won by 5!

In 1912, Lindsey moved to Bridgeport, Connecticut, where, again with Morris Herman, he opened a combination bowling and billiard parlor above Reedy's Bar on Congress Street. The parlor had 13 billiard tables and six bowling alleys.

This was the time when Mort began touring the country, betting large amounts on himself and practically never losing. He even permitted his opponents to select their favorite pair of bowling alleys for each match. "Sure it took guts," he said later, "but you'd be surprised at the psychological effect. The other fellow immediately suspected some trickery and began to sweat. Then you knew you had him."

Mort started competing seriously in bowling in 1912 when he joined a team known as the Brunswick All-Stars of New York. They won the ABC title with a 2,904 total at Chicago, Mort contributing a 557 score. In 1914 the team was barred from competing in the same tournament because Mort lived in New Haven. So, he organized his own team of local bowlers into the New Havens. They won the title in Buffalo, New York, with a 2,994 total, including a 624 score by Mort.

In 1915 Lindsey came to Ohio with the Gergman Stars of New York City and captured the Ohio crown with a 2,990 score (Lindsey: 603). That same year he married Esther D. Dugan.

From 1915 to 1925, Mort Lindsey led the ABC bowlers with an average of 201 and 47/90 (the 200 class in those days was select and small).

Once, during World War I, Lindsey was nearly arrested as a German saboteur. Traveling from Detroit, Michigan, to Windsor, Ontario, he carried a 16-pound bowling ball in a case. Police surrounded Mort suddenly when the Canadian customs man believed the object to be a bomb. It took Mort some time to convince the police that the ball was only to be used in an exhibition tour—not to blow up bridges!

He remained in Bridgeport until 1918, when he was inducted into the U.S. Navy. While still in his naval uniform, Mort won the All-Events ABC crown in Toledo, Ohio, in 1919, with a 215 average and a 1,933 total (664–579–690). He was honorably discharged as a second-class seaman late in 1919. He then opened an auto and tire accessory store in Stamford, Connecticut.

For five years Mort Lindsey worked at the store, but in 1924 opened his own eight-lane bowling alley which also had five pool and billiard tables. He managed the bowling alley until 1943, but was forced to close it when it became impossible to get enough pinboys to work. He could have kept the place going by hiring underage youngsters, but he refused.

In the years following World War I, Lindsey won several tournament victories: the New York City doubles tournament, in 1926; the New York State doubles, in 1928; the Dwyer Classic, in New York, in 1931; and the Petersen tournament, in Chicago, in 1934. He won the New York state singles and doubles title three times, and bowled 17 perfect 300 games in his career, his last in Stamford, Connecticut, in 1941. Mort also gave bowling exhibitions in the United States and Canada and made bowling films that were nationally distributed.

Mort Lindsey participated in 46 of the 55 ABC tournaments up to 1959, missing his 47th due to the illness that shortly preceded his death that year. As late as 1952, when he was 64, Mort Lindsey came from behind to win the Bowlers Journal Tournament.

HARRY LITWACK

A Modest Basketball Coach Who Left a Mark

LITWACK, HARRY "CHIEF" (born September 20, 1907, in Galicia, Austria–) American basketball coach. He coached Temple University, Philadelphia, Pennsylvania, from 1953 to 1973, with a career record of 373-193.

Harry Litwack, who arrived in the United States with his father as a youngster of five, became a star basketball player at South Philadelphia High School from 1922 to 1925. Upon graduation he entered Temple University where he not only made the team, but was captain for two years. Harry was one of only a handful of men in Temple basketball history to have been named captain for two seasons. For seven years he played for the Philadelphia SPHAs (the all-Jewish basketball team from the South Philadelphia Hebrew Association) in the Eastern and American leagues.

Harry began his coaching career at Gratz High School in Philadelphia, where he ended the season with a remarkable 15-2 record. From 1931 to 1951 he served as freshman basketball coach at Temple University without ever having a losing season. His overall record was 181-32. From 1949 to 1951 he also held down the job of assistant coach of the Philadelphia Warriors under coach-owner Eddie Gottlieb.

As Temple coach, Harry led the Owls to 13 postseason tournaments, including the 1969 National Invitation Tournament championship. His team wound up in third place in the NCAA playoffs in 1956 and 1958. In 1958 Litwack was named the New York basketball writers association Coach of the Year.

Among the achievements Harry cherished the most were the four All-Americans he produced during his career at Temple: Guy Rodgers, Hal Lear, Bill Kennedy, and John Baum.

Litwack had the reputation of being a quiet, nondescript figure who rarely made good copy for sportswriters. Litwack noted that "in 43 years of coaching and playing, I had only one technical foul called against me."

One sportswriter described him this way just after his 1969 NIT victory: "His hair is white but he still steps crisply in those Italian suits he wears, and those expensive ties he is never without, and those never-out-of-sight cigars he either has between his lips or his fingers."

Litwack has only a vague recollection of how he obtained the nickname "Chief." He explained that All-American Temple basketball star Guy Rodgers pinned it on him, "when we were in a huddle at a timeout and I explained something. He said, 'OK, chief,' and it stuck to me."

In addition to winning the 1969 NIT championship, Litwack's team that year had a 27–3 record and rolled up 25 straight wins for the longest streak in the nation that season.

In 1972, Harry Litwack retired. In that year his team had a 17–10 record for its fourteenth consecutive winning season. Harry was named to the Basketball Hall of Fame in 1975 and to the Jewish Sports Hall of Fame in Israel in July 1981. He and his wife, Estelle, have two daughters, both of whom are Temple graduates.

Since 1959, Litwack has been associated with Bill Foster, the head coach of South Carolina University, in operating the Pocono Mountain basketball camp, considered one of the finest instruction camps in the nation. Six months of the year Harry is busy with the camp, and the other six months he spends in Miami Beach, Florida, where he watches basketball on TV, plays golf, and "relaxes."

SID LUCKMAN

A Great Leader and Football Brain

LUCKMAN, SIDNEY (born November 21, 1916, in Brooklyn, New York-) American football player. The first modern T-formation quarterback, Luckman was considered the greatest long-range passer in pro football of his time. A genius at football strategy, he led the Chicago Bears, for whom he played from 1939 to 1947, to five Western Conference titles and four National Football League championships. As of September 5, 1981, he was ranked sixteenth on the list of leading lifetime passers in pro football. In 12 years with the National Football League, he attempted 1,744 passes, had 904 completions for 14,686 yards, and passed for 139 touchdowns.

Sid Luckman's father sparked his son's interest in football when he gave the eight-year-old child a football. Sid attended Erasmus High School in New York City. Despite offers of college scholarships from 40 universities, Sid planned to attend the U.S. Naval Academy in Annapolis, Maryland. But when Navy played Columbia at Baker Field in New York during Sid's senior year of high school, the Navy athletic director Rip Miller took Sid into both teams' locker rooms. "As soon as I met [Columbia coach] Lou Little," recalled Luckman, "I was impressed—the way he dressed, the way he spoke, I knew I wanted to play for him."

And that was that—almost. Sid chose Columbia, and Columbia chose Sid, but the university had no athletic scholarship program. So the new college student had to work his way through college, painting walls, and washing dishes in

fraternity houses to pay for his room and board. His college football years (1936–38) produced a disappointing 10-14-1 record but Sid was hardly to blame. In his final year, 1938, when he was named All-American, the team finished at 3-6.

Luckman became one of the best triple-threat men in college football, starring at tailback. In 1937 he returned a kickoff 82 yards against Army, boomed a 72-yard punt against Syracuse, and threw a 60-yard pass against Pennsylvania. He also connected on a 65-yard pass against Brown University in 1938. His college passing record was 180 completions (20 of which went for touchdowns) in 376 attempts for 2,413 yards, a 47.9 percentage. Said Coach Lou Little: "We would have had a very ordinary team, or less than that, without him." In truth few people realized just how good Sid Luckman was until he turned pro. Only then did he play for teams which brought out his full ability.

At certain moments in 1939 it appeared unlikely that Sid Luckman would ever become a pro football player. A routine form sent by the Chicago Bears in January of that year notified Sid that he had been selected by the club in the draft. He was asked in the letter if he was interested in playing professional football. Wrote back the diffident football star: "I have no intention of playing professional football. In fact, I have been advised against it. My plans are to enter the trucking business with my brothers."

Bears owner George Halas did not give up. He wrote Sid a lengthy letter, pleading with him to change his mind. Sid, letter in hand, went off to talk with Columbia's Lou Little to ask whether he thought this "guy Halas was on the up-and-up." Little said he thought Halas was serious and so Sid Luckman wrote back asking for an interview.

Halas had to negotiate with the Pittsburgh Steelers for Luckman. The Steelers had a draft choice before Chicago, and Halas had arranged that Pittsburgh send Sid to the Bears in exchange for another player. Though they later regretted it, the Steelers agreed. Sid became a Bear officially on July 24, 1939.

George Halas was developing a new T-formation and he thought that Luckman was the best man to run it, even though Sid had been a tailback in high school and college. Said the Bear owner, "Sid made himself a great quarterback. No one else did it for him. He worked hard, stayed up nights studying and really learned the T. Sid wasn't built for quarterback. He was stocky (5 feet, 11-½ inches, 190 pounds), not fast and not a great passer in the old tradition. But he was smart and he was dedicated." Halas once observed that Sid Luckman never called a wrong play in his career. He used to spend hours practicing pivots, feints, handoffs, and ball-handling in the dressing room, at home, in hotels on road trips, and even between seasons.

In 1940 Sid gave the T-formation permanence and credibility. In that year's title game against the Washington Redskins, the underdog Bears destroyed their opponent, 73-0. Luckman, who played only the first half because the game was so one-sided at halftime, scored one touchdown and passed for another. The day after the game, *The New York Times* said of Luckman: "No field general ever called plays more artistically or engineered a touchdown parade in more letter-perfect fashion."

That 1940 title was the first of four the Bears would win with Luckman as quarterback (they captured the championship in 1941, 1943, and 1946). Between 1940 and 1943, the Bears won four Western Division titles. From 1941 to 1944 and again in 1947, Luckman was All-Pro.

The year 1943 was Sid's greatest. On November 14, 1943, playing at the Polo Grounds in New York, he gave the greatest performance of his life. He passed for a record seven touchdowns against the New York Giants and thus surpassed the old record of six, set by Sammy Baugh. "Strictly luck," Sid said afterward. "All I could think of when that seventh touchdown went in was the day I saw Lou Gehrig (the great New York Yankee baseball star) hit four home runs in Yankee Stadium." That year Sid guided the Bears to an 8-1-1 record. The 28 touchdowns he tossed in 10 games in 1943 remained a record until the Baltimore Colts' Johnny Unitas broke it in 1959 with 32 in 12 games. In 1943, Sid also passed for five touchdowns in the NFL title game when the Bears defeated the Washington Redskins 41-21. Not surprisingly, he was named the NFL Most Valuable Player that year.

On January 4, 1944, Sid Luckman entered the U.S. Navy as an ensign in the Merchant Marine stationed at Sheepshead Bay, New York. He was assigned to an oil tanker plying the Atlantic, and served for eight months of hazardous sea duty. At times he got shore leave to play for the Bears. In 1944, the Bears finished second and then dropped to fourth in 1945, the only season that Luckman played that they had not finished second or higher.

Despite the Bears' weak 1945 season, Sid shared the passing title with Sammy Baugh and led the league in touchdown passes (14) and yardage gained (1,725). In 1946, when the Bears won the title, Sid threw 17 touchdown passes. In 1947, his final year, he threw 24 touchdown passes, his second highest annual total.

In 1949, two years after he had retired, Ed Fitzgerald of *Sport Magazine* asked Luckman whether he was religious. "Well, yes," was the reply. "I go to the temple regularly and I observe the High Holidays and I never go to bed at night without saying a little prayer." After his retirement he became an executive with a Chicago cellophane company. At the same time he helped tutor Chicago Bear quarterbacks. For his help, he was voted a share of the Bears' playoff money in 1956.

When Luckman was selected to join the Pro Hall of Fame in 1965, Lou Little, his former coach, said of Sid: "He was a great passer, of course, and a great football brain, but people forget he was a great leader. That was some gang he had to handle, those Bears. But they responded to his leadership."

Luckman is a member of the Jewish Sports Hall of Fame in Israel.

SYLVIA MARTIN

1955 and 1960 Woman Bowler of the Year

MARTIN, SYLVIA WENE (born 1930, in Philadelphia, Pennsylvania-) American bowler. Considered one of the greatest women bowlers. She was Woman Bowler of the Year in 1955 and 1960; Pennsylvania's Sportswoman of the Year in 1961; and Philadelphia's Outstanding Athlete in 1963. She has bowled three perfect (300) games in her career.

Sylvia first visited a bowling center when she was 17, but not to play, only to accompany her brother and sister. Her brother had rather patronizingly informed her that she was not big enough to bowl. The next night, petite (4 feet, 11 inches, 128 pounds) Sylvia went to the bowling center and bowled a 96 in her first game.

After a week she was able to knock down 100 pins. It took her another six years before she bowled her first perfect game. The date: March 28, 1951. The place: Philadelphia. It was the first time a woman had bowled a perfect score on the east coast of the United States.

For the next two years Sylvia ran the family grocery store during the day and practiced her bowling at night. Using an orthodox four-step approach, she became the first woman in the world to bowl more than one 300 game and the first woman to bowl two in the same season (1959).

Sylvia had 206 league averages in 1952–53 and 1953–54, then the world record league average. She also bowled 14 700 series (six in the 1954–55 season alone). She won numerous city and state bowling titles in her home state of Pennsylvania.

In March 1955, Sylvia joined the American Machine & Foundry Company's

Bowling Promotion Staff. She gave exhibitions and instruction all over the U.S.

She won the Bowling Proprietors Association of America (BPAA) All-State Individual Match Game title in 1955 in Chicago and again in 1960 in Omaha. In both those years, she was named Woman Bowler of the Year by the Bowling Writers Association of America.

In 1959 Sylvia won the Women's International Bowling Congress (WIBC) doubles, with Adele Isphording, with a 1,263 total score (each bowler bowled three games). In August of that year, Sylvia's book, *The Women's Bowling Guide,* was published.

Sylvia Wene Martin scored her second perfect game on December 11, 1959, in the finals of the World's Invitational Match Game Tournament. That marked the first time a woman had scored 300 in match game competition. Just 28 days later, on January 8, 1960, in Omaha, she did it again—her third perfect game. This time it came in the qualifying rounds of the BPAA All-State tournament which she went on to win.

After her 1960 All-Star victory she left her family's grocery store and decided to devote herself exclusively to bowling. She continued to bowl into the early 1960s and in 1965 was second in the Bowling Proprietors Association of America National Doubles tournament. Her partner was Jeanette Robinson.

In 1963 Sylvia bowled against Dick Weber, the great American bowling star. The unusual match was held on a bowling lane constructed in an American Airlines Astro-jet flying from New York to Dallas at an altitude of 25,000 feet, and going 600 miles per hour. The stunt was designed to demonstrate the size of this new cargo plane. Sylvia won the single-game match, described as "somewhat bumpy."

Sylvia retired from bowling in 1965 and was able to devote more time to her hobbies: roller-skating, playing the accordion, and sketching. In 1966 she was elected to the Women's International Bowling Congress Hall of Fame. And in May of that year she married Samuel Martin and moved to Florida.

In a 1974 list of the greatest women bowlers in history, Sylvia Wene Martin ranked fifth. In 1979 Sylvia was elected to the Jewish Sports Hall of Fame in Israel. During that year, she retired to Mesa, Arizona.

ERSKINE MAYER

The Black Sox Player Who Was Above the Scandal

MAYER, ERSKINE "SCISSORS" (born January 16, 1891, in Atlanta, Georgia; died March 10, 1957) American baseball player. The first Jewish pitcher to win over 20 games in consecutive seasons: he won 21 in 1914 and 1915. A major league pitcher for eight years, Mayer had a career record of 91–70 and an earned run average of 2.96.

Mayer's maternal grandmother converted to Judaism. His paternal grand-father wrote an opera in Hebrew. Mayer's father was a concert pianist and music teacher who played baseball in his spare time with his three children. Erskine Mayer went to Georgia Military Academy and then to Georgia Tech to study engineering. In college, he pitched for the university team.

In 1910, his final year in school, Erskine dropped out to accept an offer to pitch for the Atlanta Crackers. He was sent to Fayetteville and two years later, in 1912, the Philadelphia Phillies brought Mayer up to the major leagues. His first season, he pitched only seven games, ending at 0-1.

By 1914, Erskine Mayer was one of the National League's best pitchers. But his roommate, Hall-of-Famer Grover Cleveland Alexander, stole the glory. In that year, Alexander, the more famous pitcher, won 27 games. In 1915, one of Mayer's two 21-game seasons, he was again upstaged by Alexander, who recorded 31 victories on the mound.

Mayer married on July 4, 1915, and "after that," according to a teammate, "he had trouble finishing games." That same year, the Phillies won the National League pennant, but lost the World Series 4-1 to Boston.

The following year, 1916, Mayer slumped and his pitching record was 7-7, but the 1918 season was another good one, 16-7. He stayed with the Phillies until 1918, and then went to the Pittsburgh Pirates for whom he pitched in 1918 and 1919.

In 1919, he was the starting pitcher in one of baseball's most famous games, the 21-inning Pittsburgh Pirate victory over the Boston Braves. Mayer pitched 16 scoreless innings before being relieved. The Pirates took the game 2-0 in the 21st, but the relief pitcher, Wilber Cooper, received credit for the win.

In the middle of the 1919 season, Erskine Mayer was traded to the Chicago White Sox, the American League pennant winners that year. It was in that World Series that several Chicago players (not Mayer, though) conspired to throw the World Series to Cincinnati, thus unleashing the infamous "Black Sox scandal." Mayer appeared twice in the Series and was 0-1.

After the scandal, Mayer became disgusted with the sport. He made one appearance in 1920 and then retired from baseball to pursue a career as a sales manager.

DANIEL MENDOZA

Father of Modern Boxing

MENDOZA, DANIEL (born July 5, 1764, in London, England; died September 3, 1836) English boxer. The most celebrated Jewish sportsman of his time, he was England's sixteenth heavyweight champion (and thus world champion). Mendoza revolutionized boxing in England, introducing the "Mendoza School" (or the "Jewish School"), with its science of footwork, sparring, new punches, and strategy, replacing the brutal slugging that had passed for sport until then.

Mendoza is considered the father of modern, scientific boxing because of the defensive moves he devised that enabled him to fight against much heavier opponents. He became the first boxer to receive royal patronage, and his acceptance by royalty helped elevate the position of the Jew in English society. After defeating the best fighters around, he was recognized as world champion and reigned as such from 1791 to 1795.

In 1812, Pierce Egan, the author of *Boxiana*, a study of boxing in that period, noted that although Daniel Mendoza was not "the Jew that Shakespeare drew, yet he was that Jew." And then he goes on to say, "In spite of his prejudice, he [the Christian] was compelled to exclaim—Mendoza was a pugilist of no ordinary merit."

Born to Jewish parents in Whitechapel (a section of London), and the recipient of a Jewish education, Mendoza spent his life defending Judaism—often with his bare fists. After his Bar Mitzvah, he wanted to become a glazier, but he whipped the glazier's son in a fight and lost his job. Then, he worked in a fruit and vegetable shop. His next job was in a tea shop where, while defending the owner from a disgruntled client who appeared ready to spring at the owner, Mendoza attracted a crowd. The famous boxer Richard Humphreys, known as the "Gentleman Boxer," witnessed the scene and offered himself as Mendoza's second in the fight. Word spread about the young man's talents, and the following Saturday Mendoza was matched against a professional fighter. Mendoza, who soon became known as "The Star of Israel," won the fight for which he was paid five guineas.

Mendoza became a salesman for a tobacconist, but he was forever getting into fights. Always believing he was the injured party, he was ready to battle against brutality and injustice of any kind. In 1790 he won his first professional fight, a match which eventually won him the patronage of the Prince of Wales. Daniel was the first boxer to earn this honor. He was proud of this honor and he was proud of his heritage, for he proudly billed himself as "Mendoza the Jew."

Promising his wife that he would give up the ring, Mendoza stipulated only one condition: a fight with Richard Humphreys—by now his archrival. He had received bodily punishment in previous fights, and therefore had worked out a new style of defense, one using sidestepping, a straight left and special guarding techniques. Some had complained that Mendoza, rather than standing up in true

British bulldog style and hammering away at an opponent until he dropped, had adopted the cowardly manner of retreating and running away from his opponent.

Mendoza got his chance to fight Humphreys and to test his style. The fight was set for January 9, 1788, at Odiham in Hampshire, and the Jews of England, eager for a champion and a hero, bet much money on the contest. Humphreys won in 15 minutes (many fights at this time were recorded this way), and the Jews despaired.

Humphreys' patron, a Mr. Bradyl, received a message from the victor: "Sir, I have DONE the Jew, and am in good health." Signed, Richard Humphreys.

A second fight between the two rivals was held on May 6, 1789, at Stilton. Mendoza's training quarters were at the Essex home of Sir Thomas A. Price. Mendoza won this second fight, which was attended by nearly 3,000 spectators, and England had a new hero. Daniel Mendoza's name was added to the scripts of numerous plays, songs were written about him, and he could fill a theater for appearances earning 50 pounds. In time, Mendoza would appear three times a week. The two men fought a third time at Doncaster on September 29, 1790, and Mendoza won easily.

In the early 1790s, fighting was so highly regarded that Mendoza was induced to open the small theater at the Lyceum in the Strand, in London, for the purpose of public exhibitions of sparring and teaching interested dandies of London's society.

By defeating Bill Warr on Bexley Common on November 12, 1794, Mendoza became English heavyweight champion. He held the title until his defeat, on April 15, 1795, by John Johnson. The latter won by grabbing Mendoza's shoulder-length hair and battering him senseless in the ninth round.

Mendoza continued to fight. On March 21, 1806, he took on Harry Lee at Grimsted-Green in Kent. In the 53rd round, Mendoza was declared the winner. On July 4, 1820, Mendoza met Tom Owen at Barnstead Downs: the 56-year-old Mendoza lost when the younger man was declared the winner in the 12th round; an anonymous poet (signed only W.W.) lamented his fading glory in the pages of a magazine in Edinburgh on October 8, 1820: "Is this Mendoza?—this the Jew of whom my fancy cherished so beautiful a waking dream, a vision which has perished? . . ."

Mendoza was only 5 feet, 7 inches tall, weighing 160 pounds, but he had an enormous chest. He always fought larger men. He commented on his new technique to combat those larger fighters in an 1820 address: "I think I have a right to call myself the father of the science, for it is well known that prize fighting lay dormant for several years. It was myself and Humphreys who revived it in our three contests for supremacy, and the science of pugilism has been patronized ever since."

Daniel Mendoza became a wealthy man, but his generosity landed him in debt. He wrote *The Art of Boxing* in 1789 and *The Memoirs of the Life of Daniel Mendoza* in 1816. After his boxing career ended in 1795, he ended up in a debtors' prison. He did some teaching, theatrical touring, became a recruiting sergeant, caterer, process server, and pubkeeper. Just before his death he had been running an inn. He died in poverty, leaving a wife and 11 children.

In 1965, he was one of the inaugural group chosen for the Boxing Hall of Fame in the United States.

Daniel Mendoza is a member of the Jewish Sports Hall of Fame in Israel.

WALTER MILLER

The Jockey Who Loved Baseball

MILLER, WALTER "MARVELOUS" (born 1890, in New York City-). Considered the greatest jockey of the early twentieth century. During a four-year period he rode 1,094 winners. His best season record of 388 winners, achieved when he was only 16 years old, stood for 46 years.

Walter Miller came from an Orthodox Jewish family. One day in 1904, Walter's father, a wealthy butcher, took the youngster to the racetrack. Fascinated by what he saw, the 14-year-old frequently skipped school to see the races. When Walter's father realized that the boy had been smitten by horses, the older Miller consented to his son's becoming an apprentice to a trainer.

The 98-pound Walter rode his first race in 1904 on a filly named May J. The horse's odds were 3,000-to-1 and Miller was forgiven for not winning. A few days later though, he won for the first time, riding a 60-to-1 shot to victory.

At the time Miller loved baseball almost as much as riding. He once captained a racetrack baseball team scheduled to play a semipro outfit on a field near Sheepshead Bay. While teammates and opponents waited impatiently for him, Miller finally drove up to the field in a flashy runabout drawn by a high-stepping horse. He and his valet alighted, and the valet helped him don his spanking new uniform; the valet would also minister to Walter between pitches. Viewing himself as a great moundsman, Miller was in fact quite the opposite. He once even tried out for John McGraw's New York Giants, but McGraw thought Miller too small.

Baseball's loss was horse racing's gain. In the fall of 1904 Walter went to California to ride for Sunny Jim Fitzsimmons. Sunny Jim recalled that Miller liked baseball as much as riding at the time: "I used to have to go across the street from the track to take him out of a baseball game so he could ride his horses."

While his baseball playing was nondescript, his riding was spectacular. In Walter's four years of riding, he came home first 1,094 times in an era when most jockeys failed to go to the post 500 times in a year. Once, in a span of two days, he rode eight straight winners. In 1906 he won five straight races, and he once went five for six.

In 1905 Walter had 178 firsts in 888 mounts. He scored his greatest successes under the colors of the James R. Keene stable.

Just two years after learning to ride, in 1906, he made track history, becoming the first jockey ever to ride more than 300 winners in one year. That same year Miller also raced 300 seconds and showed 199 times in a total of 1,384 races. His 388 victories (in 1906) remained the most wins in one year until 1952 when Willie Shoemaker rode 485 firsts.

Riding 1,384 times meant that Miller rode about five races every day of the racing season from March 1, 1906, to the year's end. His most prestigious victories that year were in the Brooklyn Handicap, Dwyer, Alabama, Preakness, Toboggan, Belmont, Futurity, Saratoga Cup, and the Travers races.

In 1907 he won the national riding title for the second straight year, with 334 victories in 1,194 races. At that time he was earning more than $50,000 a year. In 1908 Walter had a total of 870 mounts, with 194 winners. Over half the horses Miller rode throughout his career finished in the money. Miller is a member of the Jockey Hall of Fame (inducted in 1957).

Eventually his problem was that of size, the plague of many jockeys. Walter grew too large, attaining a height of 5 feet, 8 inches, and weighing 160 pounds. To ride at the increased weight, he went to Europe. But by 1912, Miller had returned to the U.S., stopped riding entirely, and was playing semipro baseball in Emeryville, California.

Miller's greatest fan was his mother. For two years, she accompanied him to the track, and backed each of his mounts with a $10 bet. In 1908, she told a confidant that she had lost $8,200 gambling—obviously by betting on horses ridden by jockeys other than her son.

Charlie Miller, a racing expert who was no relation of Walter, analyzed Miller's winning technique: "It was Walter's wonderful knack of making his horse break instantly from the tape which enabled him to secure an unbeatable advantage. With a quick eye, he never lost sight of the starter, sat bolt upright in the saddle, giving his horse an almost free reign, and seemed to sense the start an instant before it happened. For a few seconds, Miller rode like a demon. Then, having secured the rail position, he took his mount up for a breathing spell, but always remained in front."

Later in his life, Miller pursued a business career. He operated a florist's shop, became a jockey's agent, and was proprietor of a bar called "The Jockey" on the Boulevard Montparnasse in Paris. He also owned a man's haberdashery. In 1945 he became seriously ill and required surgery. A few months later, he suffered a mental breakdown from which he has never recovered. He has been hospitalized ever since.

It was announced in December, 1982, that Miller was to become a member of the Jewish Sports Hall of Fame in Israel in the spring, 1983.

RONALD MIX

The Pro Who Was Proud to Be Called a Jewish Football Player

MIX, RONALD (born March 10, 1938, in Los Angeles, California-) American football player. An offensive lineman for the San Diego Chargers, he was unanimously chosen to the all-time AFL team by the Pro Football Hall of Fame. In 1979, he became the second AFL player to be admitted to the Pro Football Hall of Fame.

Ron Mix grew up in the suburb of Hawthorne, California. He was raised by his mother after his father deserted the family when Ron was a small child. Ron wanted to be a baseball player, but a coach advised him that he did not have the potential to be a good one.

Early in his high school career Ron, who weighed 115 pounds, was described as "skinny and not very fast," but by his senior year his weight was up to 180 pounds, and he had earned an athletic scholarship to the University of Southern California.

Mix played on losing teams in his first two seasons at USC. Because of a vision problem, he was given contact lenses and moved to tackle. His football career took a sudden leap forward. In 1959, the USC Trojans, which Ron co-captained, were 8–2 and he won All-America and All-Pacific honors. Ron was also voted USC's outstanding lineman of that year.

In 1960, the National Football League's prestigious Baltimore Colts and the Los Angeles Chargers of the newly-formed American Football League vied for Ron Mix's signature. Had Carroll Rosenbloom, the Jewish owner of the Colts, known that Mix was Jewish, presumably he might have offered the California lineman enough money to sign on.

Rosenbloom and the Colts offered Mix $8,500 while the Los Angeles Chargers came through with a $12,000 proposition and so, as Mix noted, "It was one of my easier decisions. It was not sentiment, but economics that dictated matters. Baltimore has a large Jewish population. But scouting reports rarely include a man's religion." Mix, the first quality player to be signed by the American Football League, planned to play for just two years and then become a teacher. The gridiron soon won out over the classroom.

In Mix's second year with the Chargers, the team moved to San Diego, where it became one of the powers of the new league under coach Sid Gillman. San Diego won the Western Division title five times in the league's first six years. In 1963, the "skinny kid" weighed 250 pounds. He made the All-AFL team as tackle and guard, and the Chargers won the league title with a crushing 51–10 victory over the Boston Patriots.

Ron was an aggressive and highly-skilled lineman. "When you're running behind Mix," observed Paul Lowe, the San Diego Charger running star who had been a collegiate opponent of Ron's at Oregon State, "it's like you're a little kid and your big brother is protecting you from the wolves." "Big brother's" skill as an offensive lineman was proven by the record: In his entire pro career Ron was assessed only two holding penalties. During that career, Mix played in seven All-Star games.

Meanwhile, Ron studied law at night and wrote articles on football for several publications. Partly because of those law studies, and partly because of his rugged style of play on the football field, he was known as the "intellectual assassin."

Despite his strong reservations about his sports career, he was proud of being a Jewish sports hero. "I only *disliked* pro ball," he noted after retiring from the pros. "I *hated* football in college." "To some people I guess I represent a kind of racial hero," Ron once declared to a sportswriter. "Sure, it would be best if people would say, 'That's Ron Mix, a human being who made good.' But until that time in history comes around, I'm proud when they say, 'There's Ron Mix, a Jewish football player who made good.'"

Sport Magazine wrote in 1967 that "his technique, desire, strength, and

balance still impress. He's known as a 'pop-out' blocker, the kind who gets his man with a quick initial thrust. He can get to the outside linebacker or defensive end in a hurry. At times he could deal with three men in one play; he could also block the corner man, stay on his feet, and get the safety as well."

In 1970, Ron Mix retired and announced that he planned to finish law school and run for public office. The Chargers, in a fitting tribute, retired his jersey number 74. Ron completed his law studies and passed the California Bar that year, but did not enter politics. The Oakland Raiders succeeded in luring him back to the gridiron and he played for them in 1971.

In 1973, he rejoined the Chargers as executive counsel. A year and a half later, he became the general manager of the Portland team in the short-lived World Football League.

In 1979, Mix was inducted into the Pro Football Hall of Fame, only the sixth offensive lineman to be so honored. Ron observed that "as an offensive lineman it's nice to get some attention.... All that running and lifting weights—it was a lot of hard work. This makes it all worth it."

Asked if any other Jew had been admitted to the Pro Football Hall of Fame, Mix commented, "I don't know, but I think we own the ground and lease to the place." The fact is that of the 88 players inducted by 1981, only two were Jewish: Sid Luckman and Ron Mix.

Mix is also a member of the Jewish Sports Hall of Fame in Netanya, Israel. Presently, he is a practicing attorney in San Diego.

CHARLES MYER

The Indian Who Refused to Play in Dallas

MYER, CHARLES SOLOMON "BUDDY" (born March 16, 1904, in Ellisville, Mississippi; died October 31, 1974) American baseball player. Considered one of the greatest Jewish second basemen in American baseball. Won the American League batting title in 1935. Hit .300 or better for nine seasons. In a 17-year major-league career, he had 2,131 hits, 850 runs batted in, and a batting average of .303.

While playing college baseball at Mississippi A & M, Myer had an offer to join the Cleveland Indians organization. He accepted and was ordered to report to Dallas, Cleveland's minor league team in the Texas League. Myer was determined to play in the major leagues, and refused to play for Dallas. Although the Indians were upset by his attitude, they brought him up to the majors briefly. Very shortly thereafter they released him as a free agent. Buddy Myer then signed with New Orleans, a minor league team in the Southern League. That year (1925) he hit .336 and drove in 44 runs, interesting several major league clubs in him.

One day two scouts, Joe Engel of the Washington Senators and Jack Doyle of the Chicago Cubs, observed Myer playing for New Orleans. Spotting Engel, Doyle asked the Senators' man what he was doing there. "Not a thing," lied Engel, who had his eye on Myer. Engel excused himself for a moment to buy a drink, and managed to get Myer's signature on a Senator contract in the interim. The two scouts then watched as Myer did some smart hitting and fielding; then Doyle decided that he wanted a "drink." He returned angry and called Engel a double-crosser. "Nothing here worth looking at?" roared the Senators' scout to the happy Engel.

Myer went on to play with the Senators for 15 seasons. In 1926, the Senators were convinced that Myer was a weak shortstop and sold him to the Boston Red

Sox where he played during the 1927 and 1928 seasons. Myer did so well with Boston (in 1927, he hit .288; in 1928, .313) that Senator owner Clark Griffith reacquired him in 1929 in a trade for five players. Instead of shortstop, Myer was shifted and became the second baseman for the Senators beginning in 1929. Washington won the American League pennant twice (1925, 1933) while Myer was playing for them.

Buddy Myer's best year was 1935 when he hit .349 to win the league batting title. He was second in total hits with 215. Clark Griffith said he would not sell Myer for less than half a million dollars, an astronomical figure at the time. Myer came in fourth for the Most Valuable Player award in the American League; Hank Greenberg took the prize that year.

A persistent stomach ailment cut short Myer's career, and he eventually retired in 1941. He established a new career for himself, becoming a banker in New Orleans.

LAURENCE E. MYERS

The First Amateur Runner to Break 50 Seconds . . . With One Shoe On

MYERS, LAURENCE E. "LON" (born February 16, 1858, in Richmond, Virginia; died February 15, 1899) American track star. Considered the greatest short-distance runner of the nineteenth century, he was the first to run the quarter mile in less than 50 seconds. From 1880 to 1888, Myers held the world record for the 100-yard, 440-yard, and 880-yard dashes. His best event was the quarter-mile; he lowered the world record from 50.4 to 48.8 seconds. At one time or another over a 21-year period, Myers held all the American records for races from 50 yards to one mile.

During Lon Myers' teenage years, he moved from Richmond to New York where the doctors advised him to exercise to improve his health. A weakling type, Lon had disproportionately long legs. But the 5 foot, 7¾ inch frame bearing his 112-pound weight was well-suited to running. He began to run seriously in November 1878, at age 20.

In September 1879, Myers set the first of his many world records, breaking the quarter-mile record with a 49.2 second time. He thus became the first amateur to break 50 seconds, accomplishing this while running the last 90 yards of the 440-yard race without wearing one of his shoes. In that same year Myers also won the AAU titles in the 220-yard, 440-yard, and 880-yard events.

In 1881 he was one of the best amateur runners. He won a series of AAU titles, and lowered his quarter-mile record to 48.6 seconds. He set a new record in the half-mile as well with a 1:56 time.

When Myers toured England, the *London Globe* said : "His mode of progression is elegant in the extreme, his action being perfectly free, his stride long, and full of power." He was so warmly received that he wrote a New York newspaper: "I am quite sure I could be Lord Mayor of London, if I was large enough, when the next elections take place."

In November 1882, Myers ran in a series of three races with the great middle and long-distance English runner, W. G. George, to determine who was the world's greatest runner. The tremendous amount of publicity surrounding the contests produced huge crowds. The first race was held at the Polo Grounds in New York in cold weather. Myers won the 880-yard race. But the Englishman took the second contest, the mile, and the third, the three-quarters of a mile. In 1884 Myers journeyed to England to challenge George to a rematch, but the Englishman refused. Myers remained determined to defeat his rival.

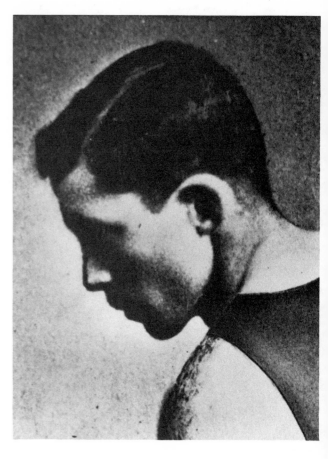

In 1885, Myers became a professional. The following year he and George ran in a three-race exhibition: 880 yards, one-half mile, and one mile. This time Myers won all three races. In Australia, a year later, the two staged another exhibition, and again Myers swept the entire program. If W. G. George was the undisputed middle and long-distance champion of the nineteenth century, Lon Myers had proven that he was the best at short distances.

Myers remained a bachelor all his life. From the cash gifts he received upon retiring as an amateur in 1885, he went into the bookmaking profession, which was then legal. He died of pneumonia when he was only 41 years old.

Lon Myers is a member of the Jewish Sports Hall of Fame in Israel.

HARRY NEWMAN

Outstanding College Football Player of 1932

NEWMAN, HARRY (born September 5, 1909, in Detroit, Michigan-) American football player. He played for Michigan from 1930 to 1932 as quarterback. In 1932, he was first team All-America and winner of the Douglas Fairbanks Trophy as outstanding collegiate player of the year. Between 1933 and 1935, he played pro ball with the New York Giants.

Newman's father died when he was 19 years old, so his mother had to finance his college education on her own. Newman enrolled at the University of Michigan in 1929.

In 1930, Michigan's coach suggested that Harry take instruction from Benny Friedman, the former Michigan quarterback, at a summer camp. The results were rewarding. Newman's quarterbacking that year helped Michigan achieve a 5-3-1 season. They shared the Big Ten Conference title with Northwestern University.

In 1931, Newman, as a sophomore, helped Michigan share (with Northwestern and Purdue) in the winning of the Big Ten Conference title with an 8-0-1 record. In 1932, Michigan's Wolverines won the conference title on their own with an 8-1-1 record. Newman was outstanding, scoring 57 of the 83 points Michigan racked up against Big Ten opponents. In Michigan's last three games, he scored all the points. Of a possible 480 minutes of play, Newman was in on all but 43 minutes!

Grantland Rice, picking Harry Newman for his 1932 All-American team, called him "one of the most effective, triple-threat backs the season has produced." Added Rice: "He made Michigan's run of eight successive victories possible with his forward passing, his broken field running, and his place kicking."

In 1933, his rookie season for the New York Giants, Harry led the team to an 11-3-0 record, and its first NFL title. The Giants defeated the Chicago Bears 23-21 and Newman completed 13 consecutive passes at one stage of the game. He also passed for two touchdowns.

In 1934, in a midseason game against the Green Bay Packers, Newman carried the ball 39 times for 114 yards as the Giants won 17-3. But Newman's career was prematurely shortened by an injury he sustained during a game against the Chicago Bears. A Bear end, Bill Hewitt, tackled Harry so hard that he was knocked out cold, and two bones in his back were broken. Newman missed the rest of the season. That year, the Giants were 8-5-0. They defeated the Bears in the title game by a score of 30-13, without Harry Newman playing. Newman decided to retire.

The Giants asked Newman to return midway through the 1935 season, and though Harry played, because of his injury, he had lost much of his ability. The Giants were 9-3 that season. They won the East Conference title, but lost to the Detroit Lions 26-7 in the NFL title game.

After retiring from football, Newman operated an automobile agency in Detroit.

TOM OKKER

An Agile Dutch Tennis Player

OKKER, TOM (born February 22, 1944, in Amsterdam, Holland-   ) Dutch tennis player. He is Holland's greatest tennis player and one of the best Jewish tennis players of all time. Okker was ranked fourth in the world in 1968, his highest world ranking, and second in the Grand Prix standings in 1973.

Tom Okker began playing tennis at the age of 10. He started to take the game seriously after winning a few junior championships. He began to travel to tournaments around the world and found that his game improved considerably after playing in Australia. There, he recalled, he had the best training possible, as did other young tennis hopefuls.

When Tom came to play in the seventh Maccabiah Games in Israel in 1965, he was totally unknown. He won both the singles and doubles easily. In that same year he won the Wimbledon Plate. In 1966, he was runner-up in the British Hard Court singles tournament.

In 1968, the year he turned pro, Tom made his big breakthrough in tennis. He was Italian singles champion that year as well as doubles champ (with Marty Riessen). Tom took the German doubles championships and the South African singles title as well as South African doubles title. He was also United States Indoor doubles champion. Entering the U.S. Open for the first time in 1968, he reached the finals and fought a titanic battle against Arthur Ashe. Ashe eventually won 14-12, 5-7, 6-3, 3-6, 6-3.

At 5 feet, 10 inches and 140 pounds, Okker has never displayed raw power. Okker thought that the secret of the game was to reach the ball in time to make the shot. He knew that power was important but not the only element in this game. Aware that he didn't have a big serve, he knew he had to develop other facets of his game to compensate.

In 1973, he started off winning or doing well in very few tournaments but, by the summer, became the hottest player around, winning the Dutch and Canadian Open tournaments along with tournaments in Washington (beating Arthur Ashe in the final), Seattle, Chicago (beating John Newcombe), Madrid, and London (beating Ilie Nastase). That year he won $173,550 in prize money.

For five straight years in the early 1970s, he was in the top ten. Okker's quickness and agility earned him the nickname of "The Flying Dutchman"; his nervous manner and inability to sit still won him the title of "Tom the Twitch."

His finest achievement was in winning the U.S. Open doubles with Marty Riessen in 1976. In 1977 he ranked No. 1 in mixed doubles. He teamed with John Newcombe twice to win doubles titles at the Italian Open (1973) and the French Open (1973). He reached the semifinals of Wimbledon in singles in 1978 and the quarterfinals in 1979.

In 1980 Okker had an excellent year playing doubles. He won the International Championships of the Netherlands in Hilversum, Holland, playing with Balazs Taroczy; the Egyptian Open, teamed with Egypt's Ismail El Shafei; and the Birmingham International Indoor, in Birmingham, Alabama, with partner Wojtek Fibak. He was also a finalist (with Fibak) in the Grand Prix Masters in New York and the Braniff World Doubles Championship in London. In singles that year he was a semifinalist at the Grand Prix in Basel; a quarterfinalist at the International Championships in Hilversum; and a quarterfinalist in the Tel Aviv Grand Prix.

In 1981, Tom reached the semifinals of the doubles tournament at Wimbledon (teaming with Dick Stockton). He also helped to organize the Masters program (over 35 years of age) as well as playing in its tournaments. He has been living in Engleberg, Switzerland. Tom is married and has two daughters: Nathalie, born April 22, 1971, and Esther, born November 13, 1976.

BARNEY PELTY

Noted American League Pitcher
at the Turn of the Century

PELTY, BARNEY "THE YIDDISH CURVER" (born September 10, 1880, in Farmington, Missouri; died May 24, 1939) American baseball player. Considered one of the best American League pitchers and fielding pitchers of his day. A right-hander, he played for the St. Louis Browns from 1903 to 1912, and for the Washington Senators in 1912. He played in 281 games and had a 92-118 record.

St. Louis bought Pelty from the Cedar Rapids, Michigan minor league team for a sum of $850. His first major league start came on August 22, 1903, against Boston. He won 2-1 on an eight-hitter. Because of this victory, the team considered him good luck, since he won without knowing the signals too well. When he did not pitch, he served the team in the coaching box.

Pelty pitched 22 major league shutouts, but was shutout 32 times himself. He was beaten 1-0 nine times during his career. The St. Louis Browns were such a weak team in 1905 that Pelty led the club with a 13-14 pitching record; three other pitchers on the team lost 20 games each that season.

Pelty's best season came in 1906 when he was 17-12. Against the Chicago White Sox that season, he permitted only one run in 32 innings.

Retiring from baseball, he returned to his hometown of Farmington, Missouri, and opened a notions store. He also managed semipro teams, and became involved in politics. He pitched his last game in 1937—an exhibition game against Hall-of-Famer Grover Cleveland Alexander, who beat him.

LIPMAN PIKE

Baseball's First Professional Player

PIKE, LIPMAN E. (born May 25, 1845, in New York City; died October 10, 1893) American baseball pioneer and the earliest known Jewish track champion. He became baseball's first professional when, in 1866, the Philadelphia Athletics paid him a regular salary. His career batting average in the National League: .304.

Lip Pike's parents were born in Holland; they raised their five children in Brooklyn. Lip's first appearance in a baseball game was one week after his Bar Mitzvah; he played first base for the Nationals with his brother at shortstop.

Pike played on numerous teams between 1858 and 1864. In 1865, he joined the strongest club in Brooklyn, the Atlantics, where he was used mainly as a substitute. In 1866, the Athletics noticed him and offered him the sum of $20 a week, a large amount at the time, to play third base. By accepting, Pike became baseball's first professional player. The first all-professional team was established in Cincinnati three years later.

Lip stayed with the Athletics for only one year. But he still managed to become the game's first home-run star, belting six homers in one game on July 16, 1866. The next year Pike became player-manager of the Irvington, New Jersey, team and in midseason began playing for the New York Mutuals. He was their star until the end of 1868 when he returned to the Brooklyn Atlantics.

In 1871, Pike became player-manager of the Troy, New York, team of the National Association, baseball's first professional league. His career (1871–75) batting average in that league was .321. In 1872 he played outfield for the Lord Baltimores, another National Association team.

Pike's athletic career was not confined to baseball. He had remarkable speed and ran competitively. On August 4, 1873, he won the Maryland State 100-yard championship for a $100 purse. Later that month, Pike raced against a famous trotting horse named "Clarence" and won, earning $250. For both races, his time was 10 seconds flat, better than the then-existing record.

In 1874, Lip was player-manager in Hartford, Connecticut, and the following two years played with the St. Louis Brown Stockings (in 1875, St. Louis was part of the National Association; in 1876, of the National League).

Pike moved to Cincinnati in 1877 as player-manager at the start of the season. Yielding the managership, he stayed on as an outfielder, and became the National League's second home run champion, hitting four homers that year. In those years, the ball was so dead that it barely reached the outfield when hit hard. By 1878 Pike played for the Providence (Rhode Island) Grays of the National League.

The following year Lip continued to move around. He was player-manager for Springfield, Massachusetts (of the National Association), and for part of the 1880 season, he played for Albany, New York (also with the Association). That season he had his best batting average: .356. In 1881, he became co-manager of the

Brooklyn Atlantics, then an independent team; but he ended the season with Worcester, Massachusetts, of the National League.

There he ran into difficulties. Worcester was having a poor season and the team's manager suspected that Lip was not playing his best. The manager made Pike the scapegoat and refused to let him play. A year later, Lip was allowed back, however.

In the meanwhile, he had announced his retirement and had entered the haberdashery business in Brooklyn. Pike tried to make a comeback with the original New York Mets at age 42, but he played only one game for that American Association team—and retired again. He died suddenly, in 1893, at the age of 42, a victim of heart disease.

After his death, the editor of *Sporting Life* chose him as one of the all-star outfielders for the 1870-80 era. In its obituary the *Sporting News* wrote:"[Pike] was one of the baseball players of those days who were always gentlemanly on and off the field—a species which is becoming rarer as the game grows older."

JACOB PINCUS

The Jockey Who Never
Discussed His Horses' Chances

PINCUS, JACOB "JACOB THE SILENT" (born September 13, 1838, in Baltimore, Maryland; died January 23, 1918) American jockey and trainer. A jockey who was considered the foremost American rider of his day during the 10 years prior to the American Civil War. He was the first trainer to develop and saddle an American winner of the English Derby.

At age 12, Jacob Pincus worked as an exercise boy in Charleston, South Carolina. Two years later, in New Orleans, he rode his first thoroughbred, a mare named Ida, but present-day records do not suggest how well Pincus did. From there he headed for Saratoga, New York, where he became the greatest jockey in America before weight and age forced him to give up riding.

He worked as a trainer in the South for a while, but during the Civil War he moved to New Jersey. There, he trained horses for August Belmont Sr. and Pierre Lorillard, two well-known owners and figures in New York society. In 1869, he saddled Belmont's only Belmont Stakes winner, Fenian.

Pincus haltered Lorillard's Iroquois who won the English Derby of 1881, and it was not until 1954 that another American-bred horse won the famous British race. He remained in Britain in 1882 and then returned to the U.S. where he worked for a brief time as a race starter.

From 1885 to 1887 Pincus worked for the Belmont Stables. But, England was so close to his heart that he returned there and lived in Newmarket until 1906, working as the trainer of a small stable during that time.

Pincus earned the nickname "Jacob the Silent" because he would never discuss his horses' chances. After his retirement, he would often visit the New York racetracks. August Belmont Sr. provided Pincus with a pension for life.

MAURICE PODOLOFF

First President of the National Basketball Association

PODOLOFF, MAURICE (born August 18, 1890, in Elizabethgrad, Russia-) American basketball administrator. First president of the National Basketball Association. He helped bring the NBA to national recognition by livening up the game and getting its games televised nationally, starting in 1954.

Maurice Podoloff came to the United States at the age of six. Raised in New

Haven, Connecticut, he finished New Haven's Hillhouse Hill School in 1909 and completed his undergraduate work at Yale University in 1913. Two years later he graduated from Yale Law School.

The Podoloff family owned the New Haven Ice Skating Arena. Maurice, after becoming a lawyer, became president of the American Hockey League.

In 1946, when he was president of that league, the owners of the teams being organized into the new Basketball Association of America (later the NBA) approached Maurice to become the first president of their 11-team venture. He knew most of the owners through his position as a hockey league president. Al Sutphin, then owner of Cleveland's American Hockey League team, had suggested Maurice as president of the new BAA.

Podoloff was appointed first commissioner of the BAA on June 6, 1946, at $9,000 a year. "I never cared for basketball. I never cared for hockey," he said. "I was hired to do a job."

Three years later, in August 1949, Podoloff presided over the merger of the BAA and the NBA.

In those days the NBA was a far cry from the popular league it was to become. Recalled Podoloff: "We had fouling, stalling, people were leaving the arenas in the last few minutes until that little guy [Danny Biasone, then owner of the Syracuse Nats] came up with his brainchild in 1954: the 24-second clock." Podoloff contends that had it not been for Biasone, the NBA would not have lasted another five years.

Until then, a team could hold on to the ball indefinitely, slowing up the game, and losing crowd interest. A special owners meeting was called in Syracuse. Biasone split the Nats into two teams for a practice game using a stopwatch, and permitting the players only 24 seconds to shoot.

The owners liked the idea and instructed Podoloff to have a 24-second clock made. Walter Brown, owner of the Boston Celtics, volunteered to get his own clock made, but Podoloff decided he would try to get one of his own. Said Podoloff: "My brother Nate knew a clock man, Bob Rosten in New York, and he got a clock made up for $300, and it worked perfectly. I ordered enough clocks for everybody in the league. Walter Brown paid $1,200 for his clock, and it wouldn't even start."

After the introduction of the 24-second clock, Podoloff was able to convince television to carry the NBA games nationally on a regular basis. "If it wasn't for the 24-second clock," he says, "we never would have had TV; the games would have dragged too long with no excitement at the end." NBA games were shown for the first time on national TV in 1954.

Podoloff, who was elected in 1973 to the Basketball Hall of Fame, tried personally to get Danny Biasone, the father of the 24-second rule, into the Hall of Fame, "but," says Maurice, "he missed by two votes."

After 17 years in the job, Podoloff retired as NBA president following the 1963 season. He has been living in the Sound View Specialized Care Center, a low red-brick nursing home in West Haven, Connecticut. The home overlooks downtown New Haven, where Maurice grew up.

He told Dave Anderson of *The New York Times* in May 1977 that he had entered the nursing home "with a nervous breakdown but I got all over that." He said that he did not watch basketball games on TV. "I don't like the game," he said frankly. "I never liked the game."

EDWARD REULBACH

The Only Man to Ever Pitch
Two Shutouts in a Doubleheader

REULBACH, EDWARD MARVIN "BIG ED" (born December 1, 1882, in Detroit, Michigan; died July 17, 1961) American baseball player. One of the National League's best pitchers in his day. He pitched 13 years in the major leagues and was the only man ever to pitch two shutouts in a doubleheader. His career pitching record was 181-105.

Reulbach, a right-hander, played for the Chicago Cubs from 1905 to 1913 and during that time the Cubs won the National League pennant three times (in 1906, 1907, and 1908), and the World Series in 1907 and 1908.

Achieving the mark of a great pitcher more than once, Ed Reulbach won 20 or more games in 1906 (20-4), 1908 (24-7), and—pitching for Newark of the

Federal League—1915 (21–10). The year 1907 was another good one: he won 17 and lost 4, playing for the Chicago Cubs.

In 1908, Ed Reulbach pitched that double shutout in a doubleheader against Brooklyn (he had pitched two full games in a single day without yielding a run). Those two games were part of a string of four straight shutouts he pitched, equaling a National League record. Reulbach pitched 42 shutouts in his major league career. In World Series play, he was 2–1, with one victory in both the 1906 and 1907 Series.

He played on the same Cub teams as the famous pitcher Mordecai (Three Finger) Brown and the legendary double-play combination of Joe Tinker, Johnny Evers, and Frank Chance.

After retiring from baseball, Reulbach worked for the Walsh Construction Company of New York for 20 years. In the years preceding his death he was employed in the company's equipment department. In the last few years of his life he lived in Glens Falls, New York.

AL ROSEN

He Wanted to Be a Jew of Whom All Could Be Proud

ROSEN, AL (born March 1, 1925, in Spartanburg, South Carolina–) American baseball player. Picked by Arch Ward, originator of the All-Star game, as his all-time All-Star third baseman. The first unanimous selection as Most Valuable Player when he won the award in 1953. He played with the Cleveland Indians from 1947 to 1956. In 1950, he hit 37 home runs to lead the American League. Between 1950 and 1954, he knocked in over 100 runs in each season. He led the league in runs batted in both in 1952 and 1953. He had a career batting average of .285 in 1,044 games.

Al's mother encouraged him to indulge in sports. When the boy suffered from violent asthma attacks, his mother, following doctors' advice, encouraged him to play outside as much as possible. "When he was little," Al's mother recalled, "I'd watch him playing with the other boys, gasping as if each breath would be his last." The asthma, which he had until age 16, eventually cured itself.

The Rosen family settled in Miami, Florida. At age 14, Al went to a baseball school, earned some money playing semipro softball, and was All-City third baseman at Miami High School. He won a scholarship to Florida Military Academy where he played football, basketball, and baseball and even boxed. He won the middleweight title in the Florida high school tournament, but baseball was his great love.

In 1941, at age 16, Al Rosen won a tryout with the Cleveland Indians' Class A farm team at Wilkes-Barre, Pennsylvania. Showing a weak bat, he was offered $75 a month to play Class D ball with Thomasville in the North Carolina State League. Shocked at how little money he had been offered, he chose instead to enter first the University of Florida, and then the University of Miami. Between baseball seasons he earned his degree. While at the University of Miami, he played end on the football team and won the Florida intercollegiate boxing title. He obtained his lifetime nickname of "Flip" as a softball pitcher, because of the way he "flipped" the ball to the batter.

In 1942 Rosen joined the Boston Red Sox system, and left soon thereafter for military service in World War II. Serving in the U.S. Navy, he spent time on Okinawa. In 1946, he was discharged as a lieutenant.

Between 1946 and 1949, he had a great batting record in the minors, playing with several teams in the Cleveland chain. In 1947 he hit .349 with Oklahoma in the Texas League; at one point he hit seven doubles in a row, and was named best player in the league.

In 1948, he accomplished something few others have done: he hit five straight

homers for Kansas City. He won a brief trial in the majors with the Indians that year, but was shipped back to Kansas City, where he hit .327, 26 homers and was voted Rookie of the Year. He had one more chance with Cleveland that year and was again disappointed. His march up the ladder was slow, in part because his fielding was weak.

In Al's third attempt at the majors—in 1950—he succeeded. In his first month up, he hit eight homers and by July 4th had 25. That year he hit .287; he slugged 37 homers, knocked in 116 runs, and won Rookie of the Year honors. In 1951, he drove in more than 100 runs, but his batting average dropped to .265, and his home run total to 24. In 1952, Rosen returned to the groove, with 28 homers and 105 RBIs.

"As far as I'm concerned," observed Marty Marion, a former major league shortstop, "I have yet to see a better clutch hitter" [than Al Rosen]. Rosen's manager, Al Lopez, noted: "After a pitcher gets him out, he'll come back to the bench and say, 'I'll get him next time.' And by golly, he does."

In 1953, Ed Sullivan, the *New York Daily News* columnist and TV star, wrote that Al Rosen was of Jewish parentage, but a practicing Catholic. "At the plate, you'll notice he makes the sign of the cross with his bat." Denying the story, Rosen said that he had made a superstitious "x" on the plate before coming to bat since he was a youngster. He insisted that he was a proud Jew.

Indeed, Rosen wanted his name to be even more Jewish than it was—Rosenthal or Rosenstein. He wanted no mistake about what he was. "And," said the third base star, "when I was up there in the majors, I always knew how I wanted it to be about me. I wanted it to be, 'Here comes one Jewish kid that every Jew in the world can be proud of.'" Rosen refused to play baseball on the Jewish high holy days. In 1953, he might have won the batting title had he played those days and gotten a few hits.

His .336 batting average that year fell just short of the top mark. He lost the batting title on the last day of the season, missing out by just .001. He did win the home run crown with 43 homers and the RBI title with 145 in 1953. And he was the unanimous choice for Most Valuable Player in the American League in 1953. From 1952 to 1955, Rosen played in the All-Star games.

In the 1954 All-Star game, he tied two All-Star records: two homers and five RBIs. (The American League won that year 11–9.) That same year he was switched from third to first base, and his batting average fell to .300, due in part to an injured index finger. Rosen was injury-prone throughout his career: he broke his nose 13 times (often from ground balls, and once in a college boxing match).

Between 1954 and 1956 he was hampered often by injuries. Feeling unable to play at the level he wished, he retired, and entered a brokerage firm. Cleveland tried to entice him back, but he refused.

From 1968 to 1977, Rosen was a member of the board of directors of the Cleveland Indians as well as part-owner. Then from 1977 to 1979 he was general manager and part-owner of the New York Yankees. When Yankee owner George Steinbrenner brought Billy Martin back to replace Bob Lemon as manager, Rosen resigned and joined the Bally International Casino in Atlantic City, New Jersey.

In October 1980, Rosen resigned from Bally's Park Place Casino Hotel where he had been executive vice president and soon thereafter was named to replace Tal Smith as president and general manager of the Houston Astros. On January 5, 1981, Rosen underwent successful open-heart surgery in Houston.

Al Rosen is a member of the Jewish Sports Hall of Fame in Israel.

AARON ROSENBERG

All-American Football Star of the Early Thirties

ROSENBERG, AARON "ROSY" (born August 26, 1912, in Brooklyn, New York; died September 1, 1979) American football player. He played guard for the University of Southern California in the early 1930s and at the time was considered the greatest guard in football. In 1932 and 1933 he made a number of All-American teams.

Aaron Rosenberg's father was a tailor in Brooklyn. When Aaron was seven, he was hit by an auto, and his family moved to Los Angeles to help Aaron recuperate.

Aaron played football for his high school team and for four consecutive years made the All-Los Angeles city high school team.

Rosenberg enrolled at the University of Southern California (USC) in 1930, a time when the school was a major football power. While Aaron was a sophomore, USC pulled off a great upset, defeating Notre Dame at South Bend, Indiana, 16-14, thus ending a string of 26 straight wins for the Irish. USC had a 9-1-0 record that year, and scored a 21-12 triumph over Tulane in the Rose Bowl. The next year the USC Trojans were 9-0-0, trouncing Pittsburgh 35-0 in the Rose Bowl.

By 1933 the USC team, with Aaron Rosenberg now playing guard, had won 27 straight games before Stanford defeated it 13-7. For that Stanford game Rosenberg had to wear a mask to protect his broken cheekbone. USC ended the season (Rosenberg's senior year) at 10-1-1.

Rosenberg was large (6 feet, 200 pounds), and possessed great speed. He often blocked two or three men on a single play.

Grantland Rice, the sportswriter, picked Rosenberg for All-America in 1933. Wrote Rice: "Howard Jones [the USC coach] calls him the best guard he ever coached. He [Rosenberg] undoubtedly was the best running guard in football and because of his great defensive skill Jones gave him a roving assignment behind Southern California's six-man line. Playing in a line with two inexperienced tackles this year [1933], he still held the Southern California defense together. He was the spearhead of the Southern California running game and his effective blocking was responsible for much of [quarterback Cotton] Warburton's success as a ball carrier."

After football, Rosenberg became one of the movie industry's top producers. He got his start during his summers in college when he worked on the production side in Hollywood. He became an assistant director after college, continuing in that job from the mid-1930s until World War II when he did service as a naval officer.

Aaron Rosenberg returned to Hollywood after the war as an associate producer. He became a full producer for Universal Studios late in the 1940s.

Among the 30 films he produced between 1949 and 1973 are: *Johnny Stool Pigeon,* his first in 1949: *The Iron Man,* 1951; *The Glenn Miller Story,* 1954; *The Benny Goodman Story,* 1956; *Mutiny on the Bounty,* 1962; *Tony Rome, Caprice,* 1967; *The Detective, Lady in Cement,* 1968; and *The Boy Who Cried Werewolf,* 1973.

Rosenberg died of a massive stroke at age 67 while playing golf in Torrance, California.

MAXIE ROSENBLOOM

The Boxer Who Slapped His Way to Fame

ROSENBLOOM, MAXIE "SLAPSIE MAXIE" (born September 6, 1904, in New York City; died March 6, 1976) Light heavyweight boxing champion from 1930 to 1934. Overall record: 206 victories (18 by knockout), 35 losses, 35 draws, 20 no-decisions, 2 no-contests. In 16 years of fighting he was knocked out only twice.

Maxie Rosenbloom, who never went beyond the fifth grade and spent part of his childhood in a reformatory, began boxing in the Union Settlement House in New York. He had his first pro fight at age 19, when he scored a third-round knockout.

At first Maxie would slug it out with opponents, then he switched to a hit-and-run style. It was because the boxer would often slap his opponents with open gloves that sportswriter Damon Runyon nicknamed him "Slapsie Maxie." When asked why he fought that way, Rosenbloom said, "I always hated to hit hard."

Maxie earned undisputed claim to the light heavyweight crown on June 25, 1930, when he defeated Jimmy Slattery in Slattery's home town of Buffalo, New York, in 15 rounds. He beat Slattery a second time in Brooklyn, New York, on August 5, 1931, also in 15 rounds.

During his four and one-half years as champion, Rosenbloom fought 106 times, an average of once every 15 days. In eight bouts his title was on the line.

Although Maxie was considered a clever boxer, he was an especially weak hitter. His hit-and-run tactics were not universally appreciated. To "Love in Bloom," a popular song of the day, sportswriter Dan Parker wrote a parody based on Maxie's movements in the ring. It went in part: "Can it be the cheese that fills the breeze with rare and magic perfume? Oh no, it isn't the cheese, it's Rosenbloom."

John Kieran, a former sports columnist for *The New York Times,* once wrote that "anyone who gets into the ring with Rosenbloom is slapped with great frequency and a moderate amount of vigor. Whether or not this furious slapping is to be regarded as a high form of pugilistic artistry is another question."

Rosenbloom's 15-round, 1933 decision over Adolph Heuser, Germany's light heavyweight champ, at Madison Square Garden in New York, was considered an important factor in Germany's decision to prohibit its athletes from competing with Jewish athletes. The Germans were unwilling to take a chance that their claim of Nazi superiority over "non-Aryans" might be called into question by a German competitor losing to a Jewish athlete.

Maxie lost his title to Bob Olin on November 16, 1934, in a lackluster decision that was booed by the fans who came to Madison Square Garden that night. The fight had been held under the rules of the New York State Athletic Commission which had restricted hitting with an open hand. Hence, no slaps for Maxie.

After Rosenbloom's fight career ended in 1939, he opened a nightclub in California, but the club did not fare well. Rosenbloom then pursued an acting career. His first role was in a Carole Lombard picture, and over the years he appeared—most often as a gangster or a punch-drunk fighter—in about 100 films, including *The Kid Comes Back*, in 1938; *Each Dawn I Die*, in 1939; *The Boogie Man Will Get You*, in 1942; and *Irish Eyes Are Smiling*, in 1944.

Rosenbloom once explained that he landed his first acting role because Carole Lombard wanted him to teach her to box "to help her in fights with Clark Gable [her husband]."

Maxie earned a fortune during his career, but money seemed to have little value to him. "I don't think he was ever inside a bank," said a close friend. Frank Brachman, who managed Rosenbloom, said the most frequent messages he had from his fighter were telegrams which read, "Send more dough."

In 1937 Rosenbloom married the former Muriel Fader, but the partnership ended in divorce eight years later, and from that time on, Rosenbloom's reputation became that of a playboy. He neither drank nor smoked, but he was an avowed womanizer.

As an entertainer, Maxie was quite successful. His broken syntax, and his sharp wit made him particularly appealing. He once joked that he had quit the ring because "Joe Louis wouldn't fight me. I guess he was afraid of me—afraid he'd kill me."

"Slapsie Maxie" Rosenbloom was elected to the Boxing Hall of Fame in 1972, just a few years after his mental and physical health began to deteriorate. The doctors attributed the decline to his having taken too many punches to the head during his fight career. This, they believed, resulted in brain damage.

FANNY ROSENFELD

A Canadian Track and Field Star Who Would Not Intermarry

ROSENFELD, FANNY "BOBBIE" (born December 28, 1903, in Katrinaslov, Russia; died in December, 1969) Canadian track and field star. In 1950 she was chosen Canada's female athlete of the half-century by the sportswriters of Canada. In the 1928 Amsterdam Olympics, she won a gold medal for Canada on the lead-off leg of the 400-meter relay team that set a world record of 48.4. She also captured a silver medal in the 100-meter sprint.

Soon after she was born in Russia, Fanny and her family emigrated to Canada. During the difficult journey, Fanny contracted smallpox. Her family settled in

Barrie, Ontario, where her father went into the junk business. Fanny learned how to play softball and hockey on corner lots with the boys.

She showed exceptional athletic talent while in her teens. When she was 16, a track meet was held in Barrie to celebrate the end of World War I. Groans went up from the other girls entered in the same sprints as Fanny, because they knew that the results were a foregone conclusion. So Fanny gave them a three-yard head start—and still she managed to beat everyone, going away.

Fanny received her nickname "Bobbie" after she arrived home one day with her long hair cut off or "bobbed" so that it would not bother her in sports—a change of hair style which caused only anguish to her mother.

Once, while at an informal track meet held during a picnic, a friend persuaded Bobbie to enter the 100-yard dash. She did. And despite her bulky, unsuitable bloomers, she outran the reigning Canadian champion. In 1920, Constance Hennessey, a founder of the Toronto Ladies Athletic Club, described Bobbie as someone who "didn't look powerful but was wiry and quick. Above all she was aggressive, very aggressive physically."

In 1922, the Rosenfelds moved to Toronto. There Bobbie took courses in stenography and eventually worked as a stenographer for a local chocolate factory, Patterson's. She played on the factory's women's teams and became an outstanding athlete in softball and ice hockey.

At the same time, Bobbie, then 19, took up track and field. By the mid-1920s, she had won Canadian titles and set national records. In September 1925, she tied the world record of 11.0 for the 100-yard dash. That same year she was Patterson's Athletic Club's only entrant in the Ontario Ladies Track and Field Championships. At that meet she won the discus, 220-yard dash, low hurdles, and long jump, and placed second in the 100-yard dash and javelin.

She held a variety of Canadian national records in the standing long jump, the running long jump, the eight-pound shot, the discus, and the javelin. Still she also participated in other sports. In 1924 she won the Toronto Ladies Grass Court Tennis Title.

In 1928, women's track and field appeared on the Olympic program for the first time. Bobbie was chosen to represent Canada in three events. She won a gold medal in the 400-meter relay. A controversy arose over whether Bobbie had won the 100-meter dash: the American runner, Elizabeth Robinson, was awarded first place though the Canadian fans were convinced that Bobbie had won. Bobbie took a silver medal. Unfortunately, photo finishes were not in use at the time. At the Games, Rosenfeld took a fifth in the 800-meter race.

After the 1928 Olympics, Bobbie returned to softball and hockey for a while. In the winter of 1929, Rosenfeld got her revenge, beating Elizabeth Robinson in the 100-meter race at the Millrose Games in New York. She called this the most satisfying victory in her career. But, catastrophe struck that year: arthritis forced her into bed and onto crutches for the ensuing 18 months. At one stage, the doctors even considered amputating one foot at the ankle, but a family doctor resisted and the foot was saved. However, Bobbie's track career was over.

In 1931, Rosenfeld returned to playing softball and hockey, but another bout with arthritis in 1933 ended her active participation in sports.

Though she never married, she did have one love affair which was doomed by religion. For a long time, she dated a young man from a Christian family, but eventually they parted, since neither his family nor hers would approve their marriage.

In the spring of 1937, Bobbie began writing for the *Toronto Globe and Mail*. Her column, "Feminine Sports Reel," focused on women in sports in Toronto, but also commented on Canadian sports in general.

Rosenfeld retained a refreshing sense of humor about herself and her misfortunes. "If I had stayed in Russia," she once said, "my running prowess might have won me the distinction of having invented the human foot." When she was asked if the arthritic problems that plagued her in her final years were due to her intensive sports activity, she commented, "It is probably the result of reaching for another bottle of beer or something." While watching a baseball game, she yelled at a player who was hesitating in a tight play, "Play the bag, play the bag, any old bag but me."

Bobbie Rosenfeld did not hesitate to attack the sports establishment in her columns. She severely criticized the female selections for the British Empire track and field teams in 1937, complaining that certain topflight athletes had not been chosen because they were not personal friends of the nominating committee members.

She stopped writing about sports in 1957 and switched to the *Globe and Mail* promotion department. She was public relations manager when she retired in 1966. Soon thereafter, her health deteriorated quickly and she died three years later. In 1974, an article in *Canada's Sporting Heroes* warmly remembered Bobbie: "From her first emergence as an athletic marvel, she was described in the press as 'refreshing and irreverent.' From the start, Bobbie Rosenfeld balanced intense competitive fire with an instinctive comic sense; she lived out her pain-wracked life with the same flair she had when she first burst upon the sporting scene."

Fanny Rosenfeld is a member of the Jewish Sports Hall of Fame in Israel.

BARNEY ROSS

First to Hold Lightweight
and Welterweight Crowns Simultaneously

ROSS, BARNEY (born December 23, 1909, on the lower East Side of New York City; died January 17, 1967) The world lightweight and junior welterweight champion from 1933 to 1935, world welterweight champion from 1934 to 1938, and the first boxer to hold the lightweight and welterweight crowns simultaneously. In 82 professional fights, he won 74 (24 were by knockout), lost 4 (none by knockout), drew 3 and had 1 no-decision.

He was born Barnet David Rosofsky, on Rivington Street, on the lower East Side of New York City. His parents had been Russian immigrants who had come to the United States in 1903. At the age of two he moved with his family (he was the third oldest of five children) to the Jefferson Street Jewish section of Chicago. His father Isadore, a talmudic scholar, made sure the Rosofsky's two and a half room home had an Orthodox atmosphere. He opened a grocery store across the street where he tragically met his death on December 13, 1924, when two holdup men broke into the store and killed him. Barney was just a boy of 14 at the time.

The death of his father placed a terrible burden on his mother who now had to care for four sons and a daughter. Unable to provide for their support, Barney's mother suffered a nervous breakdown. His two younger brothers and sister were placed in an orphanage. Barney and an older brother were taken in by a cousin.

Prior to the holdup, Barney had forsaken sports in school to concentrate on religious studies. But he lost all interest in religion as a result of the tragedy in his family. He had hoped to become a Hebrew teacher, but he abandoned that hope. Instead, he began to search for a way to make quick money. He wanted to bring the family together again. "Everything that happened to me afterward," he wrote, "happened because of that senseless, stupid murder."

He took on odd jobs, but consistently got into trouble with the law. (He was caught running illegal crap games, for example.) Somehow he managed to finish two years at Medill High School in Chicago, but the need for cash led him into the life of a minor racketeer. He became a messenger for the notorious Al Capone. In a rare moment of goodness, Capone gave Barney $20 and advised him to go straight, certain that that's what Barney's father would have wanted for his son.

Sensing that he had some talent for the ring, Barney took up the fight game. He didn't want his mother to know what he was up to so he changed his name to Barney Ross.

His tremendous talent began to show when as an amateur, in 1926, just before his eighteenth birthday, he walked away with the featherweight title in the New York–Chicago Golden Gloves tournament. The Chicago ghetto had given him the necessary toughness; and by the time he was 18 he had fought 250 fights as an amateur. On his eighteenth birthday, encouraged by another Jewish boxing champ, Jackie Fields, Barney Ross turned pro.

Now he learned the real techniques of the ring: how to feint, to bob, to shift, and to move in the ring. With 50 bouts under his belt, he was ready to take a crack at Tony Canzoneri, the lightweight champion. Even more satisfying, just before that fight, he managed to reunite his family. The bout was held in Chicago on June 23, 1933, and though the critics insisted that Tony had deserved to win, Ross triumphed in a ten-round decision. The new champion missed the post-fight celebration: he had to walk his mother, now a great enthusiast of her son's fight career, home from the stadium. It was Friday night, the Jewish Sabbath, and, being a religious woman, Mrs. Rosofsky would not ride.

Ross gave Tony Canzoneri a rematch in September of 1933. This bout was held in New York City's Polo Grounds. While training for the fight in Wisconsin, Barney renewed his interest in Judaism: "Before I took off for my roadwork," he recalled, "I dug out the bag of *tefilin* (phylacteries) which I hadn't touched for a couple of years, fastened the little black boxes around my arm and my head, and said my morning prayers." Barney won the rematch.

Soon after, in a Chicago synagogue, the rabbi advised Barney that, "You cannot behave badly. You cannot let bad things be written about you." Hitler, said the rabbi, was mistreating Jews in Europe. "You must set an example of decency and goodness so that the world will know what horrible lies Hitler is telling."

In the next year and a half, Ross defended his title five times. But, older and heavier, he eyed the welterweight division, confident that he could lick the reigning champ, Jimmy "Baby Face" McLarnin. McLarnin was the nemesis of Jewish pugilists: he had already knocked out a half dozen of them. A fight was arranged for May 30, 1934, at the Long Island Bowl. Interest was high. It was only the third time that a lightweight had fought a welterweight champion with the latter's title at stake. The bout went fifteen rounds and Ross took the split decision. His victory, said the *Chicago Tribune,* was "clean-cut, brilliant, methodical. The defending champion was outfought, outboxed, and outmaneuvered." Ross's manager, Sam Plan, noted after the fight, "The real secret of his success is his ability to come back after being hit and press the fighting." Writing of that first Ross-McLarnin fight, James P. Dawson of the *New York Times* described Barney as a "cagey boxer, a smashing body puncher, the possessor of an effective left hook, and with the physical equipment to withstand assault and keep coming in; he is no fluke champion."

Chicago welcomed Barney Ross home with a parade to City Hall. He was now a ring immortal, having become the first man to win both lightweight and welterweight crowns.

Ross gave McLarnin a rematch on September 17, 1934, a match that was postponed four times in 11 days, once because of the Jewish New Year, Rosh Hashana. In a bitterly-debated decision, McLarnin regained his title, although of the 28 boxing reporters on hand, 22 thought Ross should have won. Barney resigned his lightweight title shortly thereafter because of weight problems.

He and McLarnin fought for a third time, on May 28, 1935, at the Polo Grounds in New York City. This time Barney won in a fifteen-round unanimous decision. In the third round, Ross broke the thumb of his left hand and endured terrible pain through the rest of the fight.

On September 23, 1937, Barney fought a title defense against the Filipino, Ceferino Garcia, famous for his bolo punch. Three days before the fight, Ross broke his left hand on a sparring partner's skull. Having become a heavy gambler, and having lost much of his $500,000 in boxing earnings at the track, Barney had little choice but to appear in the ring against Garcia. He fought mostly with his right hand, and won easily. The hand, however, never healed properly.

On May 31, 1938, Ross took on Henry Armstrong, and for five rounds did well. Then, after the eleventh round, the referee wanted to stop the fight and award it to Armstrong. "Let me finish," Barney Ross pleaded to the referee, "It's the last favor I'll ever ask of you. I'll never fight again." He was still on his feet at the last bell, though he lost the fight. "A champion," he said, "has the right to choose how he goes out." Barney's career was over. He had fought 329 times and had never been knocked out.

Just before his last fight, Ross married a Jewish woman, Pearl Spiegel, whose

Barney Ross vs. Ceferin Garcia, 1937.

father had a clothing store in New York City. Entering into partnership with his father-in-law, Barney soon discovered that he had no business sense. The marriage did not last long and Barney left the clothing business and tried acting. This didn't work and soon thereafter he opened a cocktail lounge in Chicago. Barney then fell in love with a non-Jewish showgirl, Cathy Howlett.

When the Japanese attacked Pearl Harbor Barney was assigned to teach boxing. But he didn't feel right doing this type of service. He wanted to serve overseas.

In April 1942, at age 32 Barney Ross joined the Marines. By November he was on Guadalcanal with the Second Marine Division. The Americans were engaged in a bloody battle with the Japanese for control of this strategic Pacific island. On the night of November 19, 1942, Ross and four other Marines found themselves cut off from the main body of American soldiers. All except Ross were killed or wounded in the opening salvo, and Ross alone kept the enemy at bay with rifle fire and grenades, taking time out to pray in Hebrew. After a 13-hour battle, Ross and his buddies were relieved: 22 Japanese lay dead around Ross' defensive position. He was promoted to corporal on the spot. Other awards, including the Silver Star, would follow.

When Barney Ross came home from the war in February 1943, he was suffering from malaria, and his hair was white, having turned that way overnight. For a while he went on speaking tours, but soon the effects of malaria forced him to retire from public life. To ease his pain, he was given morphine, to which he soon became addicted. He squandered a fortune on drugs and before long his personal life was in ruins. Cathy divorced him. In 1946, Ross turned himself over to the Public Health Service narcotics rehabilitation center at Lexington, Kentucky, where after four months he was pronounced cured. This was an unusual feat for a morphine addict. In 1947 he remarried Cathy and spent the rest of his days trying to help others in similar straits. He fought dope racketeers, testified before congress, and aided victims of drug addiction. A movie, *Monkey On My Back,* with Cameron Mitchell, told the story of his life.

He died after a battle against throat cancer. Rabbi William Gold said in his eulogy, "Barney Ross was his own worst enemy. He was so generous to others that the only person he neglected was himself. He left no funds, no estates named after himself. All he left to be remembered by is a world full of friends."

Ross is a member of the Jewish Sports Hall of Fame in Israel.

ESTHER ROTH

First Israeli to Reach the Olympic Finals

ROTH, ESTHER (born April 16, 1952, in Tel Aviv–) Israeli track and field star. At age 18, she was one of the best women sprinters in the world. She held the world record (7.1) for the 60-meter indoor hurdles for one day. She broke Israeli records in numerous track and field events, including the 100- and 200-meter races, long jump and pentathlon. In 1976, she became the first Israeli to reach the finals of an Olympic event.

Esther, a sabra (native-born Israeli), was born to parents who emigrated to Palestine in 1940 from Moscow. She ran under her maiden name, Shachamorov, until she married Peter Roth in 1973.

At the Eighth Maccabiah Games in 1969, Esther won the 100-meter, 200-meter, and long jump. At the 1970 Asian Games in Bangkok, she won gold medals in the hurdles and pentathlon and a silver medal in the long jump. By age 18 she was considered a top contender for the 1972 Olympics in Munich. "It was everything I had lived for," she recalled. Yet when the time came, disaster struck her fellow-Israeli athletes, and she narrowly missed being part of those tragic events.

Palestinian Arab terrorists struck at the Munich Olympic village, taking Israeli athletes hostage. In the end, 11 Israelis were killed in the attack. Esther Roth and the rest of the women's team escaped because their quarters were in a separate building, 200 meters away from their male teammates. "It might have been easier if we had been attacked, too," she observed later. "As it was, we did not know any more about what was happening than anyone else. There was no accurate news. The loudspeakers kept making routine announcements about sporting events. They kept playing music."

She lost her coach Amitzur Shapira, who had worked with her for seven years. After the attack she said, "The dream was over." She had reached the 100-meter semifinal but, because of the raid, had to bow out. She was ready to hang up her track shoes: "Munich took something out of me," she remembered. "I didn't want to compete any longer."

But, in time, she did return to competition. She ran in the Ninth Maccabiah Games in 1973, and again she won the 100-meter, 200-meter, and long jump. At the time she was three months pregnant. "I didn't know, and the doctors didn't know. "But I won the gold medals anyway. I had a feeling I might have been, but wasn't absolutely sure. Anyway, my son, Yaron, had a gold medal even before he was born."

The 1974 Asian Games were scheduled for September of that year, but Esther Roth had a problem getting ready for the big event. She and husband Peter (her coach) had just become the parents of their first child in February, and Esther's training had to be limited because she had undergone a Caesarean delivery. "I only trained for three months after waiting three months from the time of the birth," she recalled. The results: she dominated the Games, winning three gold medals in the 200-meter dash, the 100-meter hurdles, and the 100-meter sprint.

At the 1976 Olympics in Montreal, Esther became the first Israeli to reach the finals of an Olympic event—she did so in the 100-meter hurdles. She had cruised through her preliminary heat and in the semifinal won fourth place in a photo finish. In the finals, she managed a sixth. Despite not taking one of the top medals, she did manage to set a new Israeli record of 13.04 for the event. She bettered that just two months later (12.93) in Berlin. The Montreal Olympics was the last major international competition for her. Israel's expulsion from the Asian Federation and the Israeli boycott of the 1980 Moscow Olympics kept her from engaging in major meets.

In 1977, she competed in the World Cup Games in Düsseldorf and in the Tenth Maccabiah Games. In the Maccabiah, she set records in the 100-meter hurdles, the 200-meters, and the 4 × 100-meter hurdles.

She was named Sportsman of the Year in Israel three times by the Israeli newspaper *Ma'ariv,* and once by the newspaper *Yediot Aharonot.* The 1976 Olympics showed that she was the greatest woman hurdler outside of Eastern Europe. Of those days, she recalled: "Most other athletes were training two or three times as hard as I was. It's unhealthy. They pushed themselves too hard and used dangerous artificial stimulants. I enjoy my sport. I remember in Montreal how all the other athletes were tense and nervous. They couldn't understand how I was always able to laugh and joke around."

Esther has dark skin, black hair, and brown eyes. She announced her retirement from competitive athletics in September 1979, but a month later she was persuaded to reverse her decision to compete in the Moscow Olympics the following summer. She, of course, did not participate in those Games because Israel, along with other countries, boycotted them. Her last competition was in the United States just before the Moscow Olympics.

Since then, she has devoted herself to teaching athletics in a junior high school in Kfar Saba, outside Tel Aviv. She also coaches 12- and 13-year-old hopeful track stars at the same school. She gave birth to her second child, a daughter, in February of 1982. She and her family live in Herzylia.

MARK ROTH

Bowler of the Year from 1977 to 1979

ROTH, MARK (born April 10, 1951, in Brooklyn, New York-). American bowler. He was selected Bowler of the Year three years in a row: 1977–79. The second bowler to earn more than $100,000 in a year. His consistent bowling in the late 1970s made him one of the dominant figures in the sport. By the spring of 1982, he won 26 PBA titles—the second highest number of titles ever won by a bowler.

Mark turned to bowling because he was too small for other sports. He bowled mostly at the Rainbow Lanes in Sheepshead Bay, not far from his Crown Heights home in Brooklyn, and would often spend the summer Saturday nights in the alleys alone. His mother, disturbed at his staying at the lanes until 2 A.M., tried to convince him the sport was worthless. But Mark told her that the lanes were better than the street corner.

Roth, however, did not seem to have the potential to become a great bowler. To compensate for his size, he threw the ball as hard as he could. And, since he had difficulty making spares, he began hooking the ball a great deal.

Roth would soak the ball to make it hook even more. Eventually, he learned to control the hook, but he had other problems. He took more steps than most bowlers, and his backswing was high. He did not take enough time before releasing the ball like other bowlers. He simply stood up and threw the ball.

Roth was on the bowling tour for four years before winning his first event: the King Louis, in Kansas City, in 1975. He won three tournaments in 1976, and finished second three times, becoming second highest money winner on the pro-bowlers tour. In 1977, he was the best bowler on the pro tour first winning the Showboat Invitational, and then coming up with a startling triple: first in succession in the PBA Doubles Classic (with Marshal Holman), the Fresno Open, and the Southern California Open. He led the tour in earnings that year with $105,583. His bowling average was 218.174.

In 1978 Mark won eight tournaments with a record 219.834 average for 1,047 games. He accumulated $134,500 in prize money and established a bowling record by earning money in each of the 25 tournaments in which he competed. He was named *Sporting News'* PBA Player of the Year.

In 1979 Roth again dominated the PBA tour, walking off with the most money and highest pin average. He had a record high average of 221.662, and led the tour in tournament victories, winning six, to give him a career total of 22 since 1975. Mark was named to Pro Bowling's 1979 All-America team.

Roth's critics argue that he just rears back and throws, with no real style. Other commentators have called Roth's style theatrical and swashbuckling. Roth throws the ball unusually fast, with a fury and power rarely seen in a bowling alley. These qualities have made him a distinctive bowler, which he seems to enjoy. At one time, his tight grip used to tear the skin off his right thumb, but he has since learned to protect the thumb, without losing any of the fire of his shot.

When asked to advise young pros, Roth urges them to take four or five smooth steps, to refrain from hooking the ball too much, and to keep arms straight and close to the body. After that, Roth advises youngsters to develop their own styles.

To prepare for a day at the lanes, Mark goes through a routine in his hotel room that is not to be believed. It's all designed to release emotional tension. Mark does not necessarily go through it all the time, only when he feels uptight. First, Mark emits a primitive shriek, then some guttural burbling, followed by an occasional "wahoo" and "eeiii" or two. Then he sends roundhouse punches flying in the air. For the next 30 seconds, he'll stare out the window and repeat the words, "firp, firp, firp, firp."

Then he hurtles through the air, plops on the bed, and shouts, "Let's go," into the pillow. Finally, Roth slams the pillow against the wall, feathers fluttering, walks past a maid outside the door, wishes her "Good morning!" and goes off to bowl.

In 1980, Roth played in 28 tournaments and won the PBA event in Rochester, New York. He emerged as the bowler with the second highest point average on the PBA tour, with a 216.928 average. His $101,665 earnings on the tour made him the second highest money winner for the year.

In 1981, Roth won three PBA tournaments: Las Vegas, Lansing, and Cleveland. He was third highest in earnings that year with $107,050. That marked the fifth straight season he had won over $100,000 per season. No other bowler in PBA history has gone over six figures for more than two straight years. He also had the leading PBA average in 1981, 216.699, the fifth time he led the field; the other years were from 1976 to 1979.

Thus far, Mark has collected 26 PBA titles. He is tied for second, with Dick Weber and Don Johnson, for most titles in a career. (Earl Anthony is first with 39 titles.)

ANGELICA ROZEANU

World's Greatest Woman Table Tennis Player

ROZEANU, ANGELICA ADELSTEIN (born October 15, 1921, in Bucharest, Romania–) Romanian table tennis player. Considered the world's greatest woman table tennis player in history. She captured 17 world titles, including six straight singles titles from 1950 to 1955. She also led Romania to five Corbillon Cup victories. Angelica was the first Romanian woman to win a world title in any sport. She also won the women's doubles crown twice and the mixed doubles crown three times.

At age nine Angelica Adelstein learned how to play table tennis at home in Bucharest on her dining room table. She and her brother Gaston, then 16, put up a net on the table and he taught her how to play.

Two years later, a YMCA club opened near her house, and there she began to play table tennis with strong male players. By age 15, Angelica was competent enough to win her first important event, the Romanian National Women's Championship in Chernovitz, Romania. She won that title every year thereafter until 1957 (except for the war years 1940 to 1945 when she did not compete).

The year she won her first title, 1936, she met the great Hungarian table tennis star Victor Barna, and decided to copy his backhand drive. Much later, Barna commented to a journalist that he was proud that Angelica's backhand was similar to his, but he was sure she hadn't copied it from him.

Young Angelica was an eager devotee of all sports, including tennis, cycling, and swimming. But, she came to regard table tennis as her favorite, perhaps because she excelled at it.

In 1938, she won her first major international victory, the Hungarian Open in Czegled, Hungary. But the Romanian Government, apparently for anti-Semitic reasons, refused to give her a passport that would have permitted her to participate in the world championships in London that year.

Then, in March 1938, she traveled to the world championships in Cairo. There, she reached the quarterfinals before losing to the current world champion Vlasta Risova, a Czech. By the time Angelica had returned to Romania, the Nazis had taken control of the country and one of their new anti-Jewish measures was to ban Jews from entering sports centers, effectively preventing Angelica from playing table tennis. She was unable to play throughout the war.

But after the war she again began to train, playing with male players to strengthen herself. In 1944, she married fellow Romanian Lou Rozeanu.

In 1948, she played a grueling match at the World Championships in Wembley against Giselle Farkas. Angelica followed a defensive strategy and lost by a shade. Thereafter, she decided to change her tactics from defensive to

Angelica Rozeanu (center) after winning one of her many table tennis titles. She is flanked by table tennis stars Petulec (to her right) and Szasz (to her left). Vienna, 1951.

offensive play and started to practice a surprise attack from both sides. Her strong forehand drive was now complemented by an excellent backhand.

Rozeanu reached her peak comparatively late. In 1950, in Budapest, Hungary, when she won the first of her six straight world singles titles, she was 29 years old. She also helped the Romanian team to victory in the Corbillon Cup (named after Marcel Corbillon, a past president of the French Table Tennis Federation), given to the world's best women's table tennis team.

In 1951, in Vienna, she played even better, repeating her performance and adding the mixed doubles title. In 1952, she won the world singles title in Bombay, India. That year she became Romania's national table tennis coach and held the post until 1958. In 1953 in Bucharest, she won the women's world singles title and helped Romania win another Corbillon Cup.

In 1953, on her first visit to Russia, she helped to popularize table tennis there. She returned in 1955 and 1960.

By this time, Rozeanu could play any match with confidence. Still she was nearly always nervous at the beginning of a match. But, by just playing and concentrating on the game, she became quite calm as the match progressed.

Between 1948 and 1950, Angelica was a sports reporter on the Romanian newspaper *Romania Libera*. She was also president of the Romanian Table Tennis Commission from 1950 to 1960. She was given the highest sports distinction in Romania—the coveted title of "Merited Master of Sport"—in 1954. In addition she has received four "Order of Work" honors from the government. In 1955, she was appointed a deputy of the Bucharest Municipality.

In 1956 Rozeanu played in the women's World Championships in Tokyo, where she was aiming to win an unprecedented seventh straight world title. In a tense and close match which some have called the best in the history of table tennis, Angelica lost to an unknown Japanese player, Kiyoko Tasaka. The score was 21–19, 22–20, and 32–30.

In addition to the 12,000 spectators crowded into the Tokyo Gymnasium, players and umpires who had been engaged in other matches stopped to watch the Rozeanu-Tasaka match. When the score went above 30 in the last game, the count indicator could no longer be used.

Rozeanu, calling the defeat the worst of her career, impressed the Japanese with her performance. One Japanese writer for the *Table Tennis Report Monthly Magazine* noticed the "gorgeous coat and diamond ring she wore with her manicured nails."

In 1958, the post of chairman of the National Table Tennis Federation in Romania was held by a Nazi-oriented Communist. A purge of Jewish table tennis players began. Angelica was forbidden from playing in international matches. She was accused of engaging in the "cult of personality." When the chairman himself was purged, Angelica returned to favor. In March 1960, she traveled to Russia and won three titles there, in singles, doubles, and mixed doubles.

Rozeanu divorced her husband, Lou, in 1959. In February 1960, he immigrated to Israel, hoping that Angelica and their daughter, Michaela, then 14, would follow. In August of 1960, Angelica and Michaela went to Vienna as tourists, then went directly to Israel. The Romanian government promptly recalled all the honors bestowed on Angelica. Upon arriving in Israel, she moved in with her former husband, who is presently a professor of thermodynamics at the Haifa

Technion. Although they were legally divorced, Angelica considered herself and Lou to be husband and wife. They did not feel it necessary to remarry formally, and they lived together until they separated for good in 1969.

In 1961 Angelica won the Maccabiah Games table tennis championship. She continued to win singles and doubles titles in Europe, but it became too expensive for Israel to send her abroad. In 1962 the sports authorities explained the country's difficult economic situation to her, and, angry and disappointed, Angelica decided to give up the game. By that time she had won some 100 international titles.

She became a coach for a Tel Aviv sports club, Mercaz Hapoel, but became disillusioned when, rather than serve in the top echelon of table tennis as she had in Romania (she had been a national coach in the 1950s), she was asked to give exhibitions with youngsters in different parts of the country.

In 1964, she was invited to coach the national team but the players made her uncomfortable in that role because she was a woman.

In February 1969, Angelica married Dr. Eliezer Lopacki, a Polish-born psychiatrist who came to Israel in 1950. He died in June 1979. Her daughter, Michaela, became an engineer at Elbit Computers in Haifa, where Angelica has also been working since 1969. In 1980, Angelica was chosen as one of the firm's "excellent workers." As of this writing, she holds a responsible supervisory position with the firm.

Angelica Rozeanu is a member of the Jewish Sports Hall of Fame in Israel.

LOUIS RUBENSTEIN

North America's First Famous Figure Skater

RUBENSTEIN, LOUIS (born September 23, 1861, in Montreal, Canada; died January 3, 1931) Canadian skater. North America's first famous figure skater. World figure skating champion in 1890; Canadian champion from 1883 to 1889; and American champion in 1888, 1889, and 1891. He was also North American champion in 1885.

Louis Rubenstein was the son of Polish immigrants to Canada. He won his first figure skating title, the Montreal Championship, in 1878. The following year he came in third in the same competition. Realizing that he had such hard training before him if he were going to win more skating titles, he devoted the next four years to rigorous effort on the ice.

In 1883, he won his first Canadian championship. Then, in 1884, and again in 1885, he made a successful tour of the Canadian Maritime Provinces. Rubenstein gave numerous exhibitions of his skating, and when local skaters challenged him to a contest, he won every time.

Rubenstein won his fame at the unofficial world figure skating championships held in St. Petersburg, Russia, on February 1, 1890. (The first official world championship was not held until 1896.) A sum of $400 was raised to send him to that skating event in Russia.

Arriving in Russia, Louis went from problem to problem. Beginning immediately, a 6-foot Russian policeman in uniform followed Louis around wherever he went. (One afternoon, Rubenstein managed to break free of the man by taking a brisk five-mile walk, forcing his ominous shadow, who could not stand the pace, to return to the hotel early to await Louis' return.)

Upon arrival at his hotel that first day, Rubenstein handed in his passport (as was required of all visitors) and heard nothing for a few days. Then he was summoned to a police station where an officer asked if he were Jewish. Rubenstein replied in the affirmative, and was told he would soon get his passport back. But he did not.

Two days later, while practicing, he was again summoned to a police station. When he asked for his passport, he was taken to another police office. There he was instructed to leave St. Petersburg within 24 hours. "You are a Jew," the officer declared, "and there is no necessity to further discuss the matter. We cannot permit Jews to stay in St. Petersburg."

Rubenstein, aghast at the Russian's behavior, appealed to the British ambassador, Sir R. Morier, who expressed sympathy for Rubenstein and anger at the Russians. Morier assured Rubenstein he would be able to participate in the championships if the ambassador had anything to say about it.

The following morning, roused out of bed, Rubenstein had to appear before a prefect of police. He was informed that, due to the British ambassador's intervention, he would be allowed to stay until the championship was over, but he would have to leave immediately after that. When his passport was returned, he noticed that the words "British subject" had been crossed out and in their place was "L. Rubenstein, Jew; must leave St. Petersburg by the 10th February."

The British envoy told Rubenstein that "foreign Hebrews" were not popular in Russia and he doubted that Louis would have a fair chance in the championship. Rubenstein was a master at figure skating: he could repeat a routine on the ice three or four times without blurring the original outline of the pattern. His figures were considered elegant and graceful.

The competition consisted of three events: the execution of nine compulsory figures, five figures selected by the skater, and a 10-minute freestyle performance. Only two of the nine judges were familiar with figure skating: after watching him at practice, they would offer advice to the local skaters based on what they had learned from the Canadian. Though the judges may have been partial to their own native skaters, they clearly had admiration for Louis' skills—even before he began the competition.

Rubenstein went on to defeat his competitors in St. Petersburg. The judges would have liked nothing better than to deny him first prize because he was Jewish. But, since he dominated the field, they had little choice. Louis' conviction that he was, as he put it, "the only dangerous person in St. Petersburg," was eased somewhat after the competition, because he knew now that he was soon to leave Russia. Although the Canadian skater's treatment in St. Petersburg actually came up for discussion in the Canadian Parliament shortly thereafter, nothing concrete was done about the matter. Never again would Rubenstein experience the slightest anti-Semitism; the Russian instance was unique in his career.

After tying for first place in the American championships in 1891, Rubenstein retired from competitive skating.

Louis Rubenstein continued to be involved in sports in a variety of ways. At one time or another, he was president of different Canadian organizations involved with bowling, lifesaving, skating, tobogganning, bicycling, and curling. He was a great bowler, averaging 173.4 in 129 bowling games between 1892 and 1900. The *Montreal Star,* in an article on February 6, 1895, wrote of his presidency of the Canadian Bowling Association and called him the "Father of Bowling in Canada."

It was the family business—Rubenstein Brothers Silver, Gold and Nickel Platers and Manufacturers—which made it possible, because of its success, for Louis to spend so much time in sports. The fact that Louis was a bachelor was another reason why he had so much free time. He was elected Montreal City Alderman in 1914 and held that post until his death in 1931. Louis was elected to the Canadian Hall of Fame and the Jewish Sports Hall of Fame in Israel.

ABRAHAM "ABE" SAPERSTEIN

Founder, Coach, and Owner
of the Harlem Globetrotters

SAPERSTEIN, ABRAHAM M. (born July 4, 1903, in London, England; died March 15, 1966) Founder, coach, and owner of the world-famous Harlem Globetrotters, a famous comedy basketball group. The Globetrotters developed a new, zany style of playing the game, becoming the busiest, funniest, and most remarkable basketball team in the world. Saperstein made basketball truly international through them.

The Globetrotters "threaten" Abe Saperstein with a River Jordan dunking. Summer, 1965.

At the age of five, Abe Saperstein came to the United States from England with his nine brothers and sisters. He grew up in a rough Irish neighborhood in Chicago, graduating from Lakeview High School in 1919. After playing semi-professional baseball for a while, he drifted into pro basketball although he was only 5 feet, 5 inches tall. He earned $5 per game.

In 1927, Saperstein took over an all-Negro American Legion basketball team called the Savoy Big Five, named for Chicago's Savoy Ballroom. He changed the team's name to the Harlem Globe-trotters. Then, piling his five players into a battered Model-T Ford bought from a funeral director, he took the team on the road. They played their first game on January 7, 1927, in Hinckley, Illinois, and earned the impressive sum of $75.

195

Saperstein was once asked how he came to use the name Harlem Globetrotters. "We chose Harlem," he said, "because, well, because Harlem was to the fellows what Jerusalem is to us. And Globetrotters? Well, we had dreams. We hoped to travel. We made it, all right. We made it all the way to Israel, as a matter of fact."

Saperstein not only owned the team, but was its coach, chauffeur, trainer, and physician. At times he was its only substitute player. He was often described as a roly-poly dynamo and was nicknamed "Little Caesar."

Unmatched as a coach, he was also unmatched as an impressario. As a result of his guidance, the Globetrotters became a team that performed basketball magic on the court. Every game in which they participated was like a circus. The five players were talented clowns whose handling of the ball was sheer magic. They gave the audience much to marvel at and laugh about at the same time.

"Laugh standards are the same all over the world," Saperstein once declared, "and that is our playing area. Wars, depressions, chaos, and one crisis after another are commonplace all around the world. Our fans, and there are millions of them, are looking for an escape from worry and tension when they come out to see us play and we never want to fail them."

The Globetrotters' first tour, in 1927, was a huge success. They wound up with a 101–6 record. The following year, their record was 145–13, and two years later it was 151–13. So good were the Globetrotters that finding opponents became a problem. It was then that Saperstein introduced the fancy, razzle-dazzle type of play which livened up the show, and for which the team became known.

It was only in 1940, 13 years after they began playing, that the Globetrotters started making money. "We never missed a meal," recalled Saperstein, "but we sure postponed a lot of them." The team traveled through blizzards and tornadoes, on dog sled, in jalopies, and in horse-drawn wagons. By 1950, the Globetrotters were so famous the world over, that Saperstein had to split them into two touring squads. During the winter of 1958–59, the teams posted a startling 411–0 record.

When critics began saying that the Globetrotters were capable only of clowning, Saperstein organized a series of games against college all-stars. The Globetrotters won the series 11–7.

The team traveled to 87 countries. The players—including such famous ones as Reece (Goose) Tatum and Marques Haynes—always gave the impression that they were not too serious about the game. But they really were. They were there to entertain and they did that well. Pope Pius XII said after an exhibition: "These young men are certainly very clever."

Go, Man, Go, a movie about Saperstein and the Globetrotters, was released in 1954, with Dane Clark playing the Globetrotters' founder. From 1927 to 1967 the Globetrotters played before five million fans, including 75,000 on one occasion in Berlin in 1951. The team won the world title in 1940 and the International Cup in 1943–44.

In the years before his death, Abe Saperstein took on new business ventures, but with little success. He sought franchises in Los Angeles and San Francisco to be part of the National Basketball Association, but was refused. So, in 1961, he formed his own loop, the American Basketball League.

Saperstein **not** only owned the Chicago team in the league, but served as league commissioner as well. The league, however, folded after only 18 months, with Saperstein and other club owners suffering major financial losses.

Saperstein died of a heart attack while in Weiss Memorial Hospital, in Chicago, Illinois. He had hoped to live to see the fiftieth anniversary of the Harlem Globetrotters, but he died 11 years too soon.

Abraham Saperstein is a member of the Jewish Sports Hall of Fame in Israel.

RICHARD "DICK" SAVITT

The Only Jew Ever to Win Wimbledon

SAVITT, RICHARD (born March 4, 1927, in Bayonne, New Jersey-) American tennis player. The first Jewish tennis player of impressive stature. He warranted a *Time* magazine cover story (on August 27, 1951). He was ranked in the first 10 between 1950 and 1952 and No. 3 in 1957. He was Wimbledon singles champion in 1951, the only Jew ever to win Wimbledon.

Savitt was an only child in a middle-class family, whose father was the owner of a food brokerage firm. As a boy, Dick was interested in football, baseball, basketball—but not tennis. At age 13 he began playing and ballboying at the Berkeley Tennis Club in Orange, New Jersey, where he watched some of the tennis greats like Bobby Riggs and Jack Kramer.

Dick began playing the game seriously at age 13, and in the summer of 1941, he won a local junior tournament in Maplewood, New Jersey. In 1944, his family moved to El Paso, Texas, because of his mother's poor health.

At El Paso High School Dick was a forward on the basketball team in his senior year (1945). He was also Texas State tennis champion and No. 4 in the national under-18 (junior) group. He was on the second-team, All-State basketball team as well.

After graduating from high school in 1945, he served for one year in the U.S. Navy and was stationed at the Naval Air Station in Memphis, Tennessee. He played on the third-ranking armed forces basketball team in the winter of 1945–46.

In 1946, Savitt enrolled at Cornell on a basketball and tennis scholarship, but an injured knee in his first year forced him to concentrate on tennis, rather than basketball. Savitt played tennis in an old armory in Ithaca, New York, with ROTC tanks roaring in the background. In 1947 and 1948, Dick was ranked twenty-sixth in the country in tennis.

In 1949 he won the Eastern Intercollegiate Tennis Tournament held in Syracuse, New York. He was ranked sixteenth nationally that year. In 1950, Savitt won several tournaments in the U.S., was ranked sixth in the country, and reached the semifinals of the U.S. Nationals at Forest Hills.

In 1951 Savitt monopolized the headlines of the tennis world. His play was described as "aggressive, nervous, often impatient, and always overpowering." He defeated Australia's great Frank Sedgman in five sets and Ken MacGregor in four sets on successive days to win the Australian championship in January. Savitt was the first foreigner to win the Australia championship since Don Budge of the U.S. scored his grand slam in 1938.

In July 1951, Savitt won the men's singles at Wimbledon, defeating Herb Flam in the semifinals and Ken MacGregor in the finals. *The New York Times* called Savitt the "world's number one amateur player." He did not turn pro because at that time the pro circuit was limited to a few barnstormers.

Standing 6 foot 3 and weighing 185 pounds (and slightly round-shouldered), Savitt was considered then the greatest backcourt player in the world. It was his simple, overpowering attack, smashing serve, and deep, hard-hit ground strokes that kept his opponents scrambling in the backcourt, always on the defensive. His deep-set eyes were unsmiling and intent as he concentrated on his opponents.

Had it not been for a leg infection in September 1951, he might well have added the U.S. National title at Forest Hills to his collection of victories. He lost to Vic Seixas in the semifinals.

Savitt was chosen as a member of the Davis Cup team in 1951, but after winning in the early rounds of the competition, he was bypassed and did not play in the challenge round in December. The Australians took the Davis Cup that year, and many felt that the U.S. would have won had Savitt played. Some believed that anti-Semitism was the main reason for Savitt's not playing, but he himself doubted this. Actually, when Savitt and Herb Flam made the Davis Cup squad in 1951, it marked the first time that Jewish players had accomplished this.

In February, 1952, Savitt won the National Indoor Singles title. In October of that year he announced his retirement from big-time competitive tennis in order, as he put it then, "to go to work." Some thought that Savitt had retired because he was snubbed in the Davis Cup competition of 1951. But Savitt's explanation seemed more realistic. After all, tennis in the early 1950s had few of the rewards of later years when top players made large sums of money, and it was reasonable that a young man like Savitt would decide to devote his time to the business world where money could be made. After October 1952, Savitt never returned to full-time tennis.

Dick Savitt's first full-time job was with an oil company, Texfel Petroleum of Dallas, Texas. Instead of accepting an executive job at the top, for the first two years he roamed the oil fields of Louisiana and Texas, working on an oil rig. After that, he took an administrative job, handling leasing arrangements for oil exploration. Then, in 1957, he was appointed office manager of Texfel Petroleum in New York.

Savitt continued to play tennis, but in a much more limited way. In 1957 he won the Eastern Grass Court tournament in Orange, New Jersey. In 1958 he won the Men's Indoor singles title, defeating Budge Patty in the final, and losing his only set of the tournament in that final match. Savitt won other tournaments that year in Atlanta, River Oaks, and Tulsa. He was called the "mightiest hitter in amateur tennis" (in the official U.S. Lawn Tennis Association Yearbook). In 1961 he traveled to Israel where he won the Maccabiah singles and doubles.

Savitt started playing father-son doubles tournaments in 1976 in the U.S. with his son Robert, and is still doing so. In 1981, when Dick was asked about his greatest moment in tennis, he replied: "Winning the National Father and Son Championships this summer (1981) was number one. Number two was winning Wimbledon."

Savitt has been working for Lehman Brothers as a stockbroker for the past 20 years, and for all those years has been a tennis instructor as well. He visits Israel each year and offers instruction to coaches and players.

Richard Savitt is a member of the Jewish Sports Hall of Fame in Israel.

DOLPH SCHAYES

The First Modern Basketball Forward

SCHAYES, ADOLPH "DOLPH" (born May 19, 1928, in New York City, New York–   ) American basketball player. Schayes played for the Syracuse Nationals from 1949 to 1963. When he retired, he had scored more points (19,249) than any player in the game. He was voted to the All-National Basketball Association team 12 times.

Dolph Schayes inherited both his love for sports and his height (6 feet, 8 inches) from his father, a Romanian Jew, who was an avid sports fan and 6 feet, 4 inches tall. Dolph played basketball throughout junior high school, high school, and college in his native Bronx. At age 16, he entered New York University.

Schayes became known as a good, hard-working college player, but his coach doubted that he had the physique to make it as a pro. When he graduated in 1948, he had collected All-American honors and the Haggerty award as the best player in the New York metropolitan area.

The New York Knicks nearly succeeded in signing Schayes, but Knick president Ned Irish offered him $1,000 less than Syracuse and so, in 1948, Dolph decided to sign with the Syracuse Nationals. The Nats moved all 6 feet, 8 inches and 220 pounds of him from center to forward. He became the first modern basketball forward: big, fast, mobile. His long-range, two-handed set shots and driving lay-ups were almost impossible to stop without fouling. His foul-shooting was as excellent as was his rebounding. And he was often his team's assist leader.

Schayes was named rookie of the year in 1949. He personified the spirit of the Nats; each time he scored a basket he would run to the opposite end of the court, fist clenched triumphantly above his head.

From February 17, 1952 until December 27, 1961, he played in 764 straight games, including playoffs. In 1957 he broke Minneapolis Laker George Mikan's career point total of 11,764. Schayes scored his 19,000th point in 1963. He won the rebounding title in 1951 and wound up in fourth place on the all-time rebounding list at his retirement. His record for the most free throws made (6,979) stood until 1972.

Schayes would not budge from the lineup even when injured. In 1952 he broke his right wrist, and a cast was put on, but he could not be kept off the court. "The cast made me work on my left-handed shots, which soon improved," he said. "Later, when the left wrist was cracked, my right-handed shots improved." Dolph was one of the few people who look upon a fracture as a blessing in disguise.

The Nats won only one world championship with Schayes (in 1955), but they always were in the playoffs. In 1964, the Nats left Syracuse to become the Philadelphia 76ers, and that same year Dolph became their head coach. In his first two seasons, the team was in third place in the Eastern Division. But, it won the title for the 1965–66 season. Schayes was named NBA Coach of the Year for leading the 76ers to that title, but he was fired the next year after his team failed to retain the title. (Boston defeated the 76ers in the playoff semifinals.)

From 1966 to 1970, Dolph served as supervisor of NBA referees. In 1970, he was back coaching a new NBA franchise, the Buffalo Braves. But after the opening game of his second season (1971–72), he was dismissed, primarily for not disciplining his players enough.

Schayes felt that being Jewish had little or no effect on his basketball career. "There was never any hint of anti-Semitism in pro basketball," he wrote. "Since many of the fans in the large metropolitan area were Jewish in the early days of the NBA, I was fairly well received."

In 1977, Schayes became head coach of the U.S. Maccabiah Games basketball team. With the help of his 6 foot, 11 inch son, Dan, the U.S. team upset the Israelis, 92–91, in the championship game.

Dolph Schayes is a member of the Basketball Hall of Fame and the Jewish Sports Hall of Fame in Israel. He lives in the Syracuse, New York, suburb of DeWitt.

JODY SCHECKTER

World Racing Car Champion

SCHECKTER, JODY (born January 29, 1950, in East London, South Africa–   ) World driving champion. The first South African to win the world championship, Scheckter has been called one of South Africa's greatest sports figures.

Scheckter's paternal grandfather moved the family from Russia to South Africa. Jody began racing go-carts at age 10. Jody's father owned a garage which Jody worked in, in East London, South Africa, which introduced the youngster to the taste of the auto world. Jody raced stock cars between 1968 and 1970 with great success on the local tracks.

South African stock car racing had its wild side with no holds barred. Drivers did not hesitate to bump into each other and at times pushed their colleagues off the track.

After defeating all his opponents in South Africa between 1968 and 1970, he won a "driver to Europe" grant. He raced in Europe from 1970 to 1972, progressing to Formula Ford and Formula Two racing. His aggressive driving style, in which he would continuously hog the road, irritated other drivers.

The year 1972 was one of his best. He was named Motoring Sportsman of the Year in South Africa and awarded his nation's highest sports honor, the Springbok colors. One year later he was voted the Jewish South African Sportsman of the Year and also won the American Formula 5000 championship.

Scheckter's flamboyant style was most distinctive. He seemed to be driving sideways almost as much as he drove forward. Scheckter felt that his background in stock car racing contributed to this impression since the stock or saloon cars do move more sideways. The flag stewards tended to retreat when Scheckter came through a corner and, coming out of the turn, Jody seemed to regain control of the car only at the last split second.

Scheckter, according to *The New York Times,* does not steer a car into a corner, rather he flings it at a target. Having no experience with accidents, he is considered fearless. Being hungry and ambitious, he drives at "ten-tenths of effort."

Scheckter enjoyed racing but found the commercialism troubling. By 1974 his flamboyant driving style was slightly tamed as he joined the Formula One circuit, winning the British and Swedish Grand Prix. The British Guild of Motoring Writers named him Driver of the Year, and that year he placed third in the world championship.

The following year was less successful, though Scheckter did win the South African Grand Prix as 110,000 fans cheered him on. A year later he won the Swedish Grand Prix again and came in third in the world championship.

In 1977, Scheckter recorded triumphs in Argentina, Monaco, and Canada, and was runner-up in the world championship. Once again he was chosen South African Jewish Sportsman of the Year. The year 1978 was not terribly successful for Jody, but in 1979 he won in Belgium, Monaco, and Italy, and became the first South African to win the world title.

Scheckter increasingly felt the pressures and dangers of motor-car racing and in 1980, at the age of 30, he quit. He admitted that if he had been a tennis star, he would have continued for another year to earn the additional money. "But," he noted, "motor racing is not like that. You can't go out there with all the dangers and do the job just for the money." Then he added facetiously, "I'd be very upset if I got killed doing something just for the money."

The Jewish Sports Hall of Fame in Israel announced on December 1, 1982, that he had become a member of the Hall of Fame and would be inducted in the spring, 1983.

BARNEY SEDRAN

The Best "Little Man" to Play Basketball

SEDRAN, BARNEY (born January 28, 1891, in New York City; died January 14, 1969) American basketball player. One of the best of the early pro basketball players. He and Max Friedman were known as the "Heavenly Twins." Nat Holman called Barney the best "little man" to play the game.

Barney was born on the East Side of New York to Russian immigrant parents who changed their name from Sedransky to Sedran. Since there were few baseball diamonds on the East Side, Barney, like other youngsters of the neighborhood, turned to basketball. He usually played with his four brothers.

Barney attended DeWitt Clinton High School but, at 5'4" and 118 pounds, he was not even given a tryout for the basketball team. He went on to City College, leading the basketball team there in scoring for three years, but it was only when he became a professional that his talent for the game really was noticed.

Barney Sedran was the smallest man in pro basketball, but he learned to move quickly and used the technique of feinting to avoid larger players. He often played every night of the week in three different leagues, a common practice at the time. In those years there were no backboards in basketball. Nonetheless, during the 1913–14 season, when Sedran was playing for Utica, New York, against Cohoes, New York, he managed to score 17 field goals from the 25–30-foot range, an all-time record.

Sedran helped to form the New York Whirlwinds in 1920, considered one of the best basketball teams of all time. Nat Holman and Max "Marty" Friedman were on the same team.

A major basketball event of those years was a scheduled three-game series between the Whirlwinds and the Original Celtics in New York. The first game of the series was played on April 11, 1921, and Sedran's Whirlwinds won 40–24. The five goals Barney scored made him the game's high-scorer. Three days later, the Celtics won 26–24. The third game was not played because two Whirlwind players, Nat Holman and Chris Leonard, bolted to the Celtics, which in effect marked the end of the Whirlwinds as a team. (Pro basketball in those days was much more fluid than today.) Barney played on 10 championship teams in 15 seasons as a pro player. He then coached such teams as Kate Smith's Celtics, and the Brooklyn Jewels.

When Barney's playing days were over he went into the garage business with Max Friedman.

Barney Sedran was elected to the Basketball Hall of Fame in 1962.

JULIUS SELIGSON

The First Jewish Tennis Player
to Rank in the Top Ten

SELIGSON, JULIUS (born December 22, 1909, in New York City-   ) American tennis player. The first Jewish tennis player to rank in the top 10 in the United States. In 1929 he ranked ninth in the U.S.

At the age of 10, Julius' attention shifted from baseball to tennis. One day when he passed a tennis court, he developed an immediate curiosity about the game. In those days a player had to bring his own net to play on public courts. Seligson saved his money and bought one for $4. When he brought the net home, his mother thought it was for fishing.

Julius became an outstanding tennis player by the time he reached his teens, and in 1927 Lehigh University of Bethlehem, Pennsylvania, awarded him a tennis scholarship. In his sophomore year there (1928), Seligson won the National Intercollegiate Championship. He won 65 straight collegiate matches before losing to Clifford Sutter in the finals of the 1930 Intercollegiate Championship.

Seligson learned his tennis from books, not coaches. He studied every book he could find on tennis and practiced what he read. He frequently practiced service swings in his bedroom and the broken lamps displeased his mother greatly.

Seligson always blamed his defeat in the 1929 Intercollegiate Championship on anti-Semitism. The match took place at the Merion Cricket Club in Merion, Pennsylvania. A great downpour had started, and so Seligson, figuring the matches would be rained out, went to the movies. Upon returning to the club, he was notified that he had been defaulted. The incident received publicity, with reporters noting that the decision not to permit Seligson to play had an anti-Semitic tinge to it. *American Lawn Tennis* magazine called the decision "drastic, in fact unique in the history of American tennis."

In 1928 and 1930 Seligson was runner-up in the National Indoor Singles championships. He considered his 1928 victory over John Van Ryan of Princeton, then ranked sixth, as the greatest triumph of his tennis career.

Seligson was a short man, but he compensated for it with his indefatigability and an exceptionally fine baseline game. He seemed to thrive on prolonged rallies and to hit the ball harder and harder as they progressed. His first service was solid and accurate, but his second was a weakness in his game. He rarely went to the net, mostly because he was not comfortable there; his smash was erratic. His success depended on his backhand, his excellent knowledge of tactics and his stamina.

After retiring from active tennis, Seligson became an insurance broker.

LAWRENCE SHERRY

The Pitcher Who Was
Born with Two Club-feet

SHERRY, LAWRENCE (born July 25, 1935, in Los Angeles, California-) American baseball player. A relief pitcher in the major leagues for 11 years. His career won-lost record: 53–44 with a 3.67 earned-run average. In relief he was 47–37 with 82 saves and a 3.56 earned-run average. He was with the Los Angeles Dodgers from 1958 to 1963, the Detroit Tigers from 1964 to 1967, and the Houston Astros and California Angels in 1968.

Larry Sherry was born with two club-feet and was not able to walk properly without braces until he was 12 after he had undergone a series of operations. Surprisingly, like his three older brothers, he played high school baseball, and was good at it. First, he was an infielder, but was converted to a pitcher by his coach at Fairfax (Los Angeles) High School because he lacked speed. The coach gave Larry a pair of orthopedic shoes, too.

Larry was also an All-City basketball player, but he aroused the interest of both the Los Angeles Dodgers and the Pittsburgh Pirates who thought he had great potential as a baseball player. He pitched in the minor leagues from 1953 to 1959, and each season he lost more games than he won. Nevertheless, he was brought up to the majors in July 1959.

In 1959 a miracle of sorts happened. Sherry became the Los Angeles Dodger pitching hero, literally putting the team into the World Series by himself. He had a regular season record of 7–2, and then won a playoff game, triumphed in two World Series games, and saved two more as the Dodgers defeated the Chicago White Sox four games to two. In that World Series the White Sox got only one run and eight hits off him in 12 and 2/3 innings of relief pitching. In the last 11 and 2/3 innings they didn't score a run. Sherry was named winner of the Babe Ruth Award as the outstanding World Series player that year.

Although his record of 14–10 in 1960 was not nearly as good as his 1959 season, Sherry's 13 relief victories led the National League in that department and he was considered one of the major league's most effective relief pitchers.

After he retired, Larry Sherry served a number of major league teams as a pitching instructor. He was with the Pittsburgh Pirates organization from 1975 to 1978, first as a pitching instructor in the minors in 1975 and 1976, and then as pitching coach for the Pirates in 1977 and 1978. In the 1979–80 season he was pitching coach for the California Angels. Sherry rejoined the Dodger organization in December 1980 as a minor league pitching instructor.

(Larry's brother Norm was a catcher for the Los Angeles Dodgers in the late 1950s and early 1960s.)

AL SINGER

The 1930 World Lightweight Champion

SINGER, AL "THE BRONX BEAUTY" (born September 6, 1907, in New York City; died April 20, 1961) American boxer. He was world lightweight champion in 1930. His career record: 70 fights of which he won 60 (24 by knockout), lost 8, and had 2 draws.

Al was born on Broome Street in the heart of New York's East Side. His family was Orthodox and middle class. His parents moved to the Bronx when he was quite young.

As a child Al was apprenticed to a diamond cutter. Despite the opposition of his parents, he took up boxing and had a successful career as an amateur before turning pro at age 19.

Singer went from total obscurity in the boxing world in 1927 to lightweight champion just three years later. For his first pro fight in 1927 he received $75, for his second $40.

In 1928 Al fought the former featherweight champion Tony Canzoneri and held him to a 10-round draw. It was Al's thirty-fifth pro fight. Jimmy Dawson of *The New York Times* called Singer the new Benny Leonard. A handsome man, Singer was nicknamed "The Bronx Beauty."

On July 17, 1930, more than 35,000 fans crowded into Yankee Stadium in the Bronx to watch the lightweight title fight between Singer and Sammy Mandell. Singer was 21 and had only three years of professional fights behind him. Still, he had lost only five of the 56 bouts he had fought. Mandell was 26, had been a pro for 10 years, and had won the crown four years earlier from "Rocky" Kansas.

The scheduled 15-round match was only 1:46 into the first round when Singer drove a hard left hook into Mandell's jaw that sent him to the canvas. Mandell was knocked out and Singer won the title.

Singer's reign as titleholder was the shortest in history to that date. He lost the title to Tony Canzoneri when the two fought on November 14, 1930, just three months and 28 days after the Mandell bout. Canzoneri scored a 66-second knockout in the first round.

Al Singer fought very little after that, retiring in 1931. He then went into the women's wear business. In 1935 he tried to make a comeback. However, by the end of that year he put down his boxing gloves for good. He had what is known in boxing as a "glass jaw," a problem that afflicts some boxers. A solid blow to the jaw affects their nervous system and results in a knockout.

During World War II, Al served in the army. Later, he owned several night-clubs, worked in New York's garment district, and sold mutual funds. For a time he was a judge for the New York State Athletic Commission.

HAROLD SOLOMON

Greatest Jewish Tennis Player of the 1970s and 1980s

SOLOMON, HAROLD (born September 17, 1952, in Washington, D.C.-) American tennis player. Ranked fifteenth in the world in 1974, he rose to seventh in 1980. In 1981, he slipped to twenty-second. Solomon was the greatest Jewish tennis player of the 1970s and early 1980s. Known as the "human backboard" due to his patient baseline game and unmatched ability to keep the ball in play.

Harold grew up in Silver Spring, Maryland. He comes from a tennis-conscious family, and has played the game since the age of five. Harold's father, business-man Leonard Solomon, built a tennis court in the backyard of the family home. For Harold, tennis provided a way of establishing a personal identity. "When I was a young kid," he once said, "I used to lie awake at night thinking about dying without anyone ever knowing I existed. I think now maybe people would know I lived."

It was at college that people started noticing Harold Solomon. He enrolled at Rice University in Houston, Texas, during the fall of 1970 and became a political science major. (By 1975, he had completed three years of college, but decided to discontinue his studies in favor of becoming a full-time professional tennis player.) In 1970 Harold won the Interscholastic Singles title as well as the Clay Court singles championship. In 1971, he was the top-rated player on a Rice team which won the Southwest Conference tennis title. Solomon made the All-American tennis teams in 1971 and 1973.

The year 1971 was a good one for Solomon. He played in 18 tournaments, winning seven of them. Out of a total 60 matches, he lost only 11. He won the U.S.

Amateur Clay Court singles but for the most part did not play in major tournaments. Unranked until 1971, he rose to No. 10 in the American amateur rankings that year, a rise more dramatic than any other player's in 1971.

In the spring 1972, at the end of his sophomore year in college, Solomon turned pro. He achieved a rank of sixth in the American rankings that year. In July 1974, he won his first big pro tournament beating Guillermo Vilas in the finals of the Washington Star International Tournament. In the 1974 French Open he was a semifinalist.

Two of Solomon's greatest successes came in 1975 and 1976 when he won

the South African Open. Throughout most of the 1970s Harold played for the American Davis Cup squad (from 1972 to 1975 and from 1976 to 1978). He won the Tournament of Champions in 1977.

Solomon's slow, methodical style of play has left opponents frustrated and, at times, angry. Ilie Nastase, the great tennis star of the 1970s, noted that Solomon hits so many balls "you are tired in [the] head, tired in [the] legs . . . tired." And Dick Stockton, another tennis player, once shouted to Solomon from the other side of the court, "Hit the ball like a man, Solly."

Others found playing Solomon no easier. "When you played Harold," observed Erik Van Dillen, another tennis pro, "you'd better bring your lunch and dinner—you might be out there all day." His adversaries on the court called him "The Mole" because he's so small and he just keeps digging.

Solomon has spent so much time on the tennis court with American tennis star Eddie Dibbs that the two have been dubbed the "Bagel Twins." They have practiced together, traveled together, played doubles together. Some believed they were so named because both are Jewish, but this impression is erroneous; Dibbs is not a Jew. Still, Dibbs takes credit for the nickname, explaining it in this way: losing a set 6–0 is called "the Bagel," because a bagel has a hole in it, and the hole looks like a zero. Because he often lost sets by a score of 6–0, Dibbs referred to himself as the Bagel Kid. When Solomon and Dibbs became partners, "Bagel Twins" seemed to be a fitting nickname.

In 1979, Solomon won three Grand Prix titles (North Conway, Baltimore, and Paris-Crocodile). He was runner-up in three others. But 1980 was his best year, a year in which he played in 23 tournaments, winning 64 matches and losing only 23. That year, he reached the finals at the Las Vegas tournament, beating John McEnroe in the quarters; winning the German Championships at Hamburg; and then reaching the semifinals in the French Open. 1980 was also the year in which he won the ATP (Association of Tennis Professionals) Championships in Cincinnati, Ohio, and tournaments in Baltimore and Tel Aviv. At one stage during 1980 Harold was among the top five players on the ATP computer.

In July 1980, Harold Solomon was elected to a one-year term as president of the ATP and in July 1981 was reelected for one more year. Although he was chosen by *Playgirl* magazine as one of the ten sexiest men of 1980, he is a serious person and a concerned citizen. He and his wife Jan have worked hard since 1977 for the Hunger Project, an association based in San Francisco and determined to eliminate death by starvation in the world by the turn of the century.

In 1981, Solomon had a disappointing year on the tennis tour. He reached the semifinals at the German Open in May, but suffered six first-round losses in the next 11 tournaments. As a result, his computer ranking slipped into the 20s. He still managed to earn $111,541 that year, making him the 28th highest money winner for the year. In 1982, though he was semiretired, Solomon ranked 45th in the world rankings.

MARK SPITZ

The Greatest Swimmer of All Time

SPITZ, MARK (born February 10, 1950, in Modesto, California–   ) American swimmer. He has been called the greatest Jewish athlete of all time and the greatest swimmer in the history of that sport. His reputation was acquired largely from his remarkable feat in the 1972 Munich Olympics, when he won seven gold medals, setting a new world record in each event.

Overall, between 1965 and 1972 when he retired from competitive swimming, Spitz won nine Olympic gold medals, one silver, and one bronze; five Pan-American gold medals; 10 Maccabiah gold medals; 31 national AAU titles, and eight NCAA championships. During those years, he set 33 world records. He was "World Swimmer of the Year" in 1967, 1971, and 1972.

Mark learned to swim at age six. By age eight he was practicing swimming 75 minutes a day.

In recalling those days, Mark said, "I had no idea where I was going when I started swimming. It was more or less like a social activity with my boyfriends, and I had goals to be somebody like [pro football star quarterback] Johnny Unitas."

To make it possible for Mark to attend coach George Haines' successful Santa Clara [California] Swim Club, the Spitz family moved to Santa Clara from Sacramento. Arnold Spitz wanted his son to be a winner. "Swimming isn't everything," he often said, "*winning* is." Coach Haines believed in Mark. He knew he had promise.

In his first year at Santa Clara (1964), Mark qualified for the national long course championships in the 400- and 1,500-meter freestyle events. The next year, at age 15, he won four gold medals and set four new records at the Maccabiah Games in Israel. "Coming here," Spitz said at the time, "was how it all began." He had finished only fifth in the 1,500 meters at the American nationals, but in Israel "getting all those firsts did something for me. Any kid of fifteen has to benefit." In 1966, as a high school sophomore, Mark became the third man in history to better 17 minutes in the 1,500 freestyle, and won his first national title, the 100-meter butterly.

Mark's first really outstanding year came in 1967. His achievements included: two short-course and two long-course national titles, five American and seven world records in the 100- and 200-meter butterfly races, and the 400-meter freestyle. He also won five gold medals at the Pan-American Games in Winnipeg, Canada. *Swimming World* magazine named him "World Swimmer of the Year."

At the Colorado Springs trials for the 1968 Olympics that were to be held in Mexico City, Spitz ran into much anti-Semitism from his teammates. His coach, Sherm Chavoor, said, "They tried to run him right off the team. It was 'Jew boy' this and 'Jew boy' that. It wasn't a kidding type of thing either. He didn't know how to handle it." Spitz confidently predicted that he would outswim everyone at Mexico City.

His predictions did not come true. While he won two gold medals in the relays, a silver in the 100-meter butterfly, and a bronze in the 100-meter freestyle, he finished last in the final of the 200-meter butterfly. Although Spitz was actually not well during the meet, suffering from tonsilitis and diarrhea, he nevertheless felt enormously disappointed and embarrassed. He had tried three times for a gold medal in an individual event, and three times he had failed. The only gold he came home with was earned by swimming on the Americans' unbeatable relay team.

In 1969, Spitz entered Indiana University, studying to become a dentist. His three triumphs in his freshman year helped the school retain the NCAA title. In fact, during each of Spitz's four years there, Indiana won the NCAA title.

In 1969 Mark was back in Israel participating in the summer Maccabiah Games. He won six swimming gold medals and was named the outstanding athlete of the games. In 1971, after another great year of collecting AAU and NCAA titles and world records, Spitz became the first Jewish recipient of the AAU's James E. Sullivan Award, given to the amateur athlete of the year.

In 1977, he told a reporter for an Israeli magazine: "I feel that being a Jewish athlete has helped our cause. We have shown that we are as good as the next guy. In mentality we have always been at the top of every field. I think the Jewish people have a more realistic way of looking at life. They make the most of what's happening at the present while preparing for the future."

Spitz carried his 170 pounds on a tightly-compact 6 foot, 1 inch frame. He has the ability to flex his lower legs slightly forward at the knees, which has allowed him to kick six to 12 inches deeper in the water than his opponents. His moustache, he says, keeps water out of his mouth.

At Indiana, Spitz and coach James (Doc) Counsilman had a daily routine they found humorous and relaxing: Mark would put his toes in the water and say it was too cold. Counsilman, spotting his star swimmer getting out of the water, would take a leather belt and chase him around the pool, into the stands, and finally back into the water.

At Munich, where the 1972 Olympics were held, Mark Spitz gave the greatest swimming exhibition ever witnessed. In eight days at the *Swimhalle,* he won four individual (the 100- and 200-meter freestyle and the 100- and 200-meter butterfly), and three relay gold medals, all in world record time. In trying to explain his Munich performance, Mark said, "Day in and day out, swimming is 90 percent physical. You've got to do the physical work in training, and don't need much mental. But in a big meet like this, it's 90 percent mental and 10 percent physical. Your body is ready, and now it becomes mind versus matter." Coach Sherm Chavoor, remembering that some expected Spitz to repeat his poor performance in Mexico City at Munich, said after Mark had won his seventh gold medal: "He did a pretty good job for a guy who was supposed to choke."

When 11 Israeli athletes were killed at Munich by Palestinian terrorists, Spitz was put under special security guard and then whisked away. It was felt that he might be next on the terrorists' list.

After the 1972 Olympics, Spitz retired, and there was talk of his becoming a

film star, another Johnny Weismuller perhaps, but nothing developed. Upon his return from Munich, he received so many commercial offers that it was estimated he could have made five million dollars. For the next four years he had become "a major endorsement figure" for several large companies. His duties included television commercials, personal appearances, and generally helping to promote products. He launched a short-lived show business career as well. In 1973 he married.

He was criticized sharply for exploiting his success, but scoffed at the criticism: "I was really the first one to take advantage of what's out there. I realize today that if someone had come up to me just before a race and offered me $100,000 a year for five years if I stepped down off the platform right then and there and retired, I would have done it. Right then."

In 1973, Spitz began doing some sports broadcasting. He bought a Los Angeles home with a large swimming pool—and then invested in real estate in California and Hawaii and became a real estate developer in Los Angeles and Honolulu. He did little swimming after leaving competition, preferring tennis and sailing. In October 1981, his wife, Susie, gave birth to their first child, a boy.

Mark Spitz is a member of the Jewish Sports Hall of Fame in Israel.

GEORGE STONE

The 1906 American League Batting Champion

STONE, GEORGE ROBERT "SILENT GEORGE" (born September 3, 1876, in Lost Nation, Nebraska; died January 6, 1945) American baseball player. He was the 1906 American League batting champion, hitting .358 for the St. Louis Browns. Played in the major leagues for seven years, and had a career batting average of .301.

While working as a clerk in Coleridge, Nebraska, in 1902, Stone had been playing baseball for fun on the local team. In a game with a team which included pro players from Omaha of the Western League, Stone had five hits, including three home runs. Word spread about the man with the good bat and Stone began to take baseball seriously. Soon thereafter, he played in his first professional game.

That year, George played with minor league teams in Omaha and Peoria, hitting .346 in 138 games, and leading the league with 198 hits and 34 stolen bases. He was brought up to the major leagues to play for the Boston Red Sox for a brief period in 1903, and then sent back down to the minors to play for Milwaukee. In 1904, playing for Milwaukee, he led the American Association in batting with .406 and hits (254). The Red Sox traded him to the St. Louis Browns and he played for them from 1905 to 1910.

The year 1905 was Stone's real rookie season and he did well. The left-handed outfielder led the American League in hitting for much of the season, finishing with a .296 average. He managed to lead the league in hits with 187, and total bases with 260.

Stone had an awkward batting style. Though left-handed, he usually placed the ball between second and third base, but rarely pulled the ball. "If he stood up," noted a commentator in a baseball magazine in 1909, "and pulled the ball to right field once in a while, I think that he would be the most wonderful batter that baseball ever saw."

Still, he did not fare badly. Stone's best season was 1906 when he won the American League batting title and was runner-up in hits with 208 and hit 20 triples.

The next year he had a poor start, but still finished with a .320 batting average, third best in the American League. In 1908 Stone contracted malaria and managed to play in only 148 games. In 1909 he hurt his ankle badly, sliding into first base. The ankle never healed and he finished his playing career with Milwaukee in 1911.

After retiring from baseball, Stone divided his time between his new career as a banker and an old hobby for which he now had more time: playing the violin. In 1916, he became part owner of the Lincoln (Nebraska) baseball team, but he sold his interest the following year, severing all ties with baseball.

STEVE STONE

The 1980 Cy Young Award Winner

STONE, STEVE (born July 14, 1947, in Cleveland, Ohio-   ) American baseball player. Won the Cy Young award as the best pitcher in the American League during the 1980 season. That year he won 25 games and lost seven. Prior to that, from 1971 to 1979, he had a mediocre 78-79 record pitching for the San Francisco Giants, Chicago White Sox, and the Chicago Cubs. His career record as of the end of the 1981 season was 107-93, with an earned-run average of 3.96, and 1,065 strikeouts.

An only son, Steve grew up in South Euclid, Ohio. His father fixed jukeboxes, his mother was a waitress. An all-around athlete as a youngster, Steve shot a hole in one at golf at age 11, and won the Cleveland junior tennis title at age 13. Sandy Koufax, the Dodger pitching superstar, was his idol. At Bush High School in Cleveland, where he graduated in 1965, Steve won All-State honors in baseball as a junior and captained the team as a senior. In 1965, when Steve was 18, he was the winning pitcher in a state high school All-Star game.

He graduated from Kent State in Kent, Ohio, in 1969 with a degree in history and government, and a distinguished baseball record. During his senior year Steve signed with the San Francisco Giants (February 15, 1969).

When Stone played in the minors between 1969 and 1971, he averaged virtually a strikeout per inning (399 strikeouts in 400 innings). The first year he pitched for the Fresno, California, minor league team he won 12 and lost 13 games. Once that year he struck out 17 batters in one nine-inning game. The following year Stone was 14-8, pitching for Amarillo (Texas) and Phoenix (Arizona). In 1971 Steve was 6-3 when the Giants brought him up in midseason to the majors. He finished that season, his first in the major leagues, at 5-9.

Stone married a woman he had known since high school in 1970, but they were divorced two years later.

In 1972, after a 6-8 season with the Giants, he was traded to the Chicago White Sox. Pitching for the White Sox in 1973, Stone was 6-11. After the season ended, he was traded to the Chicago Cubs for whom he pitched in 1974 (8-6), 1975 (12-8), and 1976 (3-6). Because of a sore shoulder he could pitch in only 17 games (75 innings) in 1976. He was on the disabled list from April 25 to July 2. His condition almost forced him to leave baseball.

After playing out his option with the Cubs, Stone signed with the Chicago White Sox on November 24, 1976. In the next two seasons he had 15-12 and 12-12 records, respectively. His 15 wins in 1977 was a career high until then. He played out his option with the White Sox in 1978 and signed a four-year contract with the Baltimore Orioles on November 29, 1978.

Stone was 11-7 with Baltimore in 1979, getting off to a slow start. (By July 10 he was only 6-7.) After July 10, he was 5-0.

Steve had a bonus provision in his contract whereby he would receive an

extra $10,000 in any season that he won the Cy Young Award. He did not think it was a serious proposal, but rather something his agent had just added. Stone thought a bonus for a winning season would have been more sensible. "It was," Stone said, "like an insurance salesman telling you, 'We'll give you $50,000 if an elephant falls on you.' He knows darn well an elephant isn't going to fall on you."

An elephant fell on Steve Stone that 1980 season.

He was 2–3 with a 4.74 earned run average through May 5. But he then went on to win 23 of the next 27 games with a 3.06 earned-run average and nine complete games. This included 14 straight wins in 17 starts from May 9 to July 26. That was the longest winning streak in the American League since 1974. In the All-Star game that year, Stone set down the first nine batters in order.

Steve's 25 wins led the majors in the 1980 season. He was the second straight Baltimore pitcher to win the Cy Young Award (Mike Flanagan won it in 1979). Steve also topped the league in winning percentage (.781) and was seventh in earned-run average (3.23). He was named American League Pitcher of the Year by *The Sporting News* (based on a vote of fellow-players) and was selected as the top right-hander on American League All-Star teams selected by the Associated Press and United Press International.

What was responsible for Stone's vast improvement? He attributed it to the fact that he had stopped thinking of himself as a mediocre pitcher. He revised his thought processes so that negative images of himself were eliminated. He credits Oriole pitching coach Ray Miller with two worthwhile suggestions: quickening his pace so the fielders would stay alert between pitches, and finding his best pitch—usually his curve—in the early innings and then sticking with it.

He had his own style of preparing for a pitching assignment, part of which involved superstition. Each time Steve pitched at home, he had breakfast at a local pancake house with Baltimore sportswriter Peter Pascarelli. In the afternoon before he pitched, he visualized how he would get each batter out, and then he left for the park. He would always stop at the same drive-in for a chocolate milkshake and would always listen to the same soft rock on his car stereo going from his suburban Towson home to Baltimore's Memorial Stadium.

When informed that only one American League Cy Young Award winner in the 1970s had improved his won-lost percentage the year following the award, Stone suggested, "Put me down for 30 wins and a no-hitter."

A gourmet cook for six years, Steve was a partner in Lettuce Entertain You, a chain of nine restaurants in Chicago. He sold his share because he planned to open a moderately-priced but high-class eatery called Steven, in Scottsdale, Arizona. He jokingly remarked that he hoped to trim the bill for a gourmet meal from $75 to $72 or $73. The restaurant opened in January 1981.

He developed a pain in his pitching elbow in spring training before the 1981 season began. The injury was diagnosed as tendonitis, and Stone was told to rest. He pitched only 34 innings at the start of 1981, and was 2–3 before going on the disabled list in mid-May with the sore elbow. He was still disabled in June when the baseball strike brought the entire season to a halt. While recuperating, Stone worked at his Scottsdale restaurant.

By the spring of 1982, there was no real improvement in his pitching arm. He ruled out surgery though he was told that, after 18 months of rest, his arm might be completely healed. In early June 1982, Steve Stone announced at a news conference in Baltimore that he was retiring from baseball. He hoped to work in broadcasting while running his restaurant in Arizona. He also hoped to write a book on his "psychic experiences, with baseball as a backdrop.... I believe I'm every man in every way, an average performer who achieved an extraordinary goal by the refinement of the mental processes."

By way of hobbies, Stone writes free-form poetry and has been published in *Sports Illustrated* and the *National Jewish Monthly*. He has always been a chess enthusiast.

"I've always been proud of being Jewish," he said. "If you're a good enough pitcher, they don't care if you're a Martian."

EVA SZEKELY

Hungarian Olympic Swimming Star

SZEKELY, EVA (born April 3, 1927, in Hungary-) Hungarian swimming star. She won a gold medal at the 1952 Olympics, a silver one at the 1956 Games and set 10 world and five Olympic records. She also established 101 Hungarian records and held 68 Hungarian national swimming titles.

From as early as Eva could remember, she felt like a stranger in her native Hungary. When she was 11 and studying at a German school in Budapest, Eva had many Jewish classmates. But she had trouble identifying with her co-religionists: she disliked them for showing their fear of anti-Semitism.

Eva belonged to a local swimming team just before World War II broke out, and was happy that it was her talent that counted, and not her religion. But, in 1941, at age 14, she was expelled from the team as "undesirable." For the next four years, during the war, she dreamed of becoming an Olympic swimming champion.

From 1944 to 1945 the Szekely family lived in a Swiss-run "safe house" in Budapest. Forty people lived in the two rooms of the five-storey apartment house that was considered "protected" from German intrusion. For exercise each

morning Eva would climb over others asleep on the ground floor and run up and down five flights of stairs 100 times. "I realized," she wrote much later, "that there is one thing that cannot be taken away from anybody: one's inner security, which consists of faith, discipline, willpower, knowledge, humanity, and never accepting the finality of evil."

Eva never lost faith. Although some knew that she was Jewish, and held it against her, she pursued her career in swimming, confident that she would one day reach the Olympics.

After the war, Eva began participating in international meets. In 1947, in Paris, she met Dezso Gyarmati, a Hungarian water polo star, whom she married four years later. Then her career began to turn around. The 1948 Olympics in London was her first, and she came in fourth in the 200-meter breaststroke.

In the years between Olympics, Eva was performing miracles in the swimming pool. On May 9, 1951, she set a world record of 1:16.9 for the 100-meter breaststroke.

At the 1952 Helsinki Olympics, both she and Dezso won gold medals. He, for water polo play; she, for the 200-meter breaststroke which she swam in 2:51.7, setting an Olympic record. The following year, on April 10, 1953, she set a world record of 5:50.4 for the 400-meter individual medley.

Eva and Dezso's daughter, Andrea, was born in May 1954. Two years later, leaving her behind, they went to the 1956 Melbourne Olympics just a few days after the Hungarian Revolt had started. En route they spent a night in Pakistan, and at the Karachi airport Eva had second thoughts about leaving her daughter behind. She tried to convince an American fighter pilot to take her back to Europe. He agreed to be at the airport at midnight. But, when she arrived, there was no trace of him. Standing on the middle of the runway, Eva broke into tears, and had no choice but to continue on to Melbourne.

Once in Australia, the only news that she and Dezso had was that Budapest had been devastated, that people had been shot en masse, and those still alive were starving. Despite the trauma, Dezso won a gold medal as captain of the winning water polo team and Eva took a silver medal in swimming. She did not sleep for a week and lost 12 pounds. Finally, she and Dezso received a phone call from her father in Hungary who reported that everyone in the family was fine.

Eva did not return with the Hungarian Olympic team to Hungary. Instead, she and Dezso went to Austria. Shortly thereafter the two returned to Budapest to try to bring out Andrea and Dezso's mother. It was not easy.

The new Russian puppet government in Hungary had apparently learned that Eva and her family wanted to defect. On February 20, 1957, four men dragged Dezso into a vacant Budapest building and tore at his body with cat-o-nine-tails and razor blades, leaving him for dead. But with a forged passport in hand, he, Eva, their daughter, and Dezso's mother reached the Austrian border shortly after daylight the next day. The Hungarian police stamped the passport and then suggested that this called for a drink. Fearing the police would turn them in, Dezso had no choice but to join them at a local bar. Fortunately for him, the policemen outdrank him, and so the water polo star, driving fuzzily, finally crossed the border into Austria.

Eva and Dezso came to the United States in early 1957. They lived for some time with Eva's cousin in New Jersey. In all, they were in America for one year before moving on to Naples, Italy, where Dezso found a coaching job. But difficulties with his work forced them to return to Budapest in 1958. Upon reaching Hungary, Eva retired from competition but Dezso continued to play water polo.

After retiring from active swimming in 1958, Eva trained youngsters to swim in local competition with an eye toward the Olympics. She also spent considerable time coaching her daughter Andrea.

In 1964 Eva and Dezso were divorced and she spent even more time on raising Andrea and on building her into a great swimmer. Andrea, by then age 18, reached the high point of her career when at the 1972 Munich Olympics she came in first in the semifinals in the 100-meter butterfly, establishing a world record. She finished third in the butterfly finals, winning a bronze medal. She then went ahead to win a silver medal in the 100-meter backstroke.

In June 1980, the retina of Eva's right eye was damaged. She underwent four operations in the next two months, with only local anesthetics. Though Hungarian physicians tried a variety of treatments, including the use of laser beams, they concluded that nothing could help. She went to Cologne, West Germany, where another operation was performed. This time the operation succeeded.

Eva Szekely is a member of the International Swimming Hall of Fame and of the Jewish Sports Hall of Fame in Israel.

BRIAN TEACHER

World Class Tennis Star

TEACHER, BRIAN (born December 23, 1954, in San Diego, California–) American tennis player. Won the Australian Open in January 1981. In 1981, he climbed from fifty-ninth to eighth place in the world. In 1982, Teacher was 18th in the world rankings.

Brian graduated from Crawford High School in San Diego, California, in the spring of 1972, and entered the University of California at Los Angeles in the fall of

that year. He followed in the footsteps of two other UCLA graduates—Arthur Ashe ('65) and Jimmy Connors ('71). Brian joined the pro tour in June 1976. (As of the spring 1982, he was nearing completion of a B.A. in economics from UCLA.)

In 1977 Brian Teacher managed to reach the finals in two Australian events, the South Australian and New South Wales Opens. He created an even bigger stir at the 1978 Seiko World Super Tennis tournament in Tokyo. There, he beat both Connors and Ashe at a time when few others could. He reached the finals only to lose to Bjorn Borg.

Teacher went on to claim his first Grand Prix title later in 1978, capturing the Cathay Trust Open in Taipei, Taiwan. The following year, 1979, Brian's game was disappointing, despite a win at Newport, Rhode Island, over Stan Smith at the Miller Hall of Fame Championships.

In 1980 he fared better, reaching five finals—Los Angeles, Hong Kong, Taipei, Bangkok, and New South Wales—and collecting the runner-up check at each event. Teacher made it to the final round of 16 of the U.S. Open that year, losing to Roscoe Tanner in four sets.

Brian played well in doubles in 1980, teaming with American tennis player Bruce Manson. The pair won five titles out of eight appearances in final rounds. At the end of the year, he and Manson won titles in Toronto, Cincinnati, and Palm Springs, and a fourth several weeks later in Taipei. He also teamed with Butch Walts, winning several tournaments in Frankfurt.

In 1981, Teacher reached the semifinals at Las Vegas and at Queen's Club (England), and the quarters at Frankfurt and Los Angeles; he also had a great win over Vitas Gerulaitis in Las Vegas and won the doubles title at the Association of Tennis Professionals Championship in Palm Springs (with Manson). Teacher earned $50,000 for winning the Australian Open in January 1981, the largest paycheck of his career until then. He was fifteenth highest in yearly earnings on the pro tennis tour, winning $163,646 in 1981.

In February 1979, Brian married Kathy May, an outstanding professional tennis player in her own right. (He divorced her in September 1981.) When not touring, Teacher practices under the guidance of Robert Lansdorp in Los Angeles, the same man who coached woman tennis star Tracey Austin. He is also coached by San Diego teaching pro Powell Blankenship.

Brian Teacher is tall and lean at 6 feet, 3 inches and 175 pounds. He prefers fast surfaces where he can best utilize his blistering serve and volley game. He is modest: "I'm not one of the more well-known players to the public or press," he said, "but outside of a very few guys—Borg, McEnroe, Connors, and a couple others—who is? I don't expect it, I don't really know if I would want the kind of attention they get, but I know it doesn't bother me that I don't have it now."

ELIOT TELTSCHER

Outstanding Tennis Player of the Early 1980s

TELTSCHER, ELIOT (born March 15, 1959, in Palos Verdes, California–) American tennis player. One of the outstanding Jewish tennis players of the early 1980s. In July, 1982, he was ranked seventh in the world. At the end of 1981, Teltscher was ninth best. In the four previous years he had made phenomenal progress, going from ninety-ninth place in 1977, to forty-eighth in 1978, to twenty-seventh in 1979, to tenth in 1980. In 1981 he earned $157,630, making him the eighteenth highest money winner of the pro tour. In 1982, he was ranked 16th in the world.

Eliot's mother was born in Israel and his father came there during the period of the Holocaust, joining the British Army in order to avoid being arrested. His mother attended the Reali Gymnasia High School in Haifa. Eventually, they made their way to the United States where Eliot's father became an outstanding table tennis player and a soccer judge.

Teltscher took up tennis at the age of nine when he and his older sister, Judy,

Eliot Teltscher (right) with tennis colleague Michael Grant. Israel, November 1981.

accompanied their parents to the Jack Kramer Tennis Club near their home in Palos Verdes. A sibling rivalry developed as Eliot and Judy competed against one another. He learned tennis, he later claimed, to demonstrate to Judy that he was better than she. Judy stopped playing, and Eliot went on.

Playing in his first tournament at the age of 10, he lost in an early round, which was a humbling experience. But in his second tournament he reached the finals. Eliot went to Israel at the age of 13 to celebrate his Bar Mitzvah at the Western Wall in Jerusalem. During the visit, his Israeli relatives arranged for him to play against another up-and-coming young tennis player at the Tel Aviv Country Club, a local boy named Shlomo Glickstein. Glickstein could not handle Teltscher any better then than he can now, and Eliot won easily.

In 1978, Teltscher attended UCLA on a full athletic scholarship, working out on the court at least four hours a day. He became an All-American, and turned pro after one year of college play. He is known for his speed, deceptive strength, and competitiveness. His UCLA coach Glenn Bassett, said: "Eliot believes in himself. He's very tough out there on the court."

In 1977, when he achieved a ranking of 99 in the world, he was runner-up at the Wimbledon Junior and the U.S. Open Junior competitions. His first big-time triumph came at Hong Kong in 1978. By that time he was ranked forty-eighth in the world. Ilie Nastase called Teltscher at that time "the best player I've played in the United States this year."

In 1979, when he climbed to No. 27 in the world, Teltscher won a title in Atlanta and reached the semifinals five times. In the process, he recorded victories over Jose-Luis Clerc, John McEnroe, and Jose Higueras.

In 1980, Teltscher won tournaments in Atlanta and Miami and was runner-up five other times. In New Orleans in 1980, he won the doubles with Terry Moor and was runner-up at the Japan Open.

Early in 1981 Eliot and Tim Gullikson lost the San Juan (Puerto Rico) final to the Mayotte brothers after Teltscher had routed Gullikson for the singles crown. In the spring of 1981 Eliot and Terry Moor reached the French Open doubles final. That summer, Eliot reached the semifinals of Boston's U.S. pro tournament.

OTTO WAHLE

First American Olympic Swimmer
to Place in a Distance Event

WAHLE, OTTO (born 1880 in Austria; died August 11, 1965) Austrian swimming champion. He emigrated to the United States and became the first American swimmer to win a place in a distance event in the Olympics.

Wahle was frequently the Austrian national swimming champion. He came to the U.S. at the turn of the twentieth century and lived in New York City until his death. Even after he settled in the U.S., he continued to represent Austria in Olympic competition, but wore the colors of the New York Athletic Club in American competition.

In the 1900 Paris Olympics he finished second to John Jarvis of Great Britain in the 1,000-meter race. He also took a silver medal in the 200-meter obstacle race. In 1904 he captured third place in the 400-meter race.

In 1912 Wahle coached the American Olympic swimmers who went to the Stockholm Olympics. Among his swimmers was General George S. Patton Jr. who competed in the swimming event in the modern pentathlon.

A swimmer and water polo player for the New York Athletic Club, Wahle became coach of the club at the same time that he was a member of the Amateur Athletic Union Records Committee. He served as Olympic swimming coach for the American squad in 1920 as well.

Wahle played an important part in the growth of swimming as a competitive sport in the United States, contributing many of the rules first listed in early AAU manuals. They were modeled on those of the Amateur Swimming Association of England.

Wahle's profession was accounting. He worked as an accountant with the law firm of Guggenheimer and Untermyer in New York until five years before his death in 1965.

HENRY WITTENBERG

A Great Wrestler of the 1940s

WITTENBERG, HENRY B. (born September 18, 1918, in Jersey City, New Jersey-) American wrestler. Considered one of the world's greatest wrestlers. Between 1938 and 1952, he won 400 consecutive matches. Wittenberg won a gold medal in the light heavyweight division in the 1948 London Olympics and a silver medal in the 1952 Helsinki Games.

Henry became involved in wrestling against his parents' wishes, but his father eventually became his greatest fan. As a child, Henry was interested only in chess. He captained his high school chess team and led it to a New Jersey county championship.

After enrolling at City College of New York (CCNY), in 1935, he decided to become involved in active sports. Though Henry had never wrestled before, he chose that sport, thinking that it would make him a better freestyle swimmer. But when CCNY's wrestling coach, Joe Sapora, assured him that with proper training

he would make the varsity wrestling team, Henry decided to give up swimming. The coach got more than he bargained for. In Henry's first match he broke two of his opponent's ribs.

Henry graduated in 1939 with a degree in education. At the time of his graduation, he was the runner-up in the National Collegiate Athletic Association (NCAA) 174-pound championships.

Wittenberg won his first national AAU title (in the 175-pound class) in 1940, and was victorious eight more times. During his eighth match he was carried out of the ring, not in celebration, but because he had hurt his back.

However, he won the national AAU title once again in 1941 when he was chosen AAU wrestler of the year.

The year 1941 was a busy one for Wittenberg. In June he received a Masters degree from Columbia Teachers College. He married in July. Three months later (on September 4th) he began working as a policeman in New York but his career was interrupted when he was called to serve in the U.S. Navy from September 1944 until 1947.

Between 1943 and 1952 Wittenberg captured the AAU's 191-pound division title six times. In 1947 he was runner-up for the Sullivan Award, an award given to the outstanding American amateur athlete.

In his adult years Henry continued to be a chess enthusiast and he often spoke of wrestling as a kind of "body chess" (his own phrase). He once said: "You give a man a leg as a gambit." To him, body positions in wrestling were more important than individual holds.

Wrestling helped Wittenberg in his police work. He was convinced that a policeman like a wrestler needs presence of mind more than anything else. The New York Police Department cited him for bravery five times, once for rescuing two children from a burning building, and another time for catching two armed bandits.

While wrestling in the 1948 Olympic final in London, he experienced intense pain in the chest caused by several ripped tendons. But Henry managed to conceal the injury and went on to take the gold medal. He announced his retirement after that because his police work demanded so much of his time. But soon afterward he reconsidered and rescinded the announcement.

In 1949 he was named America's best Jewish athlete, and in that same year he was promoted to sergeant on the police force.

Although Wittenberg competed in the 1950 Maccabiah Games in Israel and did well (he won a gold medal), he was still reluctant to enter the 1952 Olympics which were to be held in Helsinki, Finland. He had never competed in the world championships because his police job did not allow him enough free time. His wife, however, began dropping hints about how beautiful Finland is, and so he changed his mind, and he agreed to lead the American wrestling squad.

Wittenberg's greatest moment in Helsinki came when he defeated the Russian world champion, August Englas, in the semifinals. His victory over Englas marked one of the first times an American had beaten a Russian in international competition. Wittenberg won a silver medal.

In 1953 Henry was back at the Maccabiah Games and captured a second gold medal. Then he retired. Being a professional athlete held no attraction for him, and he once rejected an offer of $60,000 to turn pro. He openly questioned the authenticity of professional wrestling, and wanted no part of it.

Wittenberg resigned from the New York Police Department in October 1954, for a more lucrative position with a printing firm in Manhattan with which he was associated until 1967. In 1959, chosen national wrestling coach, he took America's first wrestling team to Russia, but it did not fare well. From 1959 to 1967, Henry coached wrestling at Yeshiva University in New York.

Elected coach of the U.S. Olympic team in 1967, Wittenberg took the team to the Mexico City Games the following year. There, he coached the Greco-Roman wrestlers though with little success.

Wittenberg became a professor of health education and coach of the wrestling squad at CCNY in September 1967. He taught and coached there until 1979.

He is a member of the National Wrestling Hall of Fame, the Helms Hall of Fame, and the Jewish Sports Hall of Fame (of Israel).

PHIL WOLF

Bowling Champion at Age 58

WOLF, PHIL (born November 2, 1869, in Germany; died July 7, 1936) American bowler. A member of the American Bowling Congress (ABC) tournament team champions in 1909 and 1920. In 1928, at age 58, he won the ABC all-events title with a 1,928 score. Wolf's 25-year average: 198.

Phil moved to the United States from Germany at age 14. Living in Brooklyn, his interest in bowling began when he worked as a pinboy. Within a few years he

became one of the East Coast's most respected match game competitors despite one of the most awkward deliveries of his era.

Wolf moved to Chicago in 1899. There, he made his ABC tournament debut in 1903, rolling 1,143 for six games. He attracted national attention at the 1909 ABC tournament in Pittsburgh in which he was anchorman for Chicago's famous Lipman team—a team that won the five-man crown with a 2,962 score (Wolf shot 571). In 1910 at Detroit, his team, the O'Leary's No. 2 of Chicago, shot 2,833 to finish third (Wolf had a 593 score).

It was in 1920 that Phil turned in his greatest team performance. Bowling in the ABC tournament at Peoria, Illinois, his 680 score led the Brucks No. 1 club of Chicago to a then-record 3,096 score.

He captured his third ABC title—the 1928 all-events—at the age of 59, putting together a series of 657 (team), 650 (doubles), and 630 (singles), for a total score of 1,937.

In 26 ABC tournaments, Wolf compiled an unusually high average of 194. In addition to the 1,937 he scored, he had seven 1800s in his career and an equal number of 1700s as total tournament scores.

Another champion bowler, Billy Sixty, noted that Wolf, on the alleys, had a "heart that was much like an ice cube in battle. He wasn't a stylist. He bowled out of an awkward, half-crouch, and his footwork to the foul line was more of a sneak than a run."

Wolf had little finesse as a bowler and possessed few tricks. Instead he plodded along in what bowler Billy Sixty called "cold demeanor," wearing down opponents with invariably high-scoring performances.

Phil Wolf died in Chicago on July 7, 1936, following an operation for cancer of the bladder. Twenty-five years later, in 1961, he was inducted into the Bowlers Hall of Fame.

THUMBNAIL
SKETCHES

ALBERT, MARV (born June 12, 1943, in Brooklyn, New York–) American sports announcer. One of America's most popular broadcasters. Since 1967 Marv has been the voice of the NBA's New York Knickerbockers and pro hockey's New York Rangers. He also does National Football League and college basketball television coverage. Has been called "the radio sports voice of New York City."

ALEXANDER, JOE (born April 1, 1898, in Syracuse, New York; died 1975) American football player. Playing for Syracuse University, he was an All-American guard in 1918 and 1919, and an All-American center in 1920. He played pro football with a number of teams from 1921 to 1927, especially the New York Giants. In 1925 he was on the National Football League All-Star team. In 1934 he served as assistant to coach Benny Friedman of CCNY. He was head coach of CCNY in the early 1940s before retiring to devote more time to his medical practice. He became a world-famous lung specialist.

ALLEN, MEL (born February 14, 1913, in Birmingham, Alabama–) American sports broadcaster. Famous as "The Voice of the New York Yankees." His broadcasting career began in 1939. Born Melvin Allen Israel, he used only his given names when he began to broadcast, and Mel Allen became his legal name when he entered the army in 1943. Beginning that year, he was the Yankees' chief announcer, first on radio and then on television. He also broadcast 14 Rose Bowl games, two Orange Bowls, two Sugar Bowls, 20 World Series, and 24 All-Star baseball games. In 1964, he was fired as Yankee announcer, but he returned in 1981 as "The Voice of the Yankees," announcing on cable TV. In 1980, Mel Allen became a member of the Jewish Sports Hall of Fame in Israel.

ARNOVICH, MORRIS "MORRIE" (born November 16, 1910, in Superior, Wisconsin; died July 20, 1959) American baseball player. He played for the Philadelphia Phillies from 1936 to 1940; the Cincinnati Reds in 1940; and the New York Giants in 1941 and 1946. In 590 games, he had a career batting average of .287.

Mel Allen

Richard Bergmann

BACHER, ARON "ALI" (born May 24, 1942 in South Africa–   ) South African cricket player. He played international cricket in the 1960s and in the early 1970s as a member of the South African national cricket team, retiring in 1974. He was appointed captain of the South African team for the 1970 test matches against England, the first Jew to reach that position. Bacher was an outstanding proponent of multiracial cricket and, as a physician, devoted his early years in medicine to nonwhites. When violent opposition in England arose in the early 1970s to South African apartheid in sport, South Africa ceased to participate in international cricket competition, thus cutting short Bacher's career.

BERGMANN, RICHARD "THE OLD LION" (born 1919, in Vienna, Austria; died 1970) Table tennis player. Regarded as the greatest defensive player in table tennis history. In 1937 Bergmann became the youngest player to capture the world singles title. He won seven world titles in all, including four singles championships. Small and stocky, he was famous for the nearly impossible shots he was able to make in table tennis. When the Nazis invaded Austria in 1938, he fled to Great Britain, and later moved to the United States. He is a member of Israel's Jewish Sports Hall of Fame.

BLUM, WALTER "MOUSY" (born 1934, in Brooklyn, New York–   ) American jockey. Considered one of the best jockeys of the late 1950s and early 1960s. He was American riding champion in 1963–64. Blum rode his first mount, Ricey, on May 4, 1953, and had his first victory 13 rides later. His first $100,000 stakes victory came on Royal Beacon in the 1957 Atlantic City Handicap. On June 19, 1961, he rode six horses to victory on an eight-race card at Monmouth Park. In 1963, his 1,704 mounts were the second highest ever ridden in a season. He rode 4,383 winners in a 22-year riding career, and retired after the 1975 season. When he rode his four-thousandth winner in 1974, he was only the sixth U.S. jockey to do so.

BREGMAN, JAMES STEVEN (born November 17, 1941, in Arlington, Virginia–   ) American judo champion. He won a bronze medal in the 1964 Tokyo Olympics in the middleweight division, the only American representative to win a judo medal to date. (Judo was introduced as an Olympic sport in 1964.) Bregman had trained with the top intercollegiate teams in Tokyo, then won the U.S. National middleweight title on his way to capturing the Tokyo medal.

BREWS, SIDNEY (born May 29, 1899, in Blackheath, England; died in 1972) South African golfer. Starting in 1925, he won 30 Open championships in six countries. During the 1920s and 1930s he won six South African Opens and six professional titles. A convert to Judaism, he won the Belgian Open in 1929 and the Dutch and French Opens in 1934 and 1935. He was runner-up in the 1934 British Open and won the Philadelphia Open in 1935.

BRODY, GYORGY (born July 2, 1908, in Hungary; died August 5, 1967) Hungarian water polo player. Considered one of the best water polo goalkeepers of all time. Brody appeared for the Hungarian national team 74 times.

Robert Cohen

He received gold medals at the 1932 and 1936 Olympics as a goalie for Hungary. He was on the 1928 Hungarian national championship squad and the 1934 European championship team. After the 1956 Revolution in Hungary had failed, Brody emigrated to South Africa. He died there 11 years later. Brody is a member of the Jewish Sports Hall of Fame in Israel.

BROWN, LARRY (born September 14, 1940, in Brooklyn, New York-   ) American basketball coach. He played college basketball for the University of North Carolina between 1959 and 1963. In 56 varsity games, he averaged 11.8 points per game. He began playing in the ABA in 1967, and for the next five years played for New Orleans, Oakland, Washington, Virginia, and Denver. In 376 ABA games, he averaged 11.3 points per game. In 47 playoff games, he averaged 14.3 points per game. He was an ABA All-Star guard for three years. Brown began coaching in the ABA in 1972 for the Carolina Cougars finishing first that year and third the next. Between 1974 and 1976, he coached the Denver Nuggets finishing first in the division twice, and in the league once. In 1974-75, Brown was voted Coach of the Year in the ABA. From 1976 to February 1979, he coached Denver in the NBA and his three-year record was 126-91. During that span, Brown finished first in the division twice. In 1979-80 he coached UCLA to a 22-10 season, and the team was ranked fourth in the country. UCLA lost to Louisville in the 1980 NCAA finals. In 1980-81, UCLA had a 20-7 season and was ranked third nationally. Brown returned to the NBA in 1981-82 to coach the New Jersey Nets. His 44-38 record, third in the division, was the Nets' best in six NBA seasons. They lost 0-2 in the opening round of the playoffs to Washington. Brown has never had a losing season as a coach.

COHEN, ROBERT (born November 15, 1930, in Bone, Algeria-   ) Boxing champion. Cohen is an Orthodox Jew who had studied to become a cantor. He began pro boxing in 1951 and was world bantamweight champion from 1954 to 1956. In 42 bouts he had 36 wins (14 by knockout), three losses, and three draws. He left the ring in 1959.

COSELL, HOWARD (born March 25, 1920, in Winston-Salem, North Carolina-) American sports broadcaster. Sportscaster for ABC since 1956. Called "the most dominant sports personality of his time, and perhaps all time" as well as "the most famous talker in America." In addition, he is considered broadcasting's most controversial and knowledgeable figure. Born Howard William Cohen, he first caught viewers' attention when he developed a close friendship with heavyweight champ Cassius Clay (Muhammed Ali). Cosell has covered NFL Monday-night football for ABC since 1971, handled national major league baseball coverage since 1977, and has been a sports commentator on many other shows.

DANILOWITZ, ABRAHAM PHINEAS "PINKY" (born August 1, 1908 in Krugersdorp Transvaal, in South Africa-   ) South African bowls champion. He began bowls in 1948 at age 40. His best year was 1957-58 when he won the South African singles championship. The next year, 1958, he became world champion. In that year, he broke the world record of 27 straight singles games winning 84 straight, a record which still stands. He later won the Western Transvaal bowls title twice and was runner-up in the South African singles in 1964.

DARMON, PIERRE (born January 14, 1934, in Tunis, Tunisia–   ) French tennis player. France's best player in the late 1960s. He had great success at Wimbledon in 1963 when he and Jean Claude Barclay reached the men's doubles final, which they lost to Rafael Osuna and Antonio Palafox of Mexico. He played 69 Davis Cup matches for France from 1956 to 1967 and won 47 of them. In 1957 he won the singles and doubles of the French national championships.

EPSTEIN, MICHAEL (born April 4, 1943, in the Bronx, New York–   ) American baseball player. Played nine years in the major leagues: with the Baltimore Orioles in 1966 and 1967; the Washington Senators from 1967 to 1971; the Oakland A's in 1971 and 1972; the Texas Rangers in 1973; and the California Angels in 1973 and 1974. In 907 games he had a career batting average of .244, hit 130 home runs, and had 380 runs batted in. In 1971 he tied a major league record with four home runs in four straight times at bat. In 1969 he hit 30 home runs and in 1972, 26.

FUCHS, JENO (born October 29, 1882, in Budapest, Hungary; died 1954) Hungarian fencer. He won four Olympic gold medals for Hungary in fencing. In the 1908 London Games, Jeno won the individual sabre and team sabre titles. In the 1912 Stockholm Games, he repeated those victories, going through the competition undefeated. He was named to the Jewish Sports Hall of Fame in Israel in December 1981.

GLASER, PAMELA (born August 17, 1957 in Boston, Massachusetts–   ) American karate champion. In November, 1982 she was in the headlines when a federal judge ordered that she be included on the American National Karate Team even though she had missed the tryouts because they fell on Rosh Hashana, the Jewish New Year. The Amateur Athletic Union Karate Committee had refused to change the September tryout date despite Pamela's requests. She was at the time the top-ranked American female athlete in amateur karate, holding a Second-degree Black Belt. She competed in the Kata form of karate, which involves a prearranged series of movements, blocking and striking an imaginary opponent. The federal judge had ordered that Glaser be made a full member of the American team in the Sixth World Karate Championship, which was held in Taiwan in late November, 1982. When she reached Taiwan, the American coaches, having been ordered by the court to determine whether Pam would be among those in good enough shape for the event, did not let her take part in the end. Glaser is now a junior at the University of Massachusetts. In 1979 she opened a karate school for women; she now teaches self-defense at that school and at various community centers.

Pinky Danilowitz

Pamela Glaser

GLICKMAN, MARTY (born August 14, 1917, in Bronx, New York-   ) American sportscaster. One of Brooklyn's greatest schoolboy athletes. Picked to run a leg for the powerful U.S. relay team in the 1936 Berlin Olympics, he relinquished his place on the team because of Hitler's influence. The great track star Jesse Owens replaced him. Marty became a broadcaster in 1938 and was best known as the voice of the New York football Giants, NBA basketball's New York Knicks, and later the pro football New York Jets. He coined the phrase, "Good, like Nedicks," in describing someone scoring a basket in a basketball game. Glickman retired in 1978, but in the spring of 1982 began week-end sports reporting on the six o'clock news for New York's Channel 4. After thirteen weeks he left the job.

GOMELSKY, ALEXANDER "SASCHA" (born 1926, in the Soviet Union-   ) Soviet basketball coach. Considered the father of modern basketball in the Soviet Union. After a mediocre playing career with an army team in Leningrad between 1947 and 1952, Gomelsky started to coach basketball in the Latvian Republic. After his successes there, he moved to the Z.S.K.A. team in Moscow and to the position of national coach. His first achievement was winning the silver medal in the Tokyo Olympics in 1964. On several occasions, when Soviet teams failed to win major championships, Gomelsky has been relieved of his duties as coach, but he has always been recalled and is quite popular in Russia. He was the coach of the USSR basketball team that won the controversial gold medal over the U.S. during the 1972 Munich Olympics, the first time the U.S. had been denied the Olympic gold medal in basketball. He returned as head coach of the Russian national team in 1977. Gomelsky is a member of the Jewish Sports Hall of Fame in Israel.

GUBNER, GARY JAY (born December 1, 1942, in New York City, New York-   ) American shot-put champion and weightlifter. In 1962 he set an indoor world record of 64' 11¾" (19.805 meters) in the shot. That same year he set four junior world records in the heavyweight lifting class. Then, in 1965, he set an American national press record of 412 pounds on his way to lifting 1,180 pounds, the fourth highest total in history.

GUREVITSCH, BORIS (born 1931, in the Soviet Union-   ) Soviet wrestler. He represented his country when it first participated in the Olympic Games in Helsinki in 1952. He became the first Jewish athlete from the Soviet Union to win an Olympic gold medal when he won the flyweight division (52 kilograms) in Greco-Roman wrestling. One year later, Gurevitsch won the first of his two world championship titles. He was named "Merited Master of Sports" in the Soviet Union and retired from sports at the end of the 1950s. He is a member of the Jewish Sports Hall of Fame in Israel.

GUTTMANN, BELA (born 1900, in Budapest, Hungary; died August 1981) Soccer player and coach. One of the best soccer players of the 1920s, Guttmann played for the famous Hakoah Vienna soccer team from 1922 to 1933, except for two years when he was on a Jewish soccer team in New York. He was on the Hakoah team that won the Austrian championship in 1924. After Guttman's retirement from active play in 1933, he coached for the next 30

Alexander Gomelsky

Bela Guttmann

years in 10 different countries, including the Hungarian, Portuguese, and Austrian national teams. His teams won two European cups, 10 national championships, and seven national cups. Guttmann is considered one of the greatest Jewish players and coaches of all time. He is a member of the Jewish Sports Hall of Fame in Israel.

GYARMATI, ANDREA (born May 15, 1954, in Hungary–   ) Hungarian swimmer. Her mother is Eva Szekely, the great swimmer, and her father, Dezso Gyarmati, the water polo champion. Andrea became a successful swimmer in her own right. At 14, she came in fifth in the 100-meter backstroke and butterfly in the 1968 Mexico City Olympics. She swam the world's fastest 100-meter butterfly in 1969 and was Europe's second best in the 100-meter and 200-meter backstroke and third best in the 100-meter freestyle. She won an Olympic silver medal in the women's 100-meter backstroke and a bronze medal in the 100-meter butterfly event in the 1972 Munich Olympics. She was Hungary's top sportswoman for 1972.

KLOSS, ILANA (born March 26, 1956, in Johannesburg, South Africa–   ) South African tennis player. She won the Wimbledon junior singles title in 1973, but has excelled at doubles. She was the South African doubles champion in 1974 and 1976; she won the French doubles and U.S. open doubles in 1976; the British hardcourt championships in 1976; and the 1977 U.S. clay court championship. Her usual partner was Linky Boshoff. Kloss won the German and Canadian championships in 1977.

KRAMER, BARRY (born November 10, 1942, in Schenectady, New York–   ) American basketball player. He was All-American in 1963 and 1964, first team, playing for New York University. Kramer won the Haggerty Award as the outstanding player in the New York metropolitan area. He was the country's second best scorer in 1963, averaging 29.3 points per game. During his college career, he averaged 22.5 points per game, scoring 1,667 points in 74 games. In 1964-65, he played in the NBA for the San Francisco Warriors and the New York Knickerbockers, averaging 3.6 points in 52 games. In the 1969-70 season, he played in the ABA for the New York Nets, averaging 3.9 points per game.

KRAMER, JOEL (born November 30, 1955, in San Diego, California–   ) American basketball player. He played basketball in the late 1970s at San Diego State University, where he was All-Pacific Coast Athletic Association (PCAA) First Team in his last two college seasons and PCAA Player of the Year as a senior. He has played with the Phoenix Suns since 1978 and has made his mark as a formidable rebounder.

KRONBERGER, LILY (circa 1885; born in Hungary–   ) Hungarian figure skater. Kronberger was the first skater to try an entire free skating program with musical accompaniment. In 1906, she was third in the first figure skating world championships. She came in third the following year as well. In 1908, she became world champion and repeated that feat for the next three years. In December, 1982, the Jewish Sports Hall of Fame in Israel announced that Lily would be inducted as a member of the Hall of Fame in the spring, 1983.

LASKAU, HENRY HELMUT (born September 12, 1916, in Berlin, Germany-) American track star. He won 42 American national titles, a feat matched by only a few others. A middle-distance runner in Germany, he came to the U.S. in 1940 and returned to running after the war. He took up walking and became a national champion in 1947, remaining undefeated in the sport in the U.S. until 1956. In 1950 he set a world indoor mile record of 6:19.2. In 1957 Laskau won the Maccabiah 3,000-meter walk. He later became a walking official and coach.

LEAND, ANDREA (born January 18, 1964, in Baltimore, Maryland-) American tennis player. One of the surprise amateur sensations of the 1981 tennis season. In addition to making the semifinals of the Junior Wimbledon tournament that year, she was also ranked in the top ten in the International Tennis Federation's Junior Ranking Circuit. During the summer of 1981, Andrea, then 17, won the Maccabiah singles title and the Maccabiah mixed doubles. Two months later, at the U.S. Open in New York, she reached the final 16 and then defeated Andrea Jaeger, rated second in the world at the time. Leand was the number two ranked junior in the U.S. in 1981. She entered Princeton University in the fall of 1981, and since then has been trying to combine an academic and tennis career. She turned pro in March 1982, and soon thereafter was ranked number 18 in the world.

MANDY, GYULA (born in July 1899, in Budapest, Hungary; died November, 1969) Hungarian soccer player. Born Julius Mandel, he played soccer despite a serious injury that shortened one of his legs. Mandy played on the Hungarian national team 32 times as fullback. After his playing career ended, he became one of Europe's best coaches; he coached the Hungarian national team in its heyday at the beginning of the 1950s. In 1956, Mandy was called to coach in Brazil; when he returned to Hungary, he accepted an invitation to coach the Israeli national team. In the four years he managed the team (1959–63), he created an Israeli team that was competitive with the Europeans. In 1963, Mandy returned to Hungary and acted as adviser and talent scout for the national soccer federation. He is a member of the Jewish Sports Hall of Fame in Israel.

McCOY, AL (born October 23, 1894, in Rosenhayn, New Jersey-) American boxer. He was world middleweight champion from 1914 to 1917. Born Al Rudolph, he changed his name to McCoy since he wanted to conceal his boxing career from his parents. When he won the middleweight title over George Chip on April 6, 1914, it was considered a huge ring upset. McCoy retired in 1919.

Hugo Meisl

Henry Laskau

Gyula Mandy

MEISL, HUGO (born in 1881, in Czechoslovakia; died in 1937) Czech soccer administrator. Meisl was connected with soccer from his early childhood as a player, referee, journalist, and official. He became general secretary of the Austrian Soccer Federation during the 1920s and 1930s. He managed Austria's national team which he turned into the "Wunderteam" (miracle team) in the 1930s. He was instructor and founder of the first international club competition, the Metropa Cup. Austria and many other European governments honored him for his achievements. He is considered one of the greatest soccer experts of all time. Meisl is a member of the Jewish Sports Hall of Fame in Israel.

MELNIK, FAINA (born June 9, 1945, in Bakota, Ukraine, Soviet Union–) Russian discus thrower and shot-putter. Considered one of the world's greatest female discus throwers ever. In her international debut at the 1971 European Championships, she set a world record with a throw of 64.22 meters; then a few weeks later, she improved it to 64.88 meters. In 1972 she extended the world record three times. Melnik won a gold medal at the Munich Olympics in 1972. She bettered the world record several more times. Her longest discus throw was 70.50 meters in 1976.

MIDLER, MARK (born September 24, 1931, in Moscow, Soviet Union–) Soviet fencer. Midler began fencing in 1943 and became a Merited Master of Sports. A Moscow school teacher, he first became a member of the Soviet national fencing team in 1954. In 1960, as captain of the Soviet Olympic fencing team, he won a gold medal in team foil competition. In 1964 he again won a gold medal at the Olympics in team foil, and that year he was captain of the National foil team. In December 1982 it was announced that he had been chosen as a member of the Jewish Sports Hall of Fame in Israel, and would be inducted in the spring, 1983.

OBERLANDER, FRED (born May 23, 1911, in Vienna, Austria–) Austrian wrestler. Former European wrestling champion in 1935; runner-up in 1932. He was Austrian champion in 1930; French champion eight times; and eight times British heavyweight champion (from 1939–45 and 1948). He was also Canadian heavyweight champion in 1951. Oberlander served as chairman of the Canadian Wrestling Association for some time. And, in 1974, he was named to the Canadian Amateur Sports Hall of Fame.

PRINSTEIN, MYER (born 1880, in Russia; died March 10, 1928) American track star. In the early twentieth century, he won four Olympic medals and twice held the world's record for the broad jump. At the 1900 Paris Olympics, Prinstein won a gold medal in the hop, step, and jump (now the triple jump). In the 1904 St. Louis Olympics, he repeated the feat and added the running broad jump to his list of gold medals. At the 1908 Athens Olympics, he again won the broad jump. Prinstein became a lawyer after retiring from track and field in 1910. He is a member of the Jewish Sports Hall of Fame in Israel.

ROSENBLUTH, LEONARD (born January 22, 1933, in New York City, New York–) American basketball player. All-American basketball player for the University of North Carolina between 1955 and 1957. In 1957, his senior year,

Myer Prinstein

Art Shamsky

Leon Rottman

Rosenbluth averaged 27.9 points per game and led his team to the national title. He then played for the NBA's Philadelphia Warriors during the 1958–59 season. Rosenbluth teaches American history at Coral Gables (Florida) High School, while coaching a basketball team at Deerborne, a nearby private school.

ROTTMAN, LEON (born July 22, 1934, in Romania–) Romanian canoeing champion. The most successful Jewish canoeist in the sport's history. In the 1956 Olympics, Rottman won two gold Olympic medals for Romania, the first in the 1,000-meter Canadian singles with a time of 5:05.3 and the second in the 10,000-meter Canadian singles with a time of 56:41.0. In the 1960 Games, he won a bronze in the 1,000-meter Canadian singles with a time of 4:35.87. Rottman lives in Bucharest and is a state employee.

SCHACHT, AL (born November 11, 1892 in New York City, New York–) American baseball player and entertainer. Known as the "Clown Prince of Baseball," he had a brief career as a major league pitcher, but became famous afterward as a pantomime entertainer at baseball games. Schacht's first appearance as a baseball clown came in 1914. As the announcer called out the starting pitcher and catcher, Schacht, then playing for the Newark, New Jersey, team in the minor leagues, took his place on a horse led by a black attendant. He performed during the 1930s and 1940s.

SCHAYES, DAN (born May 10, 1959, in Syracuse, New York–) American basketball player. The son of former NBA star Dolph Schayes. A first-team Jewish All-American selection at DeWitt High School, New York, he played for Syracuse University from 1978–81 and averaged 14.6 points per game in his senior year. He is 6 feet, 11 inches tall. Schayes was drafted by the NBA's Utah Jazz in the first round of the 1981 draft selections. He played on the victorious U.S. team in the 1977 Maccabiah Games and again in 1981. In his rookie year in the NBA, 1981–82, Schayes played in 82 games for the Utah Jazz, averaging 7.9 points per game, scoring 644 points, and capturing 427 rebounds.

SHAMSKY, ART (born October 14, 1941, in St. Louis, Missouri–) American baseball player. He played in the major leagues from 1965 to 1972, first for the Cincinnati Reds until 1968, and then for the New York Mets from 1968 to 1972. In eight years he played in 665 games and had a career batting average of .253, with 68 home runs and 233 runs batted in. He played the outfield and first base. In August 1966, he hit home runs in four straight times at bat to tie a major league record. Since retirement in 1972, Shamsky has booked athletes for TV commercials and broadcast for the New York Mets.

SHERMAN, ALEXANDER "ALLIE" (born February 10, 1923, in Brooklyn, New York–) American football player and coach. He quarterbacked Brooklyn College from 1939 to 1942 and then played pro football, mostly for Philadelphia until 1947. He became coach of the New York football Giants in 1961 where he remained until 1964. Under Sherman, the Giants won the Eastern division title from 1961 to 1963.

SPELLMAN, FRANK (born September 17, 1922, in Paoli, Pennsylvania-) American weightlifter. In the 1948 Olympics, Spellman, a professional photographer, won a gold medal, establishing an Olympic record of 860 pounds (390 kilograms) in the middleweight division. In December 1982, it was announced that he had become a member of the Jewish Sports Hall of Fame in Israel, and would be inducted in the spring, 1983.

SPERO, DONALD (born August 9, 1938, in Glencoe, Illinois-) American rowing champion. National single and double sculls champion in 1963. National single scull and quadruples champion in 1964. Spero has been called the best sculler ever produced in the U.S. In 1966 he won the world single sculls title. After getting his doctorate from Columbia University in physics in 1968, he became president and co-founder of the Fusions Systems Corporation in Rockville, Maryland.

TENDLER, LEW (born September 28, 1898, in Philadelphia, Pennsylvania-) American boxer. Nat Fleischer has ranked him as the ninth best lightweight of all time. Others have called him the best left-handed boxer ever to fight in the ring. His fights with Benny Leonard, then lightweight champion, on July 27, 1922 and July 23, 1923, were major ring events, but Tendler was unable to snare the title from Leonard. He also lost a fight for the welterweight title on June 2, 1924, when Mickey Walker defeated him in a 10-round decision. Experts agree that Tendler might have been lightweight champion in any era but Leonard's. Tendler's record was 59 wins (37 by knockout), 11 losses, two draws, 94 no decision fights, and one no contest, in 167 bouts. Tendler went into the hotel and restaurant business in Philadelphia and Atlantic City after leaving the ring.

VAN DAMM, SHEILA (born 1922, in Gloucester Terrace, Paddington, England-) British racing driver. European woman driving champion in 1954 and 1955. The first woman to drive for a British manufacturer. Van Damm won the Monte Carlo Rally in 1955. That was the first time a British woman had won in 23 years. In the early 1960s she ran the well-known Windmill Theatre in the Soho District of London.

WALK, NEAL (born July 29, 1948, in Cleveland, Ohio-) American basketball player. In his third year at the University of Florida, he was the outstanding rebounder in the nation with just under 20 rebounds per game. The next year, as a senior, he was the only major college player in the nation to rank among the top 10 in both scoring and rebounding. Walk was an All-American choice as well. In 1969, he was drafted by the Phoenix Suns where he played from 1969 to 1974. His best season was 1972-73 when he averaged 20.2 points per game. He averaged 16.8 points per game in 1973-74, and 15.7 points per game in 1971-72. Walk joined the New York Knickerbockers in February 1975 and played for them for the next two seasons (until 1975-76). In 1975-76 he averaged 7.4 points per game. For two years, beginning in September 1979, Walk played in Israel for Ramat Gan Hapoel. He then returned to the United States.

WEISZ, RICHARD (born 1879, in Hungary; died 1945) Hungarian wrestler. Weisz started wrestling in 1900 and became Hungarian national heavyweight champion in 1903, holding that title for the next six years. (He was an outstanding weightlifter as well.) In 1908, he won an Olympic gold medal for Hungary in the Greco-Roman heavyweight class. He had a 20-inch neck and 50-inch chest. It was announced on December 1, 1982 that Weisz was elected to the Jewish Sports Hall of Fame in Israel, and would be inducted in the spring, 1983.

WOLF, WARNER (born November 11, 1937, in Washington, D.C.–) American sports broadcaster. One of the most prominent sports personalities on local New York TV. He began on radio in 1961 as a country and western disc jockey and then worked on call-in sports shows. He became the top sports announcer in his native Washington, D.C., in the 1970s and more recently in New York. He has appeared on Monday Night Baseball, Wide World of Sports, and NCAA College Football Scoreboard. He is currently with WCBS-TV in New York, where he does the evening sports roundup. Wolf is best known for such snappy phrases as "boo of the week" or "O.K., let's go to the (video) tapes."

ZASLOFSKY, MAX (born December 7, 1925 in Brooklyn, New York–) American basketball player. In 1948, he led the NBA in scoring with a 21-point average. Zaslofsky played first for St. John's and then the NBA from 1946 to 1956, with the Chicago Stags and the New York Knicks. When he retired in 1956, he was the National Basketball Association's third highest all-time scorer with 7,990 points. The Jewish Sports Hall of Fame in Israel announced on December 1, 1982 that he had become a member of the Hall of Fame and would be inducted in the spring, 1983.

ISRAELI SPORTS
FIGURES

BERKOWITZ, MICKEY (born February 17, 1954, in Kfar Saba, Israel-   ) Basketball. A pillar on Maccabi Tel Aviv's teams that won the European Cup in 1977 and 1981. Mickey first joined the Maccabi Tel Aviv youth club at age 11 and subsequently became a major Maccabi Tel Aviv basketball star. He also played on the Israeli national team that won a gold medal at the 1974 Teheran Asian Games and a silver medal at the 1979 European championships in Torino, Italy. His highest scoring game in an international contest occurred in the 1975 European championships in Belgrade, Yugoslavia, when he scored 44 points against Turkey. He was named Israel's Sportsman of the Year in 1975.

CARMEL, ZEPHANIA (born December 21, 1940, in Baghdad, Iraq; died September 22, 1980) and **LAZAROVE, LYDIA** (born January 16, 1946, in Sofia, Bulgaria-   ) Israeli sailors. In August 1967, they were members of the world championship Israeli sailing team that won the team racing competition on the Hudson River in New York City. Carmel won the world championship in individual sailing in Sandham, Sweden, in 1969. That same year Carmel and Lazarove also won the world championship in the 420 non-Olympic sailing class in Sandham, making them Israel's first world champions in any sport. Carmel drowned in September 1980, off Bat Yam, Israel, while training on a windsurfing boat. He was 39. Lazarove is now a tourist guide. Both Carmel and Lazarove are members of the Jewish Sports Hall of Fame in Israel.

CHODOROV, YA'ACOV (born June 16, 1927, in Rishon Le Zion, Palestine-   ) Soccer. Considered the best goalkeeper in Israel's soccer history and a goalie who would meet international standards. He played more than 30 times on Israel's national soccer team from 1947 to 1967 and, in 1949, was named Israel's Sportsman of the Year. In 1951, the great English soccer team Arsenal offered Chodorov a contract but, since he was unwilling to leave Israel, he refused. He has been a tour guide for the United Jewish Appeal in Israel.

COHEN-MINTZ, TANHUM (born October 8, 1939, in Riga, Latvia-   ) Basketball. Considered one of the best basketball players Israel has produced and one of the best pivots ever in European basketball. A six-foot, eight-inch center, Cohen-Mintz played for Israel's national basketball team 89 times from 1958 to 1971 and scored 1,076 points. In 1961, he was selected Israel's Sportsman of

Mickey Berkowitz

*The basketball star shakes hands with Israeli Prime
Minister Menachem Begin on March 25, 1980 as
teammates and newsmen look on.*

Ya'acov Chodorov

Tanhum Cohen-Mintz

Elazar Davidman

the Year. In 1964, he was named to the starting five of the European All-Stars, the first Israeli to receive that honor. He is a senior officer in the Israel Defense Forces.

DAVIDMAN, ELAZAR (born December 9, 1936, in Tel Aviv, Israel–   ) Tennis. Israel's greatest men's tennis player before Shlomo Glickstein. Davidman won the Israeli International Championships in 1952 when he was only 15 years old. He was Israel's national men's champion from 1954 to 1970 and frequently defeated some of the world's top ten tennis players. In 1965, he was Israel's Sportsman of the Year. That year he won a match against the famous British tennis player, Mike Sangster, in Davis Cup play.

HERSCOVICI, HENRY (born February 12, 1927, in Bucharest, Romania–   ) Shooting. He was a distinguished shooter for the Romanian team before immigrating to Israel in 1965. During the first Asian Shooting Championship in Tokyo in 1967, Herscovici won gold and silver medals which helped him to be selected Israel's top athlete that year. He was not successful in the 1968 Mexico City Olympic Games, but four years later in Munich he came in twenty-third. Two years earlier (1970), he won two gold, one silver, and one bronze medals in the Bangkok Asian Games. From 1965 to 1982, he held five Israeli records. Herscovici has been a watchmaker for 30 years and at present owns a store in Tel Aviv.

KAUFMAN, MICHA (born January 3, 1946, in Kibbutz Yad Mordechai, Palestine–   ) Shooting. Israeli champion in shooting from 1975 to 1982. In the 1976 Olympic trials, he shot 598 out of a 600 point total—just one below the world record of 599 points. In the Olympics itself that year he placed twelfth. Kaufman is a diamond cleaver in Ramat Gan, Israel.

KLEIN, RALPH (born June 29, 1931 in Berlin, Germany–   ) Basketball. In 1939 his family fled to Hungary where he learned to play basketball, soccer, and handball. He came to Israel in 1951 and played on the national basketball team 68 times, scoring 318 points. Klein played in four European championships from 1953 to 1963. From 1977 to 1981 he coached Israel's national basketball team. He was also the coach of the great Maccabi Tel Aviv basketball teams of the 1970s and 1980s; his team won its first European Cup in 1977. As of 1982, he is the Maccabi Tel Aviv head coach.

KUSHNIR, DAVID (born June 21, 1931, in Afula, Palestine–   ) Track and Field. When Kushnir participated in the 1956 Melbourne Olympics in the broad jump, he did not fare well. But, at the 1960 Rome Olympics he came in twenty-ninth in the same broad jump competition. He has held three Israeli records in the 1970s (in the broad jump, hop, step and jump, and decathlon), but all have since been broken. Kushnir won a gold medal in the broad jump at the Maccabiah Games in 1953 and 1957. In July 1978, he won the broad jump event in the World Veterans Championship (age 40–45) held in Gatburg, Sweden. From 1970 until 1982, he has coached the Israeli national team in

Ralph Klein

David Kushnir

Shaul Ladany

Flanking Ladany (center), the winner of the Maccabiah 10,000-meter walk, are silver medal winner Reuven Peleg of Israel (left) and bronze medal winner Howard Jacobson of the USA (right). August 3, 1969.

Lydia Lazarove

track and field. He has also taught physical education in Ramat Aviv and coached track and field at Tel Aviv University since 1978.

LADANY, SHAUL (born April 2, 1936, in Belgrade, Yugoslavia-) Israeli walking champion. He set the world record in the 50-mile walk in Ocean Township, New Jersey: seven hours, 23 minutes, and 50 seconds. He won the 100-kilometer world championship in Lugano, Switzerland, in October 1972, in nine hours and 31 minutes. He won the national walking championship in Israel 24 times (from 1963 to 1982); in the U.S. six times (from 1973 to 1981); Belgium twice (1971 and 1972); Switzerland once (1972); and South Africa once (1975). He is now professor of Industrial Engineering and Management at Ben-Gurion University, Beersheba, Israel.

LAZAROVE, LYDIA *See* CARMEL, ZEPHANIA

LEIBOWITZ, BARRY (born September 10, 1945, in New York City, New York-) Basketball. One of the best of the American players to move to Israel, Barry had played for the Pittsburgh Pipers and New York Nets of the ABA before settling in Israel in 1968. He actually came to Israel for a visit, without intending to play basketball or to stay. A friend took him to a Hapoel Tel Aviv basketball scrimmage and he has been with the team since then, except for 1973–74 when he played for a Dutch team. In 1975 he scored 49 and 51 points in two European Cup games. His greatest moment in basketball came in 1979 when he was selected to captain Israel's national team in the European championships. Barry was acquired by Haifa Hapoel in August 1982.

MARCUS, DEBRA TURNER (born May 16, 1941, in Reading, England-) Israeli track star. She contracted a mild case of polio in July 1959, at age 18, and only two weeks after she got out of bed she entered the European Maccabi Championships in August in Copenhagen, Denmark, where she won the 100-meter race. Although her illness took its toll, Marcus managed to win the 100-meter race in the 1961 Maccabiah Games as well as taking a second in the 200-meter race. When she settled in Israel in 1964, she decided to retire from track. Marcus taught high school physical education in Tel Aviv for a while but then returned to running. In 1966 she won the European trials for the Asian Games in the 100- and 200-meter races. Then, at the 1966 Bangkok Asian Games, Marcus won a gold medal in the 200-meter sprint and a bronze in the 100-meters. She was named Israel's Athlete of the Year in 1966. She ran a sports program in a disadvantaged Jerusalem neighborhood from 1976–81, and more recently taught track and field at Jerusalem's Hebrew University.

MELAMED, AVRAHAM (born November 6, 1944, in Palestine-) Swimming. He participated in the 1964 Tokyo Olympics. His greatest achievement came at the Mexico City Olympic Games in 1968 when he reached the semifinals in the 100-meter butterfly. In 1966 he won a silver medal at the Asian Games in Bangkok. His best achievements in the butterfly style were 59.1 for the 100 meters and 2:12.8 for the 200 meters. He was Israel's Sportsman of the Year in 1963.

Debra Marcus

MELNIK, YONA (born May 27, 1949, in Kassel, West Germany-) Judo. Between 1968 and 1980, he was Israel's national champion 14 times in the welterweight (below 70 kilograms) division. He took up judo at age 12 at a Maccabi Sports Club near Tel Aviv. In November 1975, Melnik won the Scandinavian Open, and at the 1977 Maccabiah Games he won a gold medal; he also won the Canadian Open that year. In 1980, he came in third in the British Open and retired later that year. He manages several judo clubs and coaches children.

MERON, RAMI (born January 17, 1957, in Baku, Soviet Union-) Wrestling. In June, 1975, Meron came in sixth in the World Youth Championships in Bulgaria; then, two months later he settled in Israel. From August 1975 until 1979, he was Israel's outstanding wrestler. In September 1975, he represented Israel at the World Championships in Minsk in the Soviet Union; he came in seventh in the 68 kilogram class. The following year at the 1976 Montreal Olympics, Meron came in seventh. Then, in 1977, he came in fourth in the World Championships in Las Vegas. He owns a felafel restaurant in Tel Aviv.

PANTILLAT, YAIR (born January 10, 1939, in Tel Aviv, Palestine-) Track and Field. He participated in the Rome Olympics in 1960. That same year he was selected Israel's Sportsman of the Year. Pantillat was the first Israeli to run 800 meters in less than 1:55 (1:54.7) and the 1500-meter race in less than four minutes (3:59.8). He held the record in these races for many years.

PELED, PAULINA PEISACHOV (born April 20, 1950, in Vilnius, Lithuania-) Tennis. A junior champion in her native Lithuania, she settled in Israel in 1966 at age 16. Peled made a meteoric rise, becoming number 20 in the world in 1974. When she won the Israeli Women's International Tennis Championship that year, she was the first Israeli woman to take the title in twenty years. Following five months of military service, Paulina did quite well on the American Virginia Slims women's pro circuit in 1975 but never again reached the ranking she had in 1974. By 1978 she had dropped to 102nd in the world rankings. She now coaches tennis in Tel Aviv.

PERRY, AULCIE (born July 3, 1950, in Newark, New Jersey-) Basketball. He graduated from Bethune College, Daytona Beach, Florida, in 1974. Then, for one year, he played for the Virginia Squires of the ABA (1974-75); for three months during the next season he played for the New York Knickerbockers in the NBA. In 1976, Perry came to Israel to play basketball for Maccabi Tel Aviv. Two years later he converted to Judaism, an event that caused comment when some of Tel Aviv's opponents charged that Perry had been forced to convert in order to continue playing for Maccabi; he also became an Israeli citizen. At six feet, ten and one-half inches, he is a high-scoring (17-18 points per game each year) center and one of the team's top rebounders.

RIBNER, SHOSHANA (born February 20, 1938, in Vienna, Austria-) Swimming. One of Israel's best swimmers during the 1950s. Although her best stroke was the crawl, she also held records in the butterfly, medley swimming, and

Yair Pantillat

Paulina Peled

Aulcie Perry

backstroke between 1950 and 1960. At the 1953 Maccabiah Games, she won gold medals in the 100- and 400-meter crawl. Shoshana participated in the 1956 Melbourne Olympics. That year she was Israel's Athlete of the Year. In 1957, she won two gold medals in the Maccabiah Games, one in the relay crawl and the other in the mixed relay. She also won two silver medals in the 100- and 400-meter crawl. She now lives in Tel Aviv. Her son, Damon Fialkov, was the 200-meter backstroke champion in Israel in 1981.

SHEFA, GERSHON (born May 18, 1943, in Kibbutz Givat Haim, Palestine-) Swimming. He is the only Israeli who represented Israel at three Olympic Games, in 1960, 1964, and 1968. Shefa was the Israeli national swimming champion for 9 years, from 1959 to 1968; his best stroke was the breaststroke and he swam the individual medley. Gershon was Israeli Sportsman of the Year in 1962. He was the coach for the Israeli national swimming team six times between 1972 and 1980. He now coaches swimming at Kibbutz Givat Haim in addition to his other Kibbutz work.

SHEZIFI, HANA (born November 5, 1943, in Iraq-) Track and Field. She participated in the 1968 Mexico City Olympics. Her main success was at the Asian Games—her outstanding achievements were at Bangkok (twice) and Teheran. She won three gold and one bronze medals in all. In the 800 and 1500-meter events she set Asian records. Hana won gold medals at the Maccabiah and Hapoel Games. She won two bronze medals in the Asian championship in Seoul, South Korea, in 1975. She was Israel's Athlete of the Year in 1970.

SHMUELI, ZEHAVA (born May 19, 1955, in Rehovot, Israel-) Track and Field. She broke all the Israeli long-distance records while running between 1978 and 1982. A mother of two children, born in 1974 and 1975, she finished twenty-fifth in the New York Marathon in October 1981 (out of 2,500 women runners) with the excellent time of 2:49.51, surpassing her own Israeli record by a large margin. She is also Israeli champion in the five, 10 and 25 kilometer distances. In 1981 The *Jerusalem Post* named her Israel Sportswoman of the Year. Running in the 1982 annual Boston Marathon in April 1982, Zehava finished eighth among the hundreds of women entrants, setting an Israeli record of two hours, 44 minutes, almost six minutes better than her previous time. She teaches physical education in Ramat Hasharon where she lives.

SILVER, LOU (born November 27, 1953, in Brooklyn, New York-) Basketball. An all-Ivy forward at Harvard, Silver settled in Israel in 1975, and has been associated with Maccabi Tel Aviv and Israel's national basketball team ever since. He is known as the "brain" of both squads. Maccabi Tel Aviv's 1977 European Cup triumph owed much to Lou's shooting and passing. He has nearly completed his law studies.

SPIEGLER, MORDECHAI (born August 19, 1944, in Azbest, Soviet Union-) Soccer. He joined the boys' team of Maccabi Netanya at age eight and grew up with the Maccabi Netanya team where he eventually became a soccer hero. He

Shoshana Ribner

Hana Shezifi

Gershon Shefa

Lou Silver

Mordechai Spiegler

Nahum Stelmach

Stelmach (left), captain of the Israel national soccer team, exchanges flags with Turgay, captain of the Turkish national team on November 25, 1962.

Yuval Vishnetzir

Edward Weitz

Uri Zohar

has participated in the largest number of international games (79) and scored the largest number of goals in those games (26) of any Israeli. Spiegler was the first and only Israeli soccer player to score a goal in World Cup play (1:1—against Sweden in Mexico in 1970). He also played professional soccer in France in 1972, 1973, and 1974; in 1975, he played for the New York Cosmos. He retired in 1977 and later coached Maccabi Haifa, Hapoel Haifa, and Betar Tel Aviv. Betar convinced him to come out of retirement and he played the last 14 games of the 1981–82 season for Betar Tel Aviv. Retired once again, he planned to coach his home Maccabi Netanya club in the fall of 1982. Spiegler served as an Israeli television commentator for the 1982 World Cup games in Spain.

STELMACH, NAHUM B. (born July 19, 1936, in Petach Tikva, Palestine–) Soccer. He was a member of the Israeli national team 61 times and scored 22 goals. In 1957 and 1959 he was named Israel's Sportsman of the Year. Stelmach scored his first international goal in 1956 in a game between Israel and the Soviet Union in Ramat Gan. He later went into coaching. Stelmach was captain of the Israeli national team from 1958 to 1968 and captain of the Israeli army team in 1957.

VISHNETZIR, YUVAL (born February 6, 1947, in Menahamiya, Palestine–) Track and Field. Holder of national records in long distance runs (1,500, 3,000, 5,000, and 10,000 meters). Yuval won a bronze medal in the 1970 Asian Games in Bangkok in the 5,000-meter race, and four years later won a silver medal in the 5,000-meter race in the Teheran Games. He was among the 30 best runners in the world in the 1,500-meter race in 1975. He was Israeli champion 30 times and Israel's top sportsman in 1973.

WEITZ, EDWARD (born April 16, 1946, in Tshernigov, Soviet Union–) Weight lifting. He was the Red Army champion in the 60-kilogram class and was ranked in the first five in the Soviet Union in his division before immigrating to Israel. He won the Asian Games title in Bangkok in May 1976, for Israel, with a combined lift of 260 kilograms. At the 1976 Montreal Olympics he came in fifth out of 17 in the 60-kilogram class with a total of 262.5 kilograms. Weitz had a series of lifts of 110 kilograms in the snatch and 152.5 in the clean and jerk. That was Israel's best placing in the Olympics. He was Israel's Sportsman of the Year in 1976.

ZOHAR, URI (born January 14, 1937, in Petach Tikvah, Palestine–) Track and Field. He was an outstanding shot-putter. At the Asian Games in Tokyo in 1958, he won a bronze medal and shortly afterward at the Asian Open Games he won a gold with an Asian record 15.05-meter throw. He was Israel's Sportsman of the Year in 1958. He participated in seven Maccabiah Games, winning a silver medal in 1957. His best achievement was 16.00 meters in Zurich in 1966 in the European Maccabiah Games. In December 1980, Zohar won second place in the shot-put with a throw of 14.72 meters in the World's Veterans Games in New Zealand. He has coached track and field for the Maccabi Haifa club.

THE
MACCABIAH GAMES

As a response to the religious oppression, pogroms, and isolation they suffered, the Jews of nineteeth-century Eastern Europe formed self-defense groups for protection and gymnastic clubs to build their bodies. The athletic clubs appeared first in Constantinople in 1895 and then in Austria-Hungary and Germany. Taking Judas Maccabaeus, the Hebrew religious zealot and fighter from the second century B.C.E., as their role model, the clubs adopted the name Maccabi. By the eve of World War I, over 100 Maccabi-type clubs were in existence in Europe.

Selecting Judas Maccabaeus as their hero was not without irony. Although Maccabaeus, known as "The Hammer," was famous for his talents as a fighter, he had also opposed the Hellenization of Jewish life (Hellenization's most visible symbols were the Greek Olympiads and the cult of the physical). But, despite this, Maccabaeus was a genuine hero, leading as he did a successful revolt against the Syrians, a triumph for religious freedom that led to the recapture, cleansing, and rededication of the Temple in Jerusalem on the 25th day of Kislev in 165 B.C.E. That date in Jewish history is commemorated on Hanukkah, the Festival of Lights.

After World War I, the European Maccabi movement organized international games. In 1929, the contests were held in Czechoslovakia; in 1930, Belgium; and in 1931, Germany. In 1929, a Maccabi World Congress met, and Yosef Yekuteli, the only delegate from Palestine, proposed some kind of convocation of Jewish athletes in Palestine. The delegates unanimously accepted the idea. They had been impressed with the 1928 Olympics in Amsterdam and thought the time ripe for a "Jewish Olympics."

The first Maccabiah in Palestine was held in March and April 1932 and 390 athletes from 22 nations participated.

The American delegation, 11 men and two women, did exceedingly well, winning 13 gold and numerous silver and bronze medals. One woman fencer from Palestine took a gold medal, the only gold medal won by Palestine in the first Games in Eretz Yisrael (The Land of Israel).

The second Maccabiah, in 1935 (with 1,700 athletes from 27 countries), was larger than the first, but it was equally primitive and disorganized. The staduim was a sandpit. The program, though broader than the first Games, was not followed precisely: for example, the 5,000-meter race was run twice! But, happily for the Yishuv, the Jewish community in Palestine, many athletes from other countries did not return to their country of origin. These 1935 Games were thus known as the "Aliya" Games.

A third Maccabiah was planned for 1938, but the shadow of war descending upon Europe caused the games to be canceled. By the time the next Games were held in 1950, in the new state of Israel, the Jewish people had witnessed the Holocaust and Israel's War of Liberation. For the first time in 1950, the athletes were housed together in a military camp in Tel Aviv. Clubs from several countries that had participated in past Games, particularly those from the Arab states, did not attend, but South American countries were represented for the first time, as were Australia and India. Considering the pain and suffering endured throughout the war, even staging the games—though with only 20 countries and 500 athletes participating—was an achievement.

By 1977, 33 nations participated in the Maccabiah Games, with 2,276 athletes. That year the United States sent a contingent of 289 athletes. And, in July 1981, the number of countries involved was 35, with 3,500 athletes participating.

For the most part, the Maccabiah followed the Olympic model, but at times it initiated changes that the Olympics later adopted. For instance, basketball was a Maccabiah sport before it was included in the 1936 Berlin Olympics.

And, Debra Turner-Marcus was the first female torchbearer in the 1965 Games, a full three years before a woman had the same honor at the Mexico City Olympics in 1968.

One significant difference exists between Olympic rules and those of the Maccabiah Games: unlike Olympic athletes, a Maccabiah participant who lives in and competes for a given country can compete for another nation if and when he or she changes his or her country of residence. For instance, Tal Brody was a member of the American basketball squad that won a gold medal in the 1965 Maccabiah Games. He was also the captain of the Israeli team that triumphed over the U.S. to win a gold medal in the 1969 Maccabiah Games. David Berger, an American, won a gold medal in the 1969 Maccabiah Games in the middleweight weightlifting contest. He represented Israel in the 1972 Olympics, but tragically was one of the 11 Israeli sportsmen killed by Palestinian Arab terrorists in the Munich Olympic village.

American delegations to the Maccabiah Games have included such famous athletes as Isaac Berger (weightlifting), Lillian Copeland (track), Ernie Grunfeld (basketball), Mark Spitz (swimming), and Henry Wittenberg (wrestling).

The Maccabiah Games have witnessed some outstanding individual performances over the years:

HILARY BERGMAN, United States, won the 200-meter freestyle swimming event in 1:55.91; the 400-meter freestyle in 4:04.34; the 1,500-meter free style in 16:20.55; the 400-meter individual medley in 4:39.31; and the 400-meter freestyle relay in 3:34.36 and the 800-meter freestyle relay in 7:59.07. All these gold medals were won in the 1977 Games.

ADI BRANA, Israel, heavyweight class, won the snatch (117.5 kilograms), the jerk (142.5 kilograms), and the total (260 kilograms) in the 1977 Games.

MIRA BULVA, Israel, won the shot-put in the 1977 Games with a 42 foot, 10 and ¼ inch (13.06 meters) throw; and the discus throw in the same Games with a 143 foot, 7 and ½ inch (43.78 meters) throw.

WILLY CHEMBERLO, Israel, bantam weight class, won the snatch (82.5 kilograms), the jerk (90.0 kilograms), and the total (172.5 kilograms), also in the 1973 Games.

GARY GUBNER, United States, won the shot-put in 1961 with a 60 foot, 1 and ¼ inch (18.32 meters) throw.

YA'ACOV GUREVITZ, Israel, flyweight class, won the snatch (77.5 kilograms), the jerk (92.5 kilograms), and the total (170 kilograms) in the 1973 Games.

SHAUL LADANY, Israel, won the 3,000-meter walk in the 1969 Games in 13:35.4; the 20,000-meter walk in the 1973 Games with a 1:37:54 time; and the 50,000-meter walk in those same Games.

TERRY PERDUE, Great Britain, super-heavyweight class, won the snatch (142.5 kilograms), the jerk (170 kilograms), and the total (312.5 kilograms) in the 1973 Games.

ESTHER ROTH, Israel, won the 100-meter race in the 1973 games in 11.75; the 200-meter race in the 1977 Games in 24.03; the 100-meter hurdles in the same Games in 13.50; and the long jump in the 1969 Games with a 19 foot, ¾ inch (5.81 meters) jump.

WENDY WEINBERG, United States, won the 200-meter freestyle swimming event in 2:08.96; the 400-meter freestyle in 4:26.14; and the 800-meter freestyle in 9:03.46. She also won the 200-meter butterfly in 2:20.8. All these triumphs came in the 1977 Games.

EDWARD WEITZ, Israel, lightweight class, won the snatch (115 kilograms), the jerk (150 kilograms), and the total (265 kilograms) in the 1977 Games.

ANITA ZARNOWIECKI, Sweden, won seven gold swimming medals and one silver swimming medal in the 1973 Maccabiah Games.

At the 1981 Maccabiah Games, Andrea Leand, an internationally ranked tennis player, won the women's singles in tennis; Shlomo Glickstein won the men's singles that year and thus became the first Israeli to win a Maccabiah tennis championship. Alon Elyakim, a 19-year-old soldier, became the first Israeli to win a Maccabiah gold medal in the 400-meter race. Andres Saltzman, an American medical student from Bloomington, Indiana, set a new Maccabiah record of 52.33 seconds when he won the 100-meter freestyle swimming event, breaking Mark Spitz's 1969 52.90 Maccabiah mark. Lion Birkan, a 17-year-old Jerusalemite, won a gold medal, setting a new Maccabiah mark in the 200-meter medley. In the heats she was only fourth best, but in the final she timed 2:29.96 minutes.

The Maccabiah Games have grown steadily. In 1981, 3,500 athletes from 35 countries participated in the Games. Not only have the Games given Jewish athletes a chance to test their skills and record their achievements, but they have also provided a link between Jews in Israel and other countries.

HALL OF FAME

The Jewish Sports Hall of Fame was founded in 1979 to recognize Jewish men and women who achieve distinction in sports. Joseph M. Siegman, the Hollywood (California) television producer who was the moving force behind the creation of the organization, currently holds the post of International Chairman of the Jewish Sports Hall of Fame.

The Hall of Fame is located at the Wingate Institute for Physical Education and Sport, in Netanya, Israel, a thirty-minute drive north from Tel Aviv. In the first two years, it considered for admission only American athletes and sportsmen. As of 1981, however, the Hall of Fame allowed candidates from the entire world Jewish community. An international committee selects the inductees after carefully screening candidates. No more than ten people are inducted into the Hall of Fame each year. To be eligible, a candidate must have retired from sports.

As of June 1983 there were 66 members in the Jewish Sports Hall of Fame. Six more were to be inducted on December 1, 1983.

HALL OF FAME MEMBERS

Harold Abrahams, *Great Britain*
Track & Field.................. 1981
Mel Allen, *USA*
Sportscaster.................. 1980
Abe Attell, *USA*
Boxing........................ 1982
Red Auerbach, *USA*
Basketball.................... 1979
Victor Barna, *Hungary/Great Britain*
Table Tennis.................. 1981
Isaac Berger, *USA*
Weightlifting................. 1980
Richard Bergmann, *Austria*
Table Tennis.................. 1982
Gyorgy Brody, *Hungary*
Water Polo 1982
Angela Buxton, *Great Britain*
Tennis........................ 1981
Zephania Carmel/
  Lydia Lazarov, *Israel*
Yachting 1982
Lillian Copeland, *USA*
Track & Field 1980

Barney Dreyfuss, *USA*
Baseball...................... 1980
Charlotte Epstein, *USA*
Swimming...................... 1982
Jackie Fields, *USA*
Boxing........................ 1979
Alfred Flatow, *Germany*
Gymnastics.................... 1981
Benny Friedman, *USA*
Football...................... 1979
Jeno Fuchs, *Hungary*
Fencing....................... 1982
Marshall Goldberg, *USA*
Football 1980
Alexander Gomelsky, *USSR*
Basketball 1981
Eddie Gottlieb, *USA*
Basketball.................... 1980
Hank Greenberg, *USA*
Baseball...................... 1979
Boris Gurevich, *USSR*
Wrestling..................... 1982

(Above) Wingate Institute for Physical Education and Sport, in Netanya, Israel.

(Below) A gallery of mementoes at the Jewish Sports Hall of Fame in Israel.

SANFORD KOUFAX
"SANDY"
BROOKLYN N.L. 1955-1957
LOS ANGELES N.L. 1958-1966
SET ALL-TIME RECORDS WITH 4 NO-HITTERS
IN 4 YEARS, CAPPED BY 1965 PERFECT GAME,
AND BY CAPTURING EARNED-RUN TITLE FIVE
SEASONS IN A ROW, 1962-1966. WON 25 OR
MORE GAMES THREE TIMES. HAD 11 SHUTOUTS
IN 1963. STRIKEOUT LEADER FOUR TIMES,
WITH RECORD 382 IN 1965. FANNED 18 IN A
GAME TWICE. MOST VALUABLE PLAYER 1963.
CY YOUNG AWARD WINNER 1963-65-66.

(Above left) Bowie Kuhn, with glasses, inducts Sandy Koufax into the Baseball Hall of Fame at Copperstown, New York, on August 7, 1972. (Above right) Koufax's Baseball Hall of Fame plaque.

(Below) Entertainer Milton Berle (left) at the 1979 Jewish Sports Hall of Fame Inaugural Dinner with inductees Hank Greenberg and Jackie Fields.

*The 1980 inductees into the Jewish Sports Hall of Fame include
(left to right) Isaac Berger, weightlifting; Mel Allen, sportscasting;
Ron Mix, football; Marshall Goldberg, football; Al Rosen, baseball;
and Harry Litwack, basketball. (280-152)*

Harry Litwack and Nat Holman.

(Above, left to right) Nat Holman, Red Auerbach, Dolph Schayes, Joe Siegman (International Chairman of the Jewish Sports Hall of Fame), Hank Greenberg, Jackie Fields, Dick Savitt, Jimmy Jacobs.

(Below, left to right) Red Auerbach, Jerry Saperstein (Abe's son), Dolph Schayes, Irving Jaffee, Dick Savitt, Sylvia Wene Martin, Hank Greenberg, Nat Holman, and Joe Leonard (Benny's brother).

Bela Guttmann, *Hungary*
    Soccer 1981
Sir Ludwig Guttmann, *Germany/*
    Great Britain
    Sports Medicine 1981
Alfred Hajos-Guttmann, *Hungary*
    Swimming 1981
Hakoah-Vienna, *Austria*
    Soccer 1982
Nat Holman, *USA*
    Basketball 1979
Hirsch Jacobs, *USA*
    Horse Racing 1979
Jim Jacobs, *USA*
    Handball 1979
Irving Jaffe, *USA*
    Ice Skating 1979
Elias Katz, *Finland*
    Track & Field 1981
Agnes Keleti, *Hungary*
    Gymnastics 1981
Irena Kirszenstein, *Poland*
    Track & Field 1981
Sandy Koufax, *USA*
    Baseball 1979
Lily Kronberger, *Hungary*
    Figure Skating 1982
Benny Leonard, *USA*
    Boxing 1979
Battling Levinsky, *USA*
    Boxing 1982
Ted "Kid" Lewis, *Great Britain*
    Boxing 1982
Harry Litwack, *USA*
    Basketball 1980
Sid Luckman, *USA*
    Football 1979
Gyula Mandy, *Hungary*
    Soccer 1982
Hugo Meisl, *Austria*
    Soccer 1981
Daniel Mendoza, *Great Britain*
    Boxing 1981
Mark Midler, *USSR*
    Fencing 1982

Walter Miller, *USA*
    Horse Racing 1982
Ron Mix, *USA*
    Football 1980
Lon Myers, *USA*
    Track & Field 1980
Zvi Nishri, *Israel*
    Physical Education 1981
Myer Prinstein, *USA*
    Track & Field 1982
Al Rosen, *USA*
    Baseball 1980
Fanny Rosenfeld, *Canada*
    Track & Field 1981
Barney Ross, *USA*
    Boxing 1979
Angelica Adelstein-Rozeanu,
    Romania/Israel
    Table Tennis 1981
Louis Rubenstein, *Canada*
    Ice Skating 1981
Abe Saperstein, *USA*
    Basketball 1979
Dick Savitt, *USA*
    Tennis 1979
Dolph Schayes, *USA*
    Basketball 1979
Jody Scheckter, *South Africa*
    Car Racing 1982
Frank Spellman, *USA*
    Weightlifting 1982
Mark Spitz, *USA*
    Swimming 1979
Eva Szekely, *Hungary*
    Swimming 1981
Richard Weisz, *Hungary*
    Wrestling 1982
Sylvia Wene Martin, *USA*
    Bowling 1979
Henry Wittenberg, *USA*
    Wrestling 1979
Max Zaslovsky, *USA*
    Basketball 1982

INDEX